Note on the Author

Margaret Hickey, the former food and drink editor at *Country Living* magazine, has written for many publications, including the *Financial Times*, the *Guardian* and *The Times*. She is deputy director of Shorelines Arts Festival in Portumna and is a regular judge at the Strokestown International Poetry Festival. Her first book *Irish Days* is a collection of oral histories.

Also by the author

Irish Days

IRELAND'S GREEN LARDER

Margaret Hickey

Unbound

This edition first published in 2018

Unbound
6th Floor Mutual House, 70 Conduit Street, London W1S 2GF

www.unbound.com

The quotations from Patrick Kavanagh's *The Green Fool* and
Tarry Flynn are reprinted by kind permission of the Trustees of the Estate of the
late Katherine B. Kavanagh, through the Jonathan Williams Literary Agency. The
quotations from *An Irish Childhood* by Peter Somerville-Large are used by kind
permission of Little, Brown Group. Reproduced with permission of Curtis Brown
Group Ltd, on behalf of Peter Somerville-Large. Copyright © Peter Somerville-Large.
Excerpt from 'Swineherd' by Eiléain Ní Chuilleanáin from *Selected Poems* (2008) by
kind permission of the author and The Gallery Press. www.gallerypress.com

While every effort has been made to trace the owners of copyright material reproduced
herein, the publisher would like to apologise for any omissions and will be pleased to
incorporate missing acknowledgments in any further editions.

Text Design by PDQ

A CIP record for this book is available from the British Library
ISBN 978-1-78352-524-9 (trade hbk)
ISBN 978-1-78352-526-3 (ebook)
ISBN 978-1-78352-525-6 (limited edition)

Printed in Great Britain by Clays Ltd, St Ives Plc

1 3 5 7 9 8 6 4 2

In tribute to the countless generations of Irishwomen and Irishmen whose story of fortitude, generosity and imagination is told here.

Dear Reader,

The book you are holding came about in a rather different way to most others. It was funded directly by readers through a new website: Unbound. Unbound is the creation of three writers. We started the company because we believed there had to be a better deal for both writers and readers. On the Unbound website, authors share the ideas for the books they want to write directly with readers. If enough of you support the book by pledging for it in advance, we produce a beautifully bound special subscribers' edition and distribute a regular edition and ebook wherever books are sold, in shops and online.

This new way of publishing is actually a very old idea (Samuel Johnson funded his dictionary this way). We're just using the internet to build each writer a network of patrons. At the back of this book, you'll find the names of all the people who made it happen.

Publishing in this way means readers are no longer just passive consumers of the books they buy, and authors are free to write the books they really want. They get a much fairer return too – half the profits their books generate, rather than a tiny percentage of the cover price.

If you're not yet a subscriber, we hope that you'll want to join our publishing revolution and have your name listed in one of our books in the future. To get you started, here is a £5 discount on your first pledge. Just visit unbound.com, make your pledge and type **larder5** in the promo code box when you check out.

Thank you for your support,

Dan, Justin and John
Founders, Unbound

CONTENTS

INTRODUCTION

I first met Margaret Hickey in London, when I was at a very exciting stage in my career. I had just acquired my first restaurant, The Lindsay House in Soho, and, being a true Irishman, I made space on my walls for some photographs of literary heroes, such as Brendan Behan and James Joyce. She was an editor at the time, at *Country Living* magazine, and, being always interested in all things Irish, she wrote a profile of me – 'Young, Gifted and Green' – which highlighted my philosophy of food. I still live by it today. I was brought up in rural Ireland and I experienced from my earliest days the value of great, honest ingredients and a respect for the land, the rivers and the seas and the creatures that live in them.

When I learned that Margaret was writing a history of Ireland through food and drink, I was delighted to discover that the story of untold generations would now be told. The history of Ireland is often tragic, but even in the very worst times, the people had a resilience and a depth of character that helped them survive. The Irish spirit is proud and resourceful, and that is reflected in the ways in which food and drink is produced and how it is presented on the table. A cake of soda bread, a block of golden farmhouse butter, some prime Irish grass-fed beef, a head of green cabbage and a slab of one of Ireland's award-winning cheeses – these are the stuff that dreams are made of – each pure and untampered with.

Ireland's Green Larder is a tribute to the people of Ireland, and particularly to both small and tenant farmers, who worked hard and honestly to grow some of the best food on the planet. It's a history book with a few recipes included, it is lively and full of fascination and one I know I'll be dipping into often over the years. It's the only book on the social history of Ireland that you'll ever need!

Richard Corrigan
November 2017

CHAPTER ONE

PANORAMA

Tell me what you eat, and I will tell you what you are.
Jean Anthelme Brillat-Savarin

The island of Ireland is so small you can drive across it in a few hours and its population is much the same as that of, say, Croatia. For the greater part of its history, the religion, language and culture of Ireland's indigenous people were suppressed, and for centuries the poverty of the landless population was as acute as any in Europe. Yet over those same centuries it became the cradle of literature, music and dance, of politicians and soldiers, of philosophers and saints, of boozers and brawlers, and managed to be world class in all categories. How has this small country managed to achieve so much against all the odds? It can hardly be put down to the mythical 'luck of the Irish'.

Identifying the DNA of Irish culture is a challenge that offers many points of departure, but however you look at it, they all ultimately depend on the irreducible human needs for shelter from the storm and a crust of bread. What is put on a plate reveals much about a nation. Food in Ireland is far more than a body fuel – every cake of soda bread, every jug of buttermilk, every piece of bacon tells a story of the land and its people, a story that recedes into our unrecorded past. Stripped of all but the essential, each of us is, in essence, Lear's poor, bare, forked creature. In the Irish context, Lear could translate into Sweeney, the mad king who endured the storm and who, according to Flann O'Brien's affectionate parody in *At Swim-Two-Birds*, 'feasted on cresses and nettles'.

One aspect of that story is located along lines of latitude and longitude. The height of a mountain, the prevailing wind, rains that fall or droughts that persist, the clagginess or sandiness of the soil – externals such as these shape our lives. In many parts of Ireland, dense hedges of whitethorn and little fields bounded by unmortared rocks tell of survival wrested from tiny parcels of land, and the lichen-mottled but enduring stone of the dolmen, the round tower and the Celtic cross set you in a landscape that has changed little since the days of Brian Boru, the tenth-century High King of Ireland. The four basic farm animals of today, the cow, the sheep, the pig and the horse, are the same as they were in the seventh century.

Rural Ireland's unmediated connection with the fundamentals of life seems blessedly anomalous in the twenty-first century. If I step outside at night, here, just west of the Shannon, I see a black sky perforated by a million stars, free of light seepage from streetlamps or neon signs. Some mornings in spring, I spot a leveret helping himself to my sorrel and lettuces, within a few feet of the house, or I might disturb a pheasant, sending it clattering away into the trees. Deer are so plentiful in my patch of Ireland that they have to be culled. Elderflowers, wild garlic and blackberries can be gathered from trees and hedgerows round here with no noxious spraydrift having settled on them. In autumn, mushrooms spring up in fields and woods; even in winter the fat scarlet hips of *Rosa rugosa* or thorn trees provide food for wild creatures. Ireland is a food island of plenty.

An island of plenty for some, of course, but not for all. The single most important thing to remember about food in Ireland is that, for most of the people most of the time, there just was not enough of it to eat. The old truism that life lurches from famine to feast was particularly relevant to the Irish. Often, obscenely, people close to starvation had food but dared not eat it, because the rent money came from selling it.

An Outline

The story of food is always political and in Ireland's case intensely so. Significantly, the country never came under the thrall of the Roman Empire. Agricola, Roman governor of Britain from AD 77 to 84, had planned to conquer the Irish Celts (Scotii) for they were always a thorn in his side, regularly sending raiding parties in armed ships in search of plunder and slaves. But circumstances prevented it, and Ireland remained largely untouched by the outside world until the coming of Christianity, leaving aside occasional visiting traders, the Phoenicians among them.

In fact, until the discovery of America, Ireland was just a small island on the far west of the known world, although, out of all proportion to its size, it had had great influence on Europe during the early Christian period. Its wandering monks brought many skills to the countries in which they settled, including introducing cheese-making techniques to Switzerland and parts of France. But with the passing of those early days of Celtic Christianity, Ireland became more closed in on itself. Under the influence of various outsiders – the Vikings, the Normans and pre-eminently the British – the east and south-east coasts knew some development, but the lives of most people were untouched by great upheavals happening in Europe. Even during the nineteenth century, while much of Britain underwent convulsions that marked the change from a rural to an industrialised society, Ireland had almost no factories and the economy remained predominantly agricultural.

Accordingly, Ireland was, until very recently, one of the last outposts in Europe of a way of life that had changed little since the Middle Ages, and in some respects since prehistoric times, a palimpsest of ancient techniques and beliefs. Never having known an industrial revolution, the country until very recently had only a few cities, a scatter of towns and much of it was under grass. All is now changing at breakneck pace. Like an artefact preserved for centuries under the dark, cool blanket of the anaerobic bog, once it surfaces and is exposed, it begins to disintegrate.

Plesyd with Fleshe

Perhaps inevitably, the English who came to colonise Ireland painted the native Irish as barbaric. Here are just a few of the contemporary reports: Bartholomeus, in 1535, wrote that 'Men of Irelonde ben singularly clothed . . . and they be cruel of hert . . . angry of speche and sharpe . . . These men ben plesyd with fleshe, apples and fruite for mete and with mylke for drynke and given them more to playes and to huntynge than to worke and traveyle.'

Just as inimical and more influential was John Derricke, who in 1581 published *The Image of Ireland with the discoverie of the wood kerne*, a work consisting of woodcuts accompanied by text written in doggerel. This blatantly hostile piece of propaganda contains a widely reproduced illustration purporting to show an Irish chieftain's feast where the guests, Sir Philip Sydney among them, squat at legless tables devouring newly slaughtered meat spit-roasted over open fires nearby. A bard and a musician playing the harp provide the entertainment, while members of the chieftain's court toast their bare bottoms by the fire and dogs gnaw at bones thrown to the ground by the cooks.

Fynes Moryson, secretary to the new Lord Deputy of Ireland, Mountjoy, came to Ireland during the reign of Elizabeth I and stayed on to witness the first wave of post-Elizabethan 'planters'. He met another class of Irish at the beginning of the seventeenth century: 'Touching the Irish diet, some lords and knights and gentlemen of the English-Irish . . . have as great and for their part greater plenty than the English of flesh, fowl, fish and all things for food . . . And we must conceive that venison and fowl seem to be more plentiful in Ireland, because [the Irish] neither so generally affect dainty food, nor so diligently search [for] it as the English do.'

Moryson concludes, 'Many of the English-Irish have by little and little been infected with the Irish filthiness . . .'

The Englishman who made perhaps the greatest impact on Ireland was Cromwell, although he concentrated his efforts on the north and east of the country. He drove the native Irish westwards, to the inhospitable lands of Connacht, which were exposed to the first force of the weather coming in off the Atlantic, and with wild, mountainous land unsuitable for tillage. His famous malediction 'To Hell or to Connacht' was a grim envoi.

Many of the planters Cromwell left behind him – retired soldiers and administrators given land confiscated from the native Irish – felt they were surrounded by a subhuman species. John Dunton, an English travel writer and bookseller, travelled through Ireland in the late seventeenth century and in his *Conversation in Ireland*, written around 1703, put it bluntly: ' . . . as for the wild Irish, what are they but a generation of vermin?'

Not all the planters remained aloof. Over time many of them integrated and became attached to their adopted homeland. However, whether they showed any sympathy to Ireland or not, the new landlords needed men to work on their estates and house servants to cook the food. Even judged by the standards of the time, many of these landlords doled out harsh treatment, and the house servants, who worked long hours, were fed mostly on the leftovers from the master's table.

Arthur Young, the most respected British agriculturalist of his time, attempted in his 1780 work *A Tour in Ireland* to give some 'General Observations on the Present State of That Kingdom'. 'The landlord of an Irish estate, inhabited by Roman Catholics, is a sort of despot who yields obedience, in whatever concerns the poor, to no law but that of his own will ... A landlord in Ireland can scarcely invent an order which a servant, labourer, or cottar dares to refuse to execute. A poor man would have his bones broken if he offered to lift his hand in his own defence.' Confirmation of this is given by Lord Chesterfield, Lord Lieutenant of Ireland, who wrote in 1745, 'the poor people in Ireland are used worse than negroes by their lords and masters'.

As can be seen above, relations between the haves and have nots were almost as bad as they could be, but there were undoubtedly 'improving' landlords and it was not uncommon for the people employed on some large estates to form a loyal bond with their employers – a lifelong one in many cases. Those working in the kitchen had the chance to widen their culinary horizons vastly. Nonetheless, although it made use of native Irish ingredients, especially the superb beef and seafood, the cuisine of the Big House in Ireland was usually based on that found in large estates in mainland Britain. This history concerns itself chiefly with the food and cooking of the Irish in the hut, the farmhouse and the tenement.

Hard-won Yields

I live west of the Shannon and in my fields boulders of black limestone break the surface intermittently, while elsewhere it is boggy, so that you sink up to your ankles in mud if you attempt to walk to the far boundary after heavy rain. My farming neighbours have gone to great lengths to improve their land by drainage and fertilisation, but the purpose is to achieve better grazing. I know only one person round here who grows crops for a living, and that is my friend Dermot O'Mara, a farmer who farms organically in all but name. He would be really struggling to produce crops all year round if it weren't for his huge polytunnels.

Given land like this, logic and pragmatism dictated that, for the main part, the native Irish, especially in the west, adopted a pastoral form of agriculture. Grass grows exceptionally well in Ireland, and so it made sense to rear grass-eating animals – cattle, horses, goats, sheep. And because the winters are seldom acutely cold, many animals graze outdoors most if not all of the year.

True, right from the start, farmers grew some oats and barley, but the yields were hard won. One crop, however, grows well in almost any type of soil, even in heavy, muddy earth, and once that crop was introduced it was seized on and grown everywhere, even on parcels of land the size of a pocket handkerchief. I mean, of course, the potato, which is discussed, together with the Great Famine, deeper into this book.

From the eighteenth century on, the Irish peasant was squeezed. He did not own land but rented it. Later on, many peasants were reduced to merely buying the right to grow potatoes on it. This led to hand-to-mouth farming. Most improvements to land need to take the long view. Such schemes as digging drains, planting hedges and building ditches and walls require an investment of money and effort. For those under constant threat of dispossession, and with the certainty of rent increases if land was considered to have been 'improved', the long view did not exist.

The Irish, criticised by the English as lazy, were the very opposite, but there was a fatal lack of understanding between the two. As we shall see elsewhere, when the English interfered with the age-old ways of farming in Ireland, they often got it wrong, supposing that methods well suited to Suffolk would equally serve in Sligo.

By the eighteenth century, the gulf between the wealthy and the peasant classes was enormously wide and destined to become wider. A certain Mrs Delany, an Englishwoman who settled in Ireland around 1744, notes in her diary details of a dinner she gave for fifteen guests, consisting of three courses:

First course

Large joint of beef 'tremblante' garnished with
    small pâtés
Two soups
Pigeon pie
Stuffed veal with parsley and cream
Casserole with vin de Bourgogne

Second course

Large plate of Ham and baked tongue for the middle
2 plates of sugar
4 smaller roasts (Turkey, partridge and hare with
    accompanying side salads)
almond cake
apple pie garnished with peaches en sigovie

Third course

Mushrooms in cream
Foyes gras en ragout
Artichokes with parmesan

We trust her servants enjoyed the remnants of this extraordinary feast.

While high society strove for fashion and elegance, the peasant
classes were the most miserably accommodated in Europe. For
most city- and town-dwellers, life was frequently a hand-to-mouth
affair. Jonathan Swift writes of the drabs who passed themselves
off as country maidens, peddling dubious foods through the streets
of Dublin, hoping to make a few pence. Old street names, such as
Fishamble Lane, tell of the food markets that were held on what were
then the outskirts of the city, and these were the haunts of the poor,
who hoped to pick up some iffy food on the cheap.

Centuries later, nothing much had changed. Sean O'Casey based most of his characters on people from the tenements of Dublin who struggled to keep going on next to nothing. Dublin Coddle was a dish invented to feed hungry mouths on a handful of cheap ingredients made tasty by ingenuity and slow cooking. In Cork, too, they knew how to make do with the scraps and offal that were left when the better-off had brought away the choicer cuts. Drisheen, tripe and bodices (all will be explained in the chapter on meat) are still eaten there, and relished, too. In Limerick, Galway, Belfast – all the great centres of population – poor people learned to eke out a little to feed a lot.

Just the same, the poor of the city have always had a marvellous capacity for endurance, plus a life-saving sense of humour. Derrig Monks, a true Dubliner, told me the story of a woman in the Liberties who went to her butcher and asked him to put aside a nice pig's head for her for Saturday, 'And leave the eyes in it – that way it'll see me through the week.'

There were periods when little gave way to nothing. In the centuries before the Great Famine the people suffered lesser famines, and starvation levels were at times so bad that Jonathan Swift was moved to write his Modest Proposal, a piece of satire as trenchant today as when it was written, *A Modest Proposal for Preventing the Children of Ireland from being a Burden to their Parents or Country 1729*. The proposal was to look upon a superfluous child as a helpful addition to the larder, as a plump infant would serve well, boiled, stewed or fried!

Certain people in authority did not see starvation in Ireland as an altogether bad thing. A Special Correspondent of *The Times* wrote home in his *Letters from Ireland 1886* complaining that the farmers would not change their ways by, for example, improving their breeding stock of cattle. 'In some cases, however, they [the Irish] are being starved into improvements.' The unwritten coda is 'and a good thing, too'.

Short Rations

As we shall see, most Irish tenant farmers were occupied in producing food they dared not eat themselves. The Irishwoman who made butter knew that it must all be packed into wooden firkins and sent away, for if she put it on the table, where would the rent money come from? The labourer who helped drive cattle never ate a beefsteak in his life. Woe betide those caught poaching so much as a rabbit on the landlord's estate.

When people remark at the lack of invention in traditional Irish cooking, at the unadorned houses and lack of flower gardens, they fail to grasp the circumstances in which most people lived. Until recent times the peasant in his leaky, dark and smoky hut worked all day to gather the necessities of life for himself and his family. There was no time to create a rose garden. (And if he were mad enough to do so, his landlord would seize upon it as evidence of undisclosed wealth, and raise the rent on the very next gale day.)

The power of the landlords over life and death can hardly be overstated and the worst were the absentees, who lived in some style in London, drawing rents from their tenants through the services of an agent. The sole objective of these owners of vast estates was to keep the rents coming and when they saw a chance to make greater profit from the land by turning it over to grazing for cattle, they had no compunction about evicting families in order to free their acres for this use. The Highland Clearances in Scotland irresistibly come to mind.

My late father had a burning sense of the injustice of this: 'The Earl of Clanricarde, who owned vast estates in East Galway, was an absentee landlord living in London, gambling and drinking his money that he was screwing out of the peasants in Ireland, and if they didn't pay their rents, which were rack rents really, he would evict them –

regardless of the weather or what time. And he got away with it for a long time because nobody resisted.'

Peasant cooking has always been dominated by practical considerations. In much of China, for example, where fuel can be scarce, they cleverly took to slicing foods very finely, allowing them to be cooked in a few moments using the stir-fry technique. In rural Ireland, fuel was not exactly scarce, but it was precious because it required such labour to cut, save and eventually draw turf. It was not to be squandered, so cooking was usually done on a single heat source. The main fire for heating the house could always be divided into mini-fires in different spots on the hearth, allowing two or three dishes to be cooked at different temperatures. Baking and boiling were always the favoured methods of cooking.

Possessions, though, definitely were scarce. It was not uncommon for some members of the family to wait until others had finished with a spoon or fork before they took their turn. A peasant kitchen would be equipped with a boiling pot, a frying pan, a kettle and little else. (In some counties in Ulster, they also had wrought-iron harnen stands on which oatcakes were put to dry and harden.) Being made of iron and usually very large, these vessels were hard to manoeuvre, so instead of lifting the heavy pots every time, various iron hooks and straps suspended them from the crane, or metal arm, that swung back and forth over the fire. One of the attractions of the little house I bought in the west of Ireland was that it still had the crane set into the wall of a giant fireplace.

The stoicism with which people endured short rations is exemplified by Tomás O Crohan. Born on Great Blasket Island, in the Atlantic

Ocean, in 1856, he wrote of his life in *The Islandman*, as it is translated from the Irish. 'The poor people of the countryside were accustomed to say that they fancied they would live as long as the eagle if they but had the food of the Dingle people [considered well-fed]. But the fact is that the eaters of good meat are in the grave this long time, while those who lived on a starvation diet are still alive and kicking.' Moreover, he added, with the simple faith of his time, 'Don't you know He who puts us on short commons at one time gives us plenty at another time.'

On the Blasket Islands, people appear to have been hardy and healthy. Tomás O Crohan remembers, 'Potatoes and fish and a drop of milk – if there was any – that was our food in those days. When the potatoes failed, there would be only Indian meal, just shelled. People today couldn't make a shift to eat the bread it made, do what they would; they haven't got the teeth for it. I am sorry that I don't have the same food today, with the same jaws to eat it with and the same good health.'

Hardship seemed not to have harmed those islanders, and even in the times running up to the Famine, some malnourished young lads remained in remarkably good shape. The following tale is told by *A Cosmopolite* and was published in *The Sportsman In Ireland* in 1840:

> As the coach passed the ragged and shoeless creatures [near Killarney] one [gentleman] amused himself by throwing halfpence, and at length challenged one miserable-looking youth, who had pursued the coach, by the offer of half-a-crown if he would keep up with us a mile. The road was newly covered with broken flint, and the lad's anxiety to select the shortest way wholly overcame the caution which should have directed his steps. He had almost achieved the undertaking, when the loss of blood from his wounded feet, and want of

power to continue the exertion, overcame all his efforts
and he sunk on the road amid the violent laughter of the
liberal patron who had excited his attempt.

Even with a meagre diet, poor people managed to keep themselves in
some degree of health without recourse to a doctor.

In 1990, Anita Hayes founded the Irish Seed Savers Association,
a charity dedicated to preserving old varieties of trees, shrubs
and plants, cataloguing them and gathering seed for a heritage
bank. When I called to see her she told me how she admired
the country people's powers of observation – 'a forgotten art, a
disrespected art'.

She's right. When I first came to live in the Irish countryside,
having been a city dweller most of my life, I had no idea how sharp
were the eyes of people who walked the fields and forests at all hours
of the day and in all seasons of the year. Animals often have an instinct
for herbs to physic themselves and the wildlife observer will learn by
watching them, too. Many proprietary pharmaceuticals are derived
from plants found in the wild – digitalis from foxgloves, for instance,
and aspirin from willow. But the disrespected art is on its way out.
Unlike the old herbalists, we are losing our intimacy with the natural
world. 'I think,' said Anita Hayes, 'you lose a lot of gentleness when
you lose contact with what you eat.'

No matter how they strove to self-medicate, the peasant people
of Ireland could compensate for their poverty only so far, and child
mortality was high. Where an infant did survive, rickets was a worry,
together with other diseases linked with malnutrition. In the early
1900s, J. M. Synge observed the people of Aran. 'They used no animal
food except a little bacon and salt. The old woman says she would be
very ill if she ate fresh meat. Some years before, tea, sugar and flour

13

had come into general use. Salt fish was much more the staple diet than at present and I am told skin diseases were very common, though now rare on the islands.'

Spiritual Nourishment

A combination of political and historical forces that find no parallel elsewhere in Europe created conditions in Ireland inimical to the proper enjoyment of Irish food and the development of an intricate native cuisine. The mass of Irish people were forced to live a hand-to-mouth existence, and so they set their minds on other things. In the absence of material riches, the people tried to find their riches in music, in dance, in sport, in love of nature, in an interior, spiritual life and, above all, in words.

In *Lovely is the Lee*, Robert Gibbings, that fine writer and etcher, presents the following vignette from Clonakilty. 'I was standing outside a hardware shop noting the different local patterns of spades, some with a single step, some eared on both sides, some with straight sides, some tapering, when a woman said to me: "Have you ever read De Quincey? Hasn't he the wonderful English? My husband is inside buying rat traps."' I ask you, hadn't she the wonderful English? To my mind, that sublime collision of two unrelated spheres is the signature of the Irish national genius.

Not only playing with words, but playing with conceits is a national pastime; exaggeration is greatly in favour. My friend Merrily Harpur has a childhood memory of sitting in the kitchen with her brothers and being enthralled by an Irish girl who told them, 'Sure, my father is the fattest man in Ireland!' Naturally they were greatly struck by this. Years later they met him, a decent man, only moderately stout.

It takes much to crush the human spirit, and throughout the centuries the Irish responded to oppression by creating an extraordinarily rich body of music – reels and slow airs, jigs and hornpipes – by dancing and by reciting poetry and telling tales of heroes and the fairy people. Elaborate dishes and high cuisine were not in the frame – to keep hunger at bay was the priority.

It is only today that we in Ireland are starting to really relax about food, to relish it and play with new flavours and textures. The Ballymaloe Cookery School, for example, run by Darina Allen, is a marvellous showcase for Irish produce and culinary skills, and attracts disciples worldwide to this corner of east Cork. Yet for much of Ireland's history most people were grateful if there was enough food to keep them alive. Nowadays the pendulum has swung the other way and a great deal of food is wasted daily. Why? Because it can be. My friend Rachel Martin, who worked with refugees recently arrived in Ireland, noticed that when left to serve themselves they would fill their plates to overflowing, taking more than they could possibly eat. It is not difficult to fathom why their anxiety persisted long after their needs were met. In Ireland it may take generations to erase the old race memory of hunger.

CHAPTER TWO

BOG BUTTER AND SOUR MILK

*Three things that keep the world alive: the womb of a woman,
the anvil of a smith and the udder of a cow.*

Old Irish triad

In the days when no one could read or write, save a handful of monks
and scholars, Ireland possessed a spontaneous and vital oral tradition,
as rich as any in the known world, and the accumulated wisdom of
a people was passed on by means of storytelling, riddles, wordplay,
verse and song. Among the very earliest fragments of written Irish
are the triads – sayings that poetically proclaim a truth, expressed in
terms of the magical number three. One triad claims that the three

slender things that best support the world are the slender blade of green corn above the ground, the slender thread over the hand of a skilled woman and the slender stream of milk from the cow's teat into the pail.

In a world full of uncertainty, hardship and the dread of hunger, the cow's udder was the source of *bàn bídh*, two words that honoured milk in all its manifestations and all the precious foods made from it. *Bàn bídh* (we find a similar phrase in both Welsh and Old Norse) was what every hungry Irishman dreamed of when his belly yearned for its fill and his mouth watered at the very thought of food.

The Elizabethans translated *bàn bídh* as 'white meats', using 'meat' to denote any kind of food, not exclusively flesh. (Sweetmeats were usually meat-free dainties, although in its earliest form the mincemeat that we put in pies at Christmas did indeed consist of chopped meat, plus fruits and spices, and to this day it contains suet.) Fynes Moryson, secretary to Lord Mountjoy, the Lord Deputy of Ireland at the end of the Elizabethan era, whom we met earlier, wrote in 1606, 'They [the Irish] feed most on whitemeats, and esteem for a great dainty sour curds, vulgarly called by them bonaclabba.'

Fish was never the supreme object of desire, although in those days the seas around Ireland were billowing with fish and the rivers leaping with them. Nor was meat, the food of warriors and lords. For the hungry peasant the dream was of cream and butter, milk and cheese.

Dreams of Bonaclabba

Back in the twelfth century, a poor Irish scholar had created a testimony to the mouthwatering desirability of these white meats, the marvellous, rollicking poem, *The Vision of Mac Con Glinne*. Written by the eponymous Mac Con Glinne, it contains a wonderful account of the court of the King of Munster, a region famed for its dairy herds where the most luscious food in Ireland was to be found. Once he arrived, Mac Con Glinne relates:

The vision that appeared
Splendidly to me, I now
Relate to all;
Carved from lard, a coracle
In a port of New Milk Lake
On the world's calm sea.
We climbed that handsome boat,
Over ocean's heaving way
Set out bravely;
Our oars as we leaned
Raised the sea's harvest
Of honeyed algae.
The fort we reached was beautiful –
Thick breastworks of custard
Above the lake
Fresh butter for a drawbridge
A moat of wheaten bread
A bacon palisade.
Stately and firmly placed
On strong foundations, it seemed
As I entered
Through a door of dried beef
A threshold of well-baked bread
Walls of cheese-curd.
Sleek pillars of ripe cheese
And fleshed bacon posts
In alternate rows;
Fine beams of yellow cream
Thin rafters of white spice
Held up the house.

Money on Four Legs

Mac Con Glinne lived in a world of insecurity. Ireland, with its hundreds of miles of coast, could not prevent marauders from landing, plundering and making their escape. The south and east coasts were the hardest hit, but the pirates could also travel inland, following rivers and beating into the hinterland. The centres of calm, industry and learning that were the early monastic sites were usually hidden away in lonely spots and the monks had learned by hard experience to develop systems of self-defence against raiders.

The brothers usually kept bees (as much for the wax candles needed for church as for the honey) and some monasteries had fish ponds. Orchards had been planted and kitchen gardens established. At the heart of the farming activity were the dairy cattle, and the monks were skilled breeders, improving the stock generation by generation. A monastic site represented rich pickings for the marauders and the round towers that are found all over the land, some still in a fine state of repair even after the passage of a thousand years, bear witness to the need for defence. Faced with attack, the monks often concealed a few cows and could begin again to breed cattle for milk, meat and leather.

During the first millennium AD and beyond, people believed that a satisfactory yield of milk from one's animals could only be achieved when there was right governance in the land. A good king or ruler, they felt, ensured abundant yields in his territory, so the lord was encircled with duties and rituals he must perform to maintain fruitfulness on the land. Equally, it was acknowledged that injustice provoked 'dryness in milking'.

From the earliest times, the Irish were skilled stockmen and a great part of their livelihood depended on cattle, sheep and pigs, but very few actually owned animals in feudal times. A system called clientship operated, in which a lord handed over to the client a fief or favour, in return for which the client was bound to make certain precisely defined renders to the lord. A common practice saw the client bound to give one-third of the amount of the fief each year in the first three years: thus if the free client had received three cows in fief, the lord, by the end of the third year, would have received a total render of three cows. If the relationship was maintained for a further three years, the yearly render was then paid in the produce of the cattle – milk and calves – again up to one-third the value of the cattle; and if the relationship was maintained for yet a seventh year, this was free of render. The client never became free of his debt, and although these are the principal renders, there was an obligation to pay subordinate renders, such as flitches of bacon, sacks of malt and wheat, and supplies of pork and butter. Nevertheless, even though the odds were all stacked in favour of the lord, it was a cold world outside his protection, and so men had no choice but to take part in the system.

Without livestock, it was difficult to have any standing in rural society, for cattle were of pre-eminent importance. Land was measured in the number of cows that could graze on it. Legal compensations were measured in terms of cattle. A cow was money on four legs.

Cattle were generally pastured on the rougher land (the better being reserved for crops) and herded by youths, whose duties were to prevent calves from suckling and to protect the animals from harm. Danger might come in the form of a wolf or a savage dog, but also in human form, for cattle-raiding was a recognised form of warfare and also a form of sport for young nobles.

The *buaile* or booley was a designated place where cattle were taken in good weather, with a rude cabin for the cattleherd to sleep in. It was usually up in the rough lands or mountains away from the home farm, and was always in danger of being raided in wartime.

Eventually, the beasts were brought down when the weather worsened, but only a limited amount of winter fodder was available. Significantly, no words exist in Old Irish for hay or for the scythe. Giraldus Cambrensis writes of Ireland that 'the grass is green in the fields in winter, just the same as in summer. Consequently, the meadows are not cut for fodder, nor do they ever build stalls for the beasts.' If this is true (and much of what Giraldus writes is heavily salted from his imagination) it was not a great strategy, as a long cold winter usually led to loss of cattle, resulting in want, famine and disease. Eventually, farmers began to bring their animals inside during harsh weather. The so-called 'strong farmer', one with many head of cattle, put up shelters. The family that had one cow brought her into their own shack. Later, it became normal for animals to come into part of the house. The warm breath of the animals brought welcome heat to the draughty, ill-lit rooms where a family huddled in the depths of winter, plus the farmer knew his animals were safe from rustlers or from attack by famished predators. Nonetheless, it was a practice that visitors, particularly the English, viewed with horror and it confirmed a prejudice that the native Irish were little more themselves than the animals with which, at times, they shared living space.

In the very earliest times, cows were kept more for milk than for meat. When you are poor, you need to have a source of food that is not easily exhausted. The notion of slaughtering the most precious resource on the farm for the sake of a few meals never even arose. In India, where the cow provides milk and also, through her dried cowpats, a vital source of fuel, the Hindu religion declares her sacred, thus safeguarding the provider of food on a daily basis.

Only a rich man could afford to eat meat regularly. For the mass of the people in Ireland, beef was almost unknown. On occasion they might cull an old cow whose milk yield was becoming scanty, plus they might butcher the odd animal that was killed or maimed by accident; in these cases, the meat was shared among many. But the flesh with which the generality had the greatest acquaintance was that of the pig, and that none too often.

Evidence that cattle were kept more for their milk than their meat is provided by an analysis of Iron Age bones found at Dun Ailinne,

Co Kildare. It was concluded that cattle were kept in ancient Ireland primarily for dairying rather than for meat, because the bones of the animals fell into two main groups – bones from young animals of six months or less (more than two-thirds) and the rest elderly adult animals, most of them female. This would make sense if unwanted male calves and elderly cows running short of milk were being slaughtered.

The lush pastureland of Ireland is particularly good for milk production. Even the stony Burren of County Clare has good grass growing within the grykes between the clints – that is, in the cracks or crevices that open out between the blocks of limestone paving. This is something that Edmund Ludlow, one of Cromwell's generals, noted, when he writes of the Burren, 'of which it is said that it is a country where there is not water enough to drown a man, wood enough to hang one, nor earth enough to bury him, which last is so scarce that the inhabitants steal it from each other, and yet their cattle are very fat, for the grass growing in the tufts of earth of two or three feet square that lie between the rocks which are of limestone, is very sweet and nourishing.'

An old Irish saying goes thus: *As a caenn a bhlitear an bhó.* This translates as: 'The cow is milked from her head.' In other words, what she eats dictates the amount of milk she gives. Cows fattened in the rich pastureland of the south-west were particularly sought after. A good dairy farmer will always try to get the most from his cows, whatever his top priority: high yields or easy calving or rich yields. Today, most Irish farmers with milk quotas have switched to the high-yielding Friesian cow, but these are not native. If we think of the beasts herded by early Irish farmers, they might well resemble the little, hardy, black Kerry cows of today. A cow had to be hardy because she mostly had to survive outdoors.

The most famous cow in the early literature of Ireland belonged to St Ciaran of Clonmacnoise, his Dun Cow. In the earliest *Life* of the saint, written down around 1100, we read that Ciaran as a young boy left home to study under St Finian. Before he set off on his journey, he asked his parents for a cow to provide him with milk while at school, but they demurred. Nothing daunted, Ciaran blessed the prize cow of the herd while he was crossing his father's meadow, whereupon the cow followed him. His parents, taking this as a supernatural sign, gave him the cow. The cow and also its calf followed Ciaran to Clonard, where he marked out a grazing ground with his staff between cow and calf. Beyond this mark, the calf could not go, though the cow could lick him across the divide.

Ciaran's dun cow 'supplied an incredible amount of milk each day, sufficient to divide amongst a multitude and to feed every pupil at the school . . .' Even after it died, the cow was regarded as miraculous and its hide was preserved, the story going that any disciple of St Ciaran who died on the skin would possess eternal life.

Another saint was considered to be the best dairywoman in Ireland – Saint Brigid. One of the plagues of medieval Europe was leprosy, and milk was thought to assuage its symptoms. The tale is told of two lepers who came to St Brigid looking for charity. She had only one cow to give them, bidding the two of them to share it. The one praised her bounty, but the second made off with the cow, driving it across a section of the River Liffey that had dried up. When he was halfway across, the waters of the river rose up and drowned both man and cow. Brigid then acquired another cow, which she gave to the grateful leper, who went on his way, blessing her. Perhaps it was rather harsh on the innocent first cow, but the story is told approvingly of her sense of justice as well as generosity.

To get a notion of the scale of Irish dairy farming we could turn to a report sent in 1562 to Queen Elizabeth. She was told that Shane O'Neill the Proud had made off with 10,000 head of cattle from the territory of the O'Donnells, in other words, Donegal. Eleven years later, in 1573, Turlough O'Neill lifted 30,000 head from his kinsman, the Baron of Dungannon. And another eleven years later still, the forces of the Crown, under Lord President Norrys, joined in the sport by confiscating 40,000 from Sorley Mac Donnell. An estimate made at the time judged that Hugh O'Neill, Earl of Tyrone, had nearly half a million cattle at his disposal, including 120,000 milking cows. These figures are probably exaggerated – one side boasting, the other side inflating the numbers lost to increase the grievance. And for those loyal to the Virgin Queen, it was important to convey the magnitude of the feat they had pulled off and the subsequent riches that would accrue to the Crown. Even allowing for the figures being inflated, the numbers are vast.

But a much more important political strategy lay behind the English interest in how these white meats dominated the Irish diet. By fighting Irish men, the generals could win battles, but if they attacked the very foodstuff of the rebels (as they saw them) they could win the war. In Munster in 1580 'great preys of cattle were taken from the Irish and so has brought them to the verge of famine'. In Ulster in 1600, the Lord Deputy 'forced all the cows from the plains into the woods so that for the want of grass they would starve and O'Neill's people would starve for the want of milk'.

Having broken up and scattered the great herds, the English decided to change the feckless Irish ways. They were revolted at the thought of the Irish doing little more than 'follow a few cows grazing . . . driving their cattle continually with them and feeding only on their milk and white meats'. If only they could force the lazy Irish to give up their lackadaisical ways and instil in them the need for hard work, they would have achieved their goal. They are even explicit as to the motive behind this: ' . . . if they (the Irish) were exhausted by working in the fields and gardens, they would have less energy for raiding'.

As we shall see in the chapter on the Great Famine, the strategy of quelling the rebellious Irish by letting them feel the bite of hunger never died out. (As my friend Mary Dermody remarked to me, 'Aren't we still using hunger as a political weapon in the world?')

In *The Farm by Lough Gur*, Mary Carbery tells a touching story of an innocent life lived in the second half of the nineteenth century in Co Limerick. Here a Mrs Fogarty tells of her mother's love of cows.

> My mother became interested in Kerrys through Belinda, the black Dexter, who continued to provide her rich, creamy milk. Dexters are like Kerry cows, but their horns curve upwards. Kerrys are just as black, but their horns turn down and they are a bit smaller. They have a long history and descend directly from the herds kept by Celtic farmers.
>
> In due course the pretty bad-tempered cattle with their proud Celtic pedigree went to Laragh to form a much loved herd of little animals that had the grace and gaiety of fallow deer. Their milk, too creamy for my liking, was splashed into the thinner stuff provided by lesser cows to beef it up, so to speak.

Until not long ago, almost everyone living in the country owned a cow and milked it. It was taken for granted you had a cow, and the notion of buying milk was odd. Jimmy Murray, born in 1917, lived over the shop and pub in Knockcroghery, Co Roscommon, that his father ran before him. 'I often said that if my father came back here and looked at that shop he'd think we'd all gone crazy . . . Even people today who have cows of their own buy the milk, the pasteurised. Especially with a young family. The doctors more or less frightened the people to get pasteurised milk for the youngsters, I think, instead of straight from the cow.'

One family that didn't hesitate to drink the milk direct from the cow was the Slattery family who lived near Woodford. One of the daughters, Bernie, a second cousin of mine, explained to me, 'We used to have shorthorns and Herefords. You'd get a bucket out of them, morning and evening. The muscles in your hand! I don't know if I could do it now, but then we were doing it every day and you'd be used to it. But at the beginning, your hand would be as sore!'

Irish farmers always kept sheep and goats and as late as the eighteenth and nineteenth centuries they provided milk for those who could not afford to keep a cow. In the Book of Lismore, it is told that when St Brigid went to visit Cill Laisre, she found the monks using sheep's milk. And our twelfth-century visionary Mac Con Glinne refers in glowing terms to 'fair white porridge made with pure sheep's milk'. In fact, the habit of keeping sheep rather than cows, especially in poor areas, was so long lasting that at the turn of the twentieth century, sheep's milk was still commonly found in Tralee in Co Kerry, a traditionally poor county.

Goats were first domesticated at about the same time as sheep – 8000 BC – with the animal we recognise as a goat today deriving from a native of the mountainous regions of Asia Minor and the Middle East. The Old Irish law-texts show that the goat (gabor) was not considered all that important although one text does mention that a nanny goat and a buck-goat may be given by a lord to his client in fief. In return for the female, the client must give small quantities of products made from the sheep's milk. In return for the buck-goat, the client must, in the first year, supply three days' labour for his lord. This ancient system of fiefdom led to very careful animal husbandry, since the death or injury of an animal given in fief by one's lord was a disaster.

Sheep's milk was enjoyed, but the milk considered most nutritious was goat's – it was seen to be good for children and invalids, especially those suffering from tuberculosis, probably because the goat is immune to the disease. (Today goat's milk is enjoying a revival, as people who are lactose intolerant can often digest goat's milk products.)

It is clear that the vast majority of animals kept for milking were cows, and around the eighth century the milk yield of a cow was documented as being worth more than twelve times as much as that of a goat and thirty or more times that of a sheep.

Mass Production

At the very end of the nineteenth century creameries of a kind were set up in certain places, their object being to improve the making of butter. An anonymous Special Correspondent of *The Times* writes of what he observed in *Letters From Ireland*, 1886. 'Creameries have also been established in various places, in some of which the milk is simply put through the separator, while in others the people bring their cream, which is churned in the ordinary way. One gentleman in county Cork, who carries on dairy farming on the most approved principles, tells me that he gets £1 more per hundredweight than most of the farmers, and seeing that there must be over 200,000 cwt produced in this county in the year, it affords a slight indication of the increase in wealth rendered possible in the country by the adoption of improvements.'

The really significant changes in milk production in Ireland took place after 1973 when the country joined what is now the European Union. In place of the insecurity of a small mixed farm, farmers could concentrate on milk production with a guaranteed cheque at the end of the day. Every time they milked, they were making money, and this was such an attractive proposition that many sold off their sheep, pigs and goats, forgot about their orchards and cabbage patch and allowed the plough to go rusty. The creamery was ever-accepting, and soon the old Shorthorns and other cows, mild, brindled and familiar, were lost to the landscape, replaced by the high-yielding Friesians that now dominate Ireland's dairying.

Today on every narrow country road in Ireland you see the chilled tank of the milk lorry zooming along, collecting from every farm on its run, then taking the milk to the creamery where it is weighed, tested and stored. Milk collected from those farmers whose dairies are not totally modern is designated for drying, while the milk for immediate consumption is collected separately and handled apart. (And, it's a curious thing but true, many farmers buy milk in the carton for home use, rather than go out to the dairy with a jug and fill it.)

The counties of Munster are traditionally those with the richest milk, as Mac Con Glinne recognised in the twelfth century. The Golden Vale is how these southern and south-western counties are referred to, and the giant creameries of Ireland are sited here today.

Sweet and Sour

Milk and all its by-products formed one of the two core items in the diet of most Irish people right up until the eighteenth century. (The other was oats, with barley and wheat following behind.) It was a mainstay.

Specifically, *bàn bídh* consisted of milk in its every degree of freshness, thickness and sourness as well as buttermilk, curds, beestings (also called colostrum), butter, cream and cheese.

From as far back as we can discover, milk and its products supplied a great part of the Irish diet. It was drunk fresh (*leamhnacht*), skimmed (*draumce* more commonly *sceidín* or *bainne bearrtha*), thickened and soured (*bainne clabair*). Thick or 'ropy' milk, greatly valued, was got after the cream had been skimmed off the pans of fresh milk, which were then left to set for two or three days in the cool air of the dairy.

Whatever animal provided it, cow, sheep or goat, the whole milk was usually kept for the young, the elderly or the sick – those who were thought to need it. As children got older, say from nine or ten, they were introduced to mixed milk – one-third sour milk to the rest sweet milk; it was a mark of growing maturity and accepted and welcomed as such.

We might divide the sour milks into two types: summer and winter milks. From late spring to early autumn the milch cow gives milk from summer grass and anyone who has ever been acquainted with unpasteurised, unhomogenised milk (raw milk) will know from experience the richer taste of summer milk.

Some of this summer milk was drunk fresh but, perhaps born of necessity, the Irish peasantry had gone on to like, indeed often to prefer, soured milk and could hardly get enough of it. *Bainne clabair* (anglicised to bonnyclabber) was a thick milk and *treabhanter* (troander), was a mixture of fresh milk and buttermilk, the liquid left after butter-making is done.

If you wrinkle your nose at the mention of thick or sour milk, that is a modern reaction – to the Irish of only a couple of centuries ago, sour milk was considered very refreshing, and might easily be chosen over 'sweet' milk. If you quite like live yoghurt or lactic cheese, you'll feel sympathy with that.

There were ways of speeding up the process of souring milk. Fresh or 'sweet' milk could be poured into a vessel that had already held sour milk, or else a small quantity of milk or cream that was already sour was added to the 'sweet' milk. (In Morocco, to this day, the vessel that holds the soured milk for making *lben*, a slightly acidic whey, is never rinsed out, for it is needed to sour the next batch.)

Visitors to Ireland failed to share this taste for special forms of milk, however. Having remained all through the long, bitter campaign that ended with the defeat of Hugh O'Neill, Fynes Moryson wrote *The Commonwealth of Ireland*, in which he was thoroughly appalled by the ways of the wild, or mere, Irish: 'They are barbarous and most filthy in their diet. They scum the seething pot with a handful of straw, and strain their milk taken from the cow through a like handful of straw, none of the cleanest, and so to cleanse or rather more defile, the pot and milk.' Moryson also commented on the way they regarded 'milk like nectar, warmed with a stone first cast into the fire, or else beef-broth mingled with milk'.

In 1610 another outsider, Barnaby Rich, wrote in his *A New Description of Ireland*, 'God sends meat and the devil sends cooks. It is holden [believed] among the Irish to be a presagement of some misfortune to keep their milking vessels cleanly... Upon this conceit, all the vessels that they use about their milk are most filthily kept: and I myself have seen that vessel which they hold under the cow whilst they are in milking, to be furred half an inch thick with filth, so that Dublin itself is served every market day with such butter as I am sure is much more loathsome than toothsome.'

A voice more sympathetic than most is that of John Stevens, whose Jacobite views are expressed in *A Journal of My Travels since the Revolution*. From Limerick in 1690 he wrote that the people were 'the greatest lovers of milk I ever saw, which they eat and drink above twenty several sorts of ways and, what is strangest, for the most part they love it best when sourest'.

In fact, the Irish fondness for souring is not so strange. Sour milk and sour cream have a long and noble tradition in the cuisines of other countries. In Norway and Sweden, at breakfast time they set out jugs containing soured milk, with bowls of sugar, ginger and cinnamon beside them. Looking beyond the bounds of Europe, we see the taste for sour drinks spreads around the world. The cold soured drink that is called lassi in the Indian sub-continent finds its counterpart in similar versions called abdug in Iran, ayran in the Lebanon and various other names in other Middle Eastern countries. The soured-milk drinks that have made up an important part of the traditional diet in eastern Europe contain a micro-organism which takes its very name, *Lactobacillus bulgaricus*, from Bulgaria, where the original true yoghurt was made from sheep's milk.

Closer in taste to the bonnyclabber of the old days is buttermilk, another favourite drink and a famous thirst quencher for anyone saving the hay on a hot summer's day or working in the bogs. The workers who set off for bogs far from home brought with them a bottle or churn of buttermilk and when they arrived at the chosen spot the first job was to immerse the container in a handy drain or a boghole full of water, to keep it cool. Many would be the longing glance cast at that buttermilk, but hours had to be spent cutting or footing the turf before the nod was given to take a break.

Aside from its thirst-quenching properties, it was also seen as a sovereign cure for a hangover, and many an Irish girl washed her face in buttermilk to improve her complexion.

When no buttermilk was available for bread-making, the baker, usually the *bean an tí* (the woman of the house) or her daughter or daughter-in-law, would put a can or jug of milk near the fire, or else introduce a little sour milk, to hasten the souring process. Buttermilk is still greatly used in baking and is found on sale everywhere in Ireland.

Curds and Whey

If you have soured and skimmed milk you also have whey or *meadhg* (earlier called troander or *treabhanta*), the generic name for whey, which was drunk either sweet or sour. Considered a suitable penitential drink to be incorporated into the diets of monks and laymen who were affiliated to a religious order, it was in constant use in the monasteries and is mentioned among the foods allowed to the monks of Culdee who lived by the very strict Rule of Tallaght. From an Irish epic poem, *The Hag of Beare*, in which a woman laments her fall from on high, we learn that whey was held in low esteem.

> No storm has overthrown the royal standing stone.
> Every year the fertile plain bears its crop of yellow grain.
> But I, who feasted royally by candlelight, now pray
> In this darkened oratory.
> Instead of heady mead and wine, high on the bench
> With kings, I sup whey in a nest of hags: God pity me!

Nevertheless, whey was more than just a penitential drink. It was said to have excellent curative properties and two-milk whey – made by skimming sweet and sour milks, or sweet milk and buttermilk – was used as a folk cure for a variety of ailments, including weak stomachs and digestive complaints.

Even before the coming of the Normans, almost every *bean an tí* made curds by heating sour and sweet milk together. Little was needed to convert liquid into solid food you could chew – simply fresh milk, sour milk or buttermilk, and a source of heat. It is small wonder that it was the choice of military men. One famous instance took place in AD 942 after Muircheartach of the Leather Cloak had completed his circuit of Ireland with his warriors. When they returned to Tara, three score vats of curds were prepared for the men to feast on after their gruelling travels.

Buttermilk Curds

1100 ml buttermilk	A large pan
110 ml fresh cream	A cooking thermometer
1 tsp salt	A piece of cheesecloth

Put all the buttermilk in a large pan and warm to 60°C (140°F) over a low heat, checking with the thermometer. Keep at this heat for 15 minutes, stirring continuously. Now remove the pan from the heat and allow the buttermilk to cool to 32°C (90°F). When it has cooled, place a strainer lined with cheesecloth over a bowl. Pour the contents of the pan into the cheesecloth-lined strainer and leave to strain. Allow 6–8 hours, gently tightening the cloth round the curds as they settle, so that the whey passes through to the bowl below. When all is strained through, turn the curds into another bowl and add the cream and salt. Stir to mix thoroughly. Use butter paddles or two broad-bladed knives to shape the cheese on a plate. It is ready to eat at once.

Up until the ninth century, curds were paid as part of food rent. In the *Tripartite Life of Saint Patrick* we read of a miracle he performed that brings to mind that of the Wedding Feast of Cana. In the dead of winter, the overlord, knowing the cows were dry, nevertheless sent to Saint Patrick's foster mother a demand for food rent in the form of curds and butter. Patrick prayed for guidance. Outside the skies were overcast and snow fell so heavily that not a creature was to be seen on the Slemish Mountains. Patrick went out and fashioned a basket out of snow, which immediately turned into one of rushes, then he moulded snow into the shapes of balls and slabs, which turned into curds and butter. The overlord was staggered to receive this and ordered the basket of curds and butter to be set on the supper table for all to see. The servants watched with dread as all turned back to snow and when the lord realised he was dealing with a power greater than his own, he dropped his claim for the rent and thenceforth left that household alone.

Beestings

Also known as colostrum, beestings is the term used for the first couple of milkings from a cow that has just calved. The milk is very thick and is known to have special properties. This extract comes from Maura Laverty's *Never No More*, a novel that is stuffed with cooking tips. 'Grandmother would strain the rich yellow beestings and set them in a pie dish in the baker. They were heated very slowly until they set in a curd. We ate the curd with cream and sugar.' When they heard the cow had calved, neighbours would come over to Derrymore House with jugs in their hands. '"God bless her" were their first words as they came into the kitchen. The jugs were for their share of the beestings. The blessing was for the cow.'

It is said that one of the blessings of the good king Cormac Mac Airt's reign was that throughout his territory, regardless of their condition, cows had udders full of beestings.

Knowing I was researching for this book, Tommy Cunningham, my kind friend, gave me a two-litre carton of beestings – no mean gift for a farmer to give, as it is a precious commodity on a farm, nor is it easy to milk a cow that has just given birth. The beestings were deep cream in colour, darkening to buttercup yellow after heating. I followed three recipes: beestings puddings, beestings blancmange and beestings curds. The baked puddings turned out like Yorkshire puddings – they rose beautifully when hot, but settled into fairly solid lumps when cold and should therefore be eaten hot and newly made. The beestings blancmange consisted of sugar and new milk plus beestings. Together they made a kind of custard or blancmange that set firm and was quite chewy in texture – not as runny as custard. Lastly, I added only a small amount of the beestings to some pasteurised milk and some water, and heated them together. In no time, I could see the milk separating into curds and whey. After gentle heating, large cohesive lumps of curds were gathering, leaving a thinnish whey – not green but a whitish liquid, quite pleasant to drink. The curds had a slightly tacky consistency and I livened them up with some salt and chopped parsley.

Golden Butter

Today, hand-crafted butter is a relative rarity in Ireland and your best bet is to look for it at a farmers' market. The reasons for this are undoubtedly linked to grisly experiences in the past. Here is a poem from Tadhg Dall Ó hÚigínn, who died in 1591, and it paints a gruesome picture indeed.

The Present of Butter

A woman gave me butter now,
Good butter too it claimed to be.
I don't think it was from a cow,
And if it was, it finished me.
A beard was growing on the stuff,
A beastly beard without a doubt,
The taste was sickly, sour and rough,
With poison juices seeping out.
The stuff had spots, the stuff was grey,
I doubt if any goat produced it.

I had to face it every day,
And how I wish I had refused it!
This horror had a heavy stink
That left one fuddled, stunned and dead.
'Twas rainbow-hued, with what you'd think
A crest of plumes above its head.
'Twas made of grease and wax and fat,
O thoughts too horrible to utter!
You may be sure that after that,
I rather lost my taste for butter.

(Version by the Earl of Longford)

At the very end of the seventeenth century John Dunton, an eccentric English bookseller, came to Ireland and wrote of his experiences. In west Connaught he spent the night at the home of a poor family, and got a shock when he observed the woman of the house preparing to make butter. 'For my landlady... fell to washing her hands and arms, and immediately brings to the hearth a small wooden churn, narrow at the mouth, and bottle-bellied. She seats her... with the churn between her legs, and clasps in her right arm almost up to the arm pit, which she made use of it instead of a churn staff, and as the milk flashed out of the vessel upon her thighs, she stroked it off with her left into it again. The butter was not long coming, nor do I wonder that Irish butter should smell rank and strong if all be made after this manner, for surely the heat which this labour put the good wife in must unavoidably have made some of the essence of arms pits trickle down . . . into the churn . . .' The sight, he confided, 'made my guts wamble'.

You hear similar off-putting tales in later times, but in general Irish butter was always highly prized. In the great tapestry of Irish food history, strands of golden yellow shine through strongly. It is almost impossible to overstate the central significance of butter as we trace the history of food in Ireland – as a foodstuff, as a means of currency (if you were a poor cottier, a peasant farming a small parcel of rented land, you probably paid at least part of your rent in butter) and as one of the three principal commercial exports of Ireland throughout much of its history, the other two being cattle and linen. It is arguable that the greatest export of all was the population of Ireland itself, a haemorrhage on the country that was particularly acute from the mid-nineteenth century on.

The production of butter is, of course, intimately bound up with cattle rearing. The Irish folk-life scholar, A. T. Lucas, observed that for most of the country's history, cattle 'touched the lives of everyone from sunrise to sunset and from birth to death'. And, as the old saying goes: *An rud nach leigheasann im ná uisce beatha níl aon leigheas air* (What butter or whiskey does not cure cannot be cured).

There is something wondrous about the alchemy of butter-making. Fresh milk, warm and white from the udder, transmutes into a substance that is golden and gleaming, solid, smooth and heavy, and with keeping qualities that far outstrip those of its mother liquid. Whoever first had the notion of skimming cream from milk and then, by dint of beating, dashing, paddling and churning it, producing both butter and buttermilk, was someone of vision and persistence. To carry on beating cream, with no guarantee of reward for a sore arm and time expended was only done because that farmer had observed how cream has a tendency to thicken and deepen in colour around the edges, especially in cold weather. The lines from a poem 'Swineherd' by Eiléan Ní Chuilleanáin come to mind.

I want to lie awake at night
Listening to cream crawling to the top of the jug . . .

The history of butter-making is ancient. There are references in the Old Testament to cheese, and the making of butter surely predated this. We know that butter and oatmeal were staples of the Irish in very early times, probably as early as 3,600 BC. Before the introduction of the potato, the main diet of the peasantry consisted of oats with dairy products to help them down. Fynes Moryson, about the year 1600, wrote of the Irish, 'They swallow lumps of butter mixed with oatmeal'. In the cities, too, the diet was much the same. The streets of Dublin would resound to the cries of 'Fresh butter, fresh butter here – Here's the new milk hot from the cow, maids, come for your milk – here's fine rich cream.'

In feudal times the consumption of butter was subject to rules. It was seen as a food fit for people of some station and as a luxury food, so a mere low-ranking man was not entitled to butter when visiting, only to milk and cereals. In schools, the offspring of lords were given butter in their porridge, but the children of commoners had to do without. On one occasion, St Brigid was asked by her foster mother to fill a hamper with butter, a trick to catch her out. Brigid prayed,

> Mary's son, please help my need,
> Send butter enough for my mistress's greed.

Even though she had little milk, she set to churning and miraculously when she had finished there was enough butter to feed all the people of the province of Leinster. In honour of the saint, butter used always to be freshly churned for St Brigid's Day.

Butter was highly esteemed for its flavour, of course, but also because it represented a large investment of resources; a gallon and a half of milk produced just one pound of butter. Moreover, butter can last a good while and be stored to tide the hungry through lean months. Viking invaders were not the only ones to make forays into areas of plenty and carry off what they could. The *Annals of Connacht* record that in 1296 Aodh O Conchobhair and his allies ravaged the area around the monastic settlement at Boyle, in Co Roscommon, destroying the corn and pillaging the stores of butter. One way of preserving butter from outside threat was to bury it, well wrapped, in bogs. Finds of this bog butter come in a range of vessels, from wooden firkins and baskets to butter wrapped in cloth or animal skin or even in peeled bark, and the quantities vary from a few pounds to as much as a hundredweight. A giant ball of bog butter is on display in the Damer House, Roscrea, Co Tipperary. It looks like a spent meteorite, and is so big a group of people must have buried it – I suspect it was monks, hiding it from marauders.

Due to the anaerobic condition of the bogs, organic matter that has been submerged is preserved superbly. (In Denmark, not so long ago, they dug up several bodies that are known as the Tollund finds. Seamus Heaney wrote a sequence of poems based on them.) Accordingly, butter buried in the bogs was safe from predators and the bog acted as a modern-day refrigerator, keeping it cool. Interestingly, where bog butter has been discovered it is observed that although preserved, it has changed in its composition, being more like lard than butter. Often, the turf-cutter who found the butter would take it to the fair and sell it as grease rather than treat it as still edible.

The practice is not restricted to Ireland: other countries along the north-western fringes of Europe also made use of their bogs in this way, and in hot countries such as India and Morocco, butter was buried in moist earth to preserve it.

It is possible that the origins of this practice are other than utilitarian. E. Estyn Evans, the great scholar of folk customs and traditions, speculates that magic ritual could be at the root of burying something precious in the ground. In a pre-Christian Celtic world that was notably harsh and unpredictable, attempts had to be made to appease malevolent supernatural powers. Burying what you considered precious was an offering that, it was hoped, would be accepted and could placate those powers. By appeasing the spirits with the gift of buried butter people could buy, for a time, the health of cattle and a good supply of milk for the making of that butter.

As Ireland became more prosperous, the availability of butter was more widespread. When the Papal Nuncio, Archbishop Rinuccini, visited Ireland in 1645, his secretary wrote back to Italy, that the people were well nourished, mentioning 'Butter is used abundantly.'

From the 1690s onward, dairying took over from extensive sheep and bullock rearing. In Munster, especially around the Lee and Blackwater valleys, a system evolved that was focused on the great dairy master. The most powerful of them might become *fear mile bo* – man of a thousand cattle – and he leased anything between twenty and forty cows to a dairyman in return for a butter rent. The size of the herd never exceeded forty because that was the maximum number that could be milked by a single family.

Part of the deal was that the dairyman could dispose of any calves, kept the buttermilk and was given a rudimentary cabin and a plot on which he could raise crops. The dairy houses were also supplied with a room for keeping the milk and the necessary utensils for butter-making.

As the fattening of the cattle proceeded, they were moved from the wilder west to the east, to the bigger centres of population. Similarly, cattle were gradually moved from the uplands to the lowlands, calves reared in the wilds and mountains of Kerry travelling to the fatter lands of Cork as heifers.

From the mid-1760s, as farmers' conditions improved, due to a sustained rise in the prices to be got for butter, cheese and calves, the rent was no longer paid in butter but in cash. Small independent dairy farmers emerged, leasing land for cash, and in the process the dairy masters reverted to being plain middlemen. Cork city became the most important centre for commercial butter production in the Atlantic world, as its grass-rich hinterland with its old dairying tradition became an intensive butter-producing region.

The boom in dairying peaked in that mid-eighteenth century period then began to decline, with commercial tillage farming taking over as the prime farming activity in favourable parts of the country.

However, it did create a solid farming class in more accessible lowland regions of mid-Munster, and you can still see the solid farmhouses of some of those who prospered around that time.

In the middle of the eighteenth century, the diet of the lower classes consisted mainly of milk, butter, offal and oats with the occasional piece of meat. Fish and shellfish were part of the diet of coastal dwellers. From that period on, the diets of the poor became progressively less varied and more reliant on a few ingredients, the potato being the principal one. This is markedly different from what we find if we look at the diets of working-class people in England at the same period.

The manufacture of butter had become a little less onerous. Instead of the wearying beating by hand, churns came into widespread use. Manufactured from oak and other hardwoods, they were often large vessels, constructed from staves held in place by hoops, wide at the base, narrowing considerably towards the top, although it seems likely that there were various sizes of churn. Ripened, rather than fresh cream was preferred for butter-making, and fresh butter, lightly salted, was for immediate use, while *gruiten*, more commonly *im leasaithe*, a heavily salted butter, was only used as a last resort, since it was considered to taste bitter, due to age and an excess of coarse salt.

In the depths of winter, no butter was made, so the summer was the time when the activity was at its height, and there had long been a practice of travelling up to the mountains along with the herds in the Irish version of transhumance known as 'booleying'.

There are references long before the coming of the Normans to women going up to the herds in the mountains to make butter, and the *Life of Saint Colum* has an account of some monks climbing up into the heights, where they found youths herding their cattle. Elsewhere in the early literature, there are references to *macha samraidh*, the summer grazing place in the hills. The most usual term is *buaile*, hence the anglicisation 'booley'.

Over time, the tradition grew up that the booleying was entrusted to the young – usually young women and girls. The young people did not mind the primitive conditions of the little huts in the hills, counting it a small price to pay for extraordinary liberty. In no sense was it seen as a hardship, but was looked forward to as a time of fun and perhaps also a rite of passage, as the young people got their first taste of freedom and self-regulation. A Donegal man described how his mother first went booleying in the mid-nineteenth century: 'On a May morning the whole village accompanied the girls to the booley. Everything they would need was brought – needle and thread, soap, hairbrush. Donkeys with panniers and pack horses were used for transport. Also milking-cans, tubs and butter-churns, bed linen and stools, pots and pans, crockery, knives and spoons, wool for spinning and iron rations of flour, potatoes, oatmeal and salt fish.'

On the journey the cattle were herded along the mountain track by young boys, while each girl carried her spinning wheel, combs and knitting needles. One November day, when the potatoes were gathered and the harvest was home, they would leave the mountains and return home, and the next week would be spent in visiting the various houses of their companions at the booleying.

The butter was made in common, and when it was sold, each girl was paid according to the number of cows her family had sent up. The butter was packed into tubs (often made of sycamore) and stored in underground houses lined with flagstones to be as cold as ice-houses.

Tadhg O Buachalla from Gougane Barra reveals that even as late as the early decades of the twentieth century the practice survived in places. 'About the end of May, or early in June, when the potatoes had all been used up, and the next year's potatoes set, those who had hill-land, extending from what was arable, would take the cows up there. They might also have a couple of goats or more. Beside a rock, up in the hill, a little house would have been built, roofed with scraws [large sods of grass]. There they would make butter. Also they would boil goat's milk and crack it so as to make curds and whey.'

Butter was usually measured in terms of its most common

container, the firkin, a wooden barrel holding about four stone (25 kg) of butter. During the summer and early autumn, with milk at its most plentiful, one farm could produce enough butter to fill the firkin using only six weeks' gathering of cream. Later in the year, milk supplies dwindled and it might take several months to get enough butter to pack the firkin, so a few neighbours often joined together to make up the firkin for market and afterwards each was paid according to the amount contributed.

While this account tells of butter sales in the west of Ireland, a visitor from London observed a new zealous approach to butter-making taking place in Co Cork. A letter by 'A Special Correspondent of *The Times*' dated 1886 contains the following.

> At Bantry I visited a most prosperous butter factory, which was started about five years ago . . . Irish butter has for a long time had a bad name, chiefly owing to the carelessness and want of method with which it is made. I have heard of one old woman who said she liked to set the milk in her room, because she could skim it from her bed in the morning.
>
> The manager of the butter factory buys up the butter from the people just as it is made; the different qualities are then carefully separated, and a batch of one kind is put through four different machines, worked by an engine – two for washing, one for pressing out the water, and one for salting the butter. It is then packed into clean firkins lined with muslin and despatched to London, where the best brand is now well known and commands the highest price. They turn out nearly £2,000 worth of butter a week during the summer and a considerable quantity in the

winter, while between the cooperage and dairy work there are nearly 100 hands employed.

I saw 180 firkins of the butter which had been bought only the day before, ready to be despatched by the next train. In the same way Ireland ought to be able to supply the English market with eggs, but the people seem to be wanting in the energy and method requisite for developing such an industry.

The making of butter was usually the responsibility of the women of the household, although not always. Back in 1942, Eric Cross wrote the delightful *The Tailor and Ansty*, immortalising an elderly couple of his acquaintance, the tailor of Gougane Barra and his wife. In this household it was the Tailor, now retired and well into his seventies, who used to 'make the churn' once a week, using a type of churn that has been in use for a thousand years and more – the dash churn, wherein you work the plunger up and down, up and down until the cream 'cracks' and the butter starts to gather. As was always the custom, any visitor would be invited to take a turn at the dash, not just to lighten the load, but also for luck.

While the Tailor's butter was undoubtedly of the best, stories abound on the horrors of badly made butter. Usually the milk was set in large, wide-mouthed earthenware pans and when the cream had risen it was skimmed off. Often, it was blown off through pursed lips – a practice that would sit ill with today's hygiene regulations – and put in large crocks until churning day, by which time the cream had become a bit sour, which gave the 'country butter' its distinctive taste.

And you weren't necessarily safe when you bought butter at the shop. Within living memory, it was very common for people to take produce in to the grocer's shop and barter eggs, chickens and especially butter in exchange for goods that could not be found at home. To identify her butter, the maker would usually print a pattern on it, or wrap it in a distinctive paper.

My neighbour, the late Tommy Hanley, told me the following tale.

> One time, women would make the butter at home and they'd take it in – 7 lb or 8 lb of butter. And this old woman come in this time to the grocer's and she handed over th'butter and she said, 'There was two dead mice in the cream, but I fired them out of it and what people don't know won't harm them. Would ye ever take them and I'll have 4 lb back for myself and you can give me some tea and some sugar to go with it.' 'Oh, no problem,' says the grocer. 'Do you go and get your messages and I'll have it all ready for you when you come back.' And when she'd gone, he went to the back of the shop and he changed the paper on the butter she handed in and when she came back he gave it to her. And when she'd gone, he said, 'What you don't know won't harm ye.'

On my local supermarket shelves, the different types of 'dairy spread' outnumber those of butter by about eight to one. Here in Ireland where most of the farms have milking parlours in the yard, farmer's wives are buying hydrogenated vegetable oil, attracted by how soft and easy it is to spread and by vague promises that it is the healthy option. Meanwhile, a local shop used to keep a small stock of so-called 'country butter', blocks of buttercup yellow wrapped in parchment paper and simply labelled with the name of the maker, Barbara Harding, now sadly departed. The country butter of this cheerful farmer from north-west Tipperary was always in great demand. The reason for its popularity is not difficult to understand: her ripened butter was as yellow as 24-carat gold and so full of flavour it lingered on your palate. Barbara had ten cows, a mix of Friesian and Montbeliardes, and from the likes of Patch, Daisy, Clothilde and Ruby she got around 10,000 gallons of milk per year. The breed is important, she explained to me, because while Friesians are bred for milk and cream, the Montbeliarde are excellent for cream and butterfat. (Traditionally, Irish butter was quite low in butterfat, which explains how the peasantry could eat large quantities of it with impunity.)

Milking in the morning, Barbara would get the majority of her thirty gallons a day, around three-quarters more than in the evening, but she explained that evening milk is richer. She would skim off the cream from the unpasteurised milk, and the remaining skim milk would go, in the time-honoured way, to feed the calves.

The by-product of making the butter is the buttermilk – four litres of it per day, and maybe as much as double that at the peak of milk production.

I sampled the buttermilk at her farm and noted it had a warm straw colour (creamery buttermilk is almost white). I found it mild and refreshing, with an edge of sharpness that is very different from the much thinner, acidic buttermilk that you buy in the shops. With all the pride of a craftsman, Barbara explained, 'Everything you do with the cows reflects in the milk. If you had the cows in during the winter, feeding them silage, you'd know it in the milk. And I remember as a child, we'd be pulping mangels for the feed, and you'd taste it in the butter, I swear you could.'

Mrs Margaret Connell, old enough to be Barbara Harding's grandmother, shared her memories with me. 'Making the butter, you'd decorate it on the top. You'd take the end of the wooden pats – hands, we called them – and you'd tip a pattern round the edge and then you'd make another shape in the middle. 'Twould make it look attractive, you know. We'd never touch the butter but always use the tools.'

Austin O'Toole had more to say on the subject:

We had big enamel pans and the milk was strained into muslin. We'd be very careful about the milk, washing the cow's teats and that. They'd sit in the dairy – three or four pans, sit till the cream had come to the top. It could take twenty-four hours, or you could skim it after twelve – it would depend on the weather. My mother would skim off and store the cream in a crock, which was earthenware – big, about eighteen inches high and wide. She stored it for so many days and then poured the cream, and the skim milk was fed to the calves. Churning day would come. First we had a little roundabout churn, then we got an end-over-end barrel with a glass on the top. The lid would be screwed down and when the glass – it was bigger than a half crown – would get blobs of butter on it, we'd say it was 'broken'. You'd rock it then for a while, gather it. Then you'd strain the buttermilk away . . . The butter would take a lot of washing. You'd take all the milk out, otherwise it would get sour. Finally, a wide wooden bowl and two pats. My mother would crock all her butter, churning two or three times a week. She'd add plenty of salt and put muslin on the top and then another layer, till all was completed in the crock. Packed down nice and airtight. The cows would be dry in the winter – they'd give enough to colour your tea.

From Letterkenny, Co Donegal, comes this report of butter-making: 'If the butter was very pale and not marketable, it would be coloured. They put grated carrots into a saucepan on the fire, boiled them, strained the juice and spilled a drop or two of carrot juice over the butter and raked it. It was the loveliest you ever tasted.'

There are two main types of butter on the market today: sweet cream, which accounts for most of the butter made in Britain today, and lactic or 'ripened' butter, the style preferred on the continent. Either can be salted or unsalted. The British used to make lactic butter because 'that was the peasant way'. Most smallholdings had only a few cows, and when the cream was skimmed off, there wouldn't be enough to make butter in one day, so it was kept for up to a week, until there was enough to churn, during which time it had naturally soured or 'ripened' and acquired its distinctive flavour. As farms grew, they were able to produce enough fresh cream to churn immediately, and this bland-tasting 'sweet cream' butter became the favourite in Britain and the USA.

The real issue is one of choice. Country butter is not going to be ideal for every purpose. 'Although,' says top chef Henry Harris, 'it tastes great with bread, it has too much of a farmyard flavour for delicate cooking. Try making a beurre blanc with it, and it's like diving into cowshit!'

Of course, cream is what goes to make the highly esteemed golden Irish butter. When it was made by hand in every farmhouse, people learned by the pattern stamped on the butter who had produced each packet, and they selected their favourites, because standards certainly varied. Here Bernie Hogan, née Slattery, remembers butter-making from her childhood in the middle of the twentieth century. 'Mother had a separator, stainless steel, it was, and it'd be so clean you could see your face in it. After you'd milked, the calves would get a certain amount and then you brought in the milk and it'd go into the separator – about two buckets, eight pints or so. And cream would come out of one tube into a bowl and the skim milk, the whey, would come out into a bucket and you'd use that to feed the pigs. And you'd collect the milk over a few days and then it'd go in the churn. Mother had a stainless steel churn as well – we were very modern!'

The Slatterys had a modern churn with a handle for turning, but the old-style wooden churn consisted of a tall tapering cylinder with a vertical paddle or dash set into the lid, which had to be endlessly thumped up and down. Dorothy Hartley gives a vivid picture of one. 'Within the house I can hear the steady thump of the dasher going up and down, down and up, in the churn. For half an hour or so that sound and the bees in the clover would hold the sunlit air . . . The butter would be coming soon, she'll not be able to leave the dasher for a moment now . . .'

If you want the ultimate evocation of butter-making, turn to Ireland's great poet, Seamus Heaney, and read 'Churning Day'.

Cheese

The generic word for cheese in Irish is *cáis*, a borrowing from the Latin *caseus*, which has led some scholars to the conclusion that cheese was unknown in Ireland prior to Christianity, although the Latin borrowing may have effaced an earlier word.

The discovery of hard cheese probably came about when someone noticed that if curds were left for a while (especially with their souring agent) they began to harden and could be cut. Instead of going mouldy, the hardened curds kept well and during the hard months of winter, the cheese was heartily welcome. The monks, at the centre of calm and continuity, would be likeliest to have developed new species, new techniques, new ideas.

Some believe that it was Irish monks who, in their proselytising journeys in Europe, spread the art of cheese-making and are its true fathers. Patrick Rance, a great cheese expert, writes 'There is a strong . . . tradition that the first preaching of the Gospel here [France] was by Irish monks from the following of Columban. This Irish saint had founded a monastery (now a seminary) at Luxeuil-les-Bains . . .' Later he describes how the monks helped to clear the forest of the eastern slopes of the Vosges mountains for pasture. 'The lower farms and the chaumes, as the high pastures became known, were let to farmers or mercaires who paid at least part of their rent in the cheese the monks had taught them to make.'

Further confirmation of the influence of Irish monks on cheese-making in continental Europe is provided by the Swiss Cheese Union. Appenzell cheese, from eastern Switzerland, came about thus: the monastery of St Gallen, founded in AD 620 by the Irish monks Gall and Columban, had attracted others to settle in the vicinity. The region of Appenzell, close to St Gallen, was also slowly developing and the first recorded mention of it occurs in 1071, under its Latin name, Abbatis Cella – the cell of the abbey. The Latin words evolved quite naturally into Appenzell, and the region, always a stronghold of hunting, became more and more devoted to mountain farming, under the influence of the monastery. People had to pay dues to the monks and these were usually collected in the form of butter and cheese, as recorded in a document from 1282. So well loved was the cheese that the authorities had to stipulate that the local markets must first be supplied before a licence would be granted for its sale outside the area.

In a similar vein, a valley in the French Vosges was named Munster Valley after the foundation of a monastery there in AD 668 and speculation exists that it was so named because Irish monks founded it. Certainly, documents dating from AD 850 prove that regular farming with cheese-making was the principal economic activity in the region. Today, Munster and Munster-type cheeses are widespread, particularly in France and Germany.

Whatever the point of departure, cheese-making flourished in Ireland for many centuries. By and large, Irish cheeses were made using rennet or *binid*, commonly taken from the stomachs of calves and sheep. We find references to its use as far back as the ninth century, and by the Rule of Tallaght, which imposed a strictly vegetarian diet, the Culdee monks were forbidden to eat cheese because the rennet was extracted from the flesh of an animal. Other ways of curding milk were discovered: cheese makers used a herb called lady's bedstraw (*Galium verum*, in Irish *ru Mhuire* or *boladh cnis*), which gets its name from the belief that it was one of the herbs in the manger in Bethlehem. Or they used some other coagulating agent, such as butterwort, carrageen moss and other vegetable preparations.

It is clear that there were a variety of cheeses made in Ireland over the centuries. In the earliest written sources, we find *faiscre grotha*, the term probably applied to a cheese made out of curd and eaten fresh. It must have been small enough, for there are references to a woman being able to carry several in the folds of her cloak.

With increasing knowledge of cheese-making techniques, other types of cheese were produced. *Tanag* or *tanach* was a round, hard, dry cheese made of skimmed milk and pressed in a mould. In an undignified end (almost equal to that of the man in the Graham Greene story who was killed in Naples by a pig falling from a balcony) Queen Méabh of Connacht in her old age was struck on the forehead by a piece of *tanach*, let fly by her nephew Furbaide, and was killed.

Tath, on the other hand, was a soft cheese made from heated sour milk curds, rather like a cooked continental cheese. *Maethal* was a smooth-textured soft-bodied cheese made from buttermilk curds and must have been fairly large in size because someone of formidable girth was said to have 'buttocks like a half a *maethal*'; and *milsean* was a semi-liquid curd cheese made from whole milk set with rennet and eaten at the end of a banquet or harvest feast.

Grus was a soft curd cheese made from soured buttermilk which was kneaded but not pressed. *Mulchan* was made of buttermilk beaten to form a soft cheese which was then pressed and moulded to become another hard cheese and it was one of the last traditional Irish cheeses to die out. It was exported in large quantities, being made in Wexford right up to 1824, when an English writer, anglicising the name to Mullahawn, says it was 'a cheese made from skim milk, but of such a hard substance that it required a hatchet to cut it'.

Much was lost during the sixteenth and seventeenth centuries, more during the eighteenth, and by the early nineteenth century cheese-making was in serious decline. An observer of the time noted, 'Cheese is not an article of Irish produce: it is brought to the tables of the affluent as an indulgence.' Come the 1940s and 1950s it was almost impossible to get your hands on a farmhouse cheese. This once-important food had all but disappeared. Curds and soft cheese persisted, but so seldom was hard cheese made that the following story might actually be true. A country girl had arrived in a town and, surrounded by strange and bewildering sensations, she was on her guard. Offered a slice of cheese, she was quick to defend herself. *'Má's cailín ón dtuath mé ní íosfainn geir!'* she said, meaning 'I may be a country girl, but I do not eat tallow!'

Starting around the second half of the twentieth century, there has been a remarkable revival in cheese-making and thanks should be given to a number of cheesemakers who came originally from continental Europe, and who show such sympathy with the country that they are honorary Irish.

In the vanguard of the great cheese-making revival was the late, great Veronica Steele. She explained to me that at Maher's grocery in Cork they kept a cheese that was wrapped in strips of muslin, like bandages, and as a chunk was cut off with the cheese wire you could smell and see that it was the real thing, made from the milk of a cow and, what's more, a cow that had fed on the rich grass of Co Cork. Word got out that this cheese was no longer to be made, so Veronica determined that if no one else was making real farmhouse cheese, then she must. Together with her husband Norman, she created Milleens, a cheese so majestic that even the French, with their panoply of cheeses, felt compelled to import it.

With the talent and dedication of pioneering cheese makers in the latter half of the twentieth century, some of them Dutch, German or English, the Irish farmhouse cheese has been rescued from the brink of extinction, and the ancient tradition that had faltered was not allowed to collapse. Irish farmhouse cheeses today are in the first rank, wonderfully varied and are great ambassadors for the country.

CHAPTER THREE

BARLEY LOAVES AND OATCAKES

Bread is older than man.

Hungarian proverb

Whenever I plan to visit friends in England they always ask me to bring over some airport bread, by which they mean the wholewheat loaves, on sale in food shops in Irish airports. These neat little loaves are knobbly and nutty, with green bits (the wheatgerm) in them, and if you spread some home-churned Irish country butter on a slice you'll experience a gourmet treat. This splendid bread is made with nothing but stoneground wheatflour, wheatgerm and salt, bicarbonate of soda and buttermilk – no yeasts or sugars are involved.

One of the glories of the Irish culinary repertoire, this type of non-yeast bread is such a doddle to get right that even in our fast-moving times large numbers of people continue to make it at least once a week. The newly discovered ciabatta, chapatti, pain de campagne and pumpernickel all deserve a welcome in the nation's larders, but a fine loaf of Irish brown bread is something to be put forward with pride.

The Daily Grind

To bake bread, you need grain for flour, and from the fragments of evidence we can piece together it is clear that cereal-growing was part of the food economy of the people in Ireland from very early times – certainly by 5500 BC. Hunter-gatherers they may have been at the beginning, but the advantages of growing cereals to provide a reliable source of food were not lost on them. While the men mostly sowed the seed, and dealt with harvesting, threshing with flails and drying the grain,usually in a kiln, the women had the task of crushing the corn in a quern to turn it into meal. Take a mortar and pestle and start to grind any grain into flour and see how long you last!

To travel back to those times, all you need do is drive along the cliff road on the north coast of Co Mayo, until a glass pyramid suddenly shimmers on the skyline, signalling the presence of a museum centred on the Céide Fields. On this site the layers and accretions of centuries have been peeled back to reveal the landscape of that part of Ireland such as it was some 7,500 years ago. Just stop and think about that. The oldest Egyptian pyramid is dated 2600 BC. These structures predate that by millennia, although there is currently some dispute as to the accuracy of the dating.

The Céide Fields represent the most extensive Stone Age site in the world, and the field systems are also the oldest known on the planet. Wear something warm and windproof and go there as soon as you can!

Back in the 1930s, Patrick Caulfield, a local schoolteacher, became intrigued when he came across unusual heaps of stones that were revealed after turf had been cut in the bog. He had no doubt that these stones had been deliberately placed and that the configurations could not be random. It took his archaeologist son, Seamus, some forty years later, to fully uncover the well-made stone walls, houses and megalithic tombs that were lying beneath the bog.

The earliest researches were carried out using the simple but effective method of plunging a metal marker staff along the probable line of these walls to trace their outlines. Patrick Caulfield's apprehension that these were of great significance, his vision you might say, set in motion excavations that reveal how the first farmers up on that windswept coast all those millennia ago built a network of stone walls to enclose their fields, then used crude spades carved out of stone, bone or horn to break the earth sufficiently to sow corn.

From the Iron Age, 200 BC onward, iron sickles were brought into use, and strong, sharp blades for ploughs and harrows let grain be grown on a large scale. The early Christian era saw the monks systematising agriculture and it was in those times, after AD 700, that mills became common sights in the landscape of Ireland. The most complex piece of equipment known to the early Irish farmer was the mill, which was regarded as a great boon since it did away with the backbreaking task of grinding the threshed corn by hand, and also produced greater quantities of a superior milled flour. (Excavations have uncovered a tidal mill at Little Island, Co Cork, thought to date from as early as AD 630.) Hand-crushed grains must have produced a gritty flour, while the milled flour would have been purer, although with primitive sieving techniques there would still have been a fair admixture of stone and grit in it. Biting down unwittingly on something hard can crack a tooth and even if that misfortune was avoided, imagine how worn down the teeth of our forebears must have been.

Once the knowledge and skill had been acquired, every parish built a mill, often owned by a band of people. Throughout the west and north the mill was most usually powered by water, while in the south and east windmills were more common, Co Wexford, in particular, being famous for the windmills that thrust up from its skyline.

A story is told of the monks at Fore, Co Westmeath, whose job it was to grind corn in the hand querns. They were frustrated to see that the water trickling down the bog in the valley was too weak to turn a mill wheel, while just on the other side of the rocks were swift streams ideal for the job. After a while 'very weary they grew and complaint they had made to St Fechin', so he told them to build a mill on a hillside beyond the abbey. Wondering, they did so and by the next summer the millstones 'lay hungry waiting' and the new wheel was dusty and bone dry. At that point, St Fechin summoned the water to come and turn his mill, and it rushed down a dry watercourse, causing the mighty millwheel to groan, creak and begin to turn.

The harvesting of crops, the saving of the hay and the thrashing of the corn were such important events that no young person could fail to be impressed. Peter Somerville-Large, writing of the 1950s or so, remembers them, though at a certain remove. 'Cows were milked and fields were ploughed by the many men we employed and in the social climate of the day we were not expected to dirty our hands. Only at harvest time did we help to stook the oats or the wheat which the farm was forced to grow on thin Wicklow land because of Emergency regulations. Then we could watch the steam thresher slowly make its way up the avenue and into the long field, where for two or three days the men would work enveloped in clouds of steam. Each man had his duty, varying from watching the whirling belts to pitchforking up the corn. But we were spectators.'

My father, brought up near Woodford, Co Galway, told me how he would take grain to the mill, back in the 1920s.

> There was a flour mill about maybe five mile away, driven by a big water wheel. It was called Clarke's Mill. The donkey and cart would be brought out again, th'ould ass and cart, and there'd be a sack of wheat. You'd have to take that to the mill and when you'd get there, there'd be a line of people all waiting and your name

would be put down, but you might be there a good few hours before your corn would be ground. It was a big stone mill, with grindstones, as they call them, driven by the wheel. The water would be dammed further up and then the water let go to do the day's grinding. The wheat would be ground up between these stones and then dropped to a lower level and ground again and so on.

You'd have two bags going home. You'd have one bag of flour, pure flour, and the other bag would be what we call bran − the outside of the wheat kernels. The mill, also, it drove a sawmill. Timber would be cut up and sawn. It was all a very interesting day out.

If you want to see a watermill close up, you should hasten to Finnerty's Mills, near Loughrea, Co Galway, where they give really informative tours. (By the way, here is a little riddle for you. What goes into a bucket of water white and comes out black? Give in? A miller's boot.)

In earlier times, the miller's official reward was every fifth quart of the grain and he was kept busy after harvest time, but the poorest people waited to take their oats to the mill to be ground at Christmas. In Connemara during the late nineteenth century, the week before Christmas was the busiest in the miller's year. People lined up with their sacks and some cute fellows might try to jump the queue by winking at the miller with an implicit promise of a bottle or a plug of tobacco.

As people liked to have bread baked from freshly ground flour, it was the custom to store grain and just have a sack or two ground now and again. Providing you could keep the rats out of the stored grain, there was no harm in this system because in Ireland the winters are seldom so severe that the water freezes. Moreover, the wind blows all year round.

Holding onto the grain, though, was not so easy. An English commentator in the eighteenth century remarked on the importance of the hasty pudding. 'They [the Irish] have a custom every Mayday which they count their first day of summer to have one formal dish, which some call stirabout or hasty pudding, that is of flour and milk boiled thick and this as an argument of the good wife's good housewifery that made her corn hold out so well, as to have such a dish to begin the summer fare with . . . even in the plentifullest and greatest of houses where bread is in abundance all year long, they will not fail of this dish, nor yet even they that for the month before wanted bread.'

Farming for Grain

In the first centuries of the Christian era, the Brehon laws were greatly concerned with the minutiae of transactions between people. The devil is in the detail, they say, and these rules were very specific. The dimensions of loaves to be given as food rent were itemised as being either a woman's cake, being two fists in breadth and one fist in thickness, a man's cake, twice the size of a woman's cake, and finally a huge cake reserved by the woman of the house to offer her guests, before whom it was shameful to put a cake of bread already cut into. (Aren't we the same today? When I have guests I hate to put on the table anything but a whole loaf.)

While the early Christian monks developed and systematised agriculture, it was the Normans who introduced the idea of crop rotation over three fields. Under the Norman dispensation, which was strongest on the east and south coasts, the infield belonged directly to the lord of the manor and the land beyond was used by the farmers, cottiers and betaghs whose rent was exacted in goods and labour. One of the duties of a betagh, also called a villein, was to provide men to help sow, weed and harvest the landowner's grain. From old documents we know that in 1333 on one estate the betagh had to provide, for roughly one hectare of land, three men in autumn for a day's work at harvesting the wheat, and two men to bring in the oats. Other men were required to turn hay and cart it where it was wanted, plus others to carry the grain to the mill for grinding. As his part of the deal the local lord provided the tools needed for the job and also contributed to the cost of the harvest feast.

In those feudal times, the ruling classes very vehemently propagated the distinctions between commoner and lord. In the *Annals of the Four Masters* it is recorded with dismay that such was the shortage of labour in the year 1085, following a famine, *some rich men had to till their own land.* [My italics.] This was not only a disgrace but a dangerous state of affairs: manual labour was considered to be beneath the dignity of a ruler and to be seen engaging in physical work undermined his authority and thus destabilised the whole basis of the feudal hierarchy.

In the Norman castles, and later in the Elizabethan and Jacobean great houses, the kitchens were scenes of great plenty, with trenchers playing an important daily role. These were thick, stale slices of bread, four days old, made of wholewheat flour often mixed with barley or rye, served on platters of silver or pewter. The coarse bread soaked up the gravy and juices and at the end of the meal. The trenchers were given to the servants or to the dogs or occasionally to the poor at the gates. (Hence the expression, he's a great trencherman.) Moreover, in the great houses, the bread might now and then be enlivened by the addition of flavourings: wild garlic might be stirred into the dough, or herbs, or salmon roe, or even honey for a special sweet cake.

Even the most ascetic of monks had to eat, and according to the Old Irish *Rule of Ailbe*, the daily loaf of a monk weighed thirty ounces (850 g) and measured twelve inches (30 cm), probably in diameter. (A small loaf or bun was called a *tortine*, a diminutive from the Latin *torta*, meaning loaf, from which the French take their *tartine*.) The daily food of the ascetic Saint Ciaran was reported to consist of a barley-bun with fresh water and two roots of seaweed.

A Welcome Crop

A variety of grains and flours have been used to make bread in Ireland. An eighth-century law text *Bretha Dein Checht* lists seven types of cerealgrains. Some of these can be identified with confidence as bread wheat (*cruithnecht*), rye (*seagal/secal*) and the common oat (*coirce/corcae*), while the others are less certainly identified as spelt wheat, two-row barley, emmer wheat and six-row barley.

An old rhyme spells out the advantages of each main kind:

Rye bread will do you good,
Barley bread will do you no harm;
Wheaten bread will sweeten your blood,
Oaten bread will strengthen your arm.

In barley-growing districts, barley bread was baked, but, being coarser, it was generally less favoured than oat or wheat bread and was frequently part of the strict diets of the monastic orders. A *Life* of St Finian of Clonard tells us that on weekdays the saint partook of a piece of 'woody bread of barley' and a drink of cloudy water, while on Sundays and holy days, he ate a piece of wheaten bread with a morsel of salmon and drank a cup of mead or ale. (High living indeed.) Although barley was not so highly prized, it was still a welcome crop, and there is an old saying: *Is í an eorna nua tú a fheicáil*, which translates as 'Seeing you is like seeing the new (season's) barley.' Nowadays, barley is little used in bread-making, but is still grown because it is a staple of whiskey making, with malted barley being the 'malt' in malt whiskey/whisky.

While bread wheat, which originated in the Iran-Iraq area, is one of the world's most important food plants, Ireland is not really a suitable country in which to grow it, being too wet and cool. Rye, on the other hand, can grow in poorer soil than many cereals and can withstand cooler temperatures, being the most winter-hardy cereal and suitable for autumn sowing. The Anglo-Normans liked the taste of rye and often mixed it with wheat to make a bread known as 'maslin', which was found in the counties of Dublin, Meath, Wexford and Kildare.

Growing oats, on the other hand, is a good option in Ireland's damp, cool climate. For roughly two millennia oaten bread was most common. (According to legend, the nurse of young Colm Cille, St Columba, taught him his alphabet by shaping the letters on his oatcakes.)

In the nineteenth century, desperate families seeking to escape the famine and its aftermath stocked up for the journey with flat dry oatcakes to take on board ship. What's more, oatmeal porridge that is made extra thick and allowed to go cold can be cut into slabs to make a sustaining meal while away from home. In Scotland, kilted men going to war or on a long journey carried slabs of porridge in their sporrans. In Seamus Heaney's 'Requiem for the Croppies', men on the run, unsure of where their next meal might come from, stuffed the pockets of their greatcoats full of barley.

Wheaten bread was a great delicacy, given as tribute to chieftains and kings, and part of the celebratory food of feast days. It was always the most highly regarded.

Following their introduction by the Normans, peas and beans were grown in south-eastern counties, and when other crops failed, they would be ground up and the meal used to make a bread that was satisfactory, although never the bread of choice. The advantage of legumes and pulses is that they can be preserved, and peas and beans certainly made a contribution in the winter months when other foods were scarce, pea and bean pottages making a tasty meal, perhaps flavoured with a scrap of pig meat.

In the early nineteenth century, Indian meal, also called Indian corn or yellow meal, was imported occasionally, sometimes for use as cattle feed. After the Famine had really taken a grip, maize was shipped in from the United States by the British authorities. This maize meal was used for bread and for porridge and the people's early experiences of it were nothing short of disastrous, as we shall discover in the chapter on the potato and the Great Famine. Eventually, the people incorporated it into their baking repertoire, but other than in parts of Ulster, it is seldom seen today.

A seductive description, almost amounting to a recipe, comes from Maura Laverty's novel *Never No More* in which she describes how her grandmother made ash cakes of yellow meal during the 1920s. 'She scalded the Indian meal with salted boiling water, made it into a dough, rolled it thinly and cut it into little scones. A bed was made on the hearth by raking among the ashes on all sides. Each scone was rolled in a cabbage leaf and placed on the bed with hot ashes piled on top and left until cooked. The scorched leaf was then turned back to disclose fragrant little cakes which were delicious with rasher gravy and egg yolk.'

A Declining Tradition

Although Irish farmers always put pastoral farming above arable, Ireland managed to grow enough grain to keep going. Since might is right, the Anglo-Normans took over the best cereal-growing areas in the country, and the Irish cereal-growing tradition went into a decline. Writing in the late fourteenth century, the Catalan pilgrim Count John de Perilhos claims that no corn was sown in the O'Neill kingdom (the seat of the Earls of Tyrone, who had their main residence at Dungannon), although he mentions eating oatcakes.

As we know, the English from pre-Elizabethan times settled the best of the land in Ireland, and planted it not only with crops but with sympathisers, often confiscating estates from the native Irish and handing them over as rewards to loyal servants of the crown. The prime land around Dublin, stretching into counties Meath and Kildare, was known as the Pale, as a fence or paling was erected on parts of its perimeter. The land that was left in the west – literally beyond the Pale – was stony or boggy or both, and growing crops in it was a thankless task.

The lack of cereal-growing by the Irish was lamented by, for example, John Dymmok in his *Treatise of Ireland*, circa 1600, who linked the dearth of grain in the country to the 'wandering and idle life' of the people. However he also admitted that the heavy demands of the Irish landlords upon their tenants were the fundamental cause of the underdeveloped state of Irish agriculture. Farming is a long-term business, and no man dared risk making improvements to land – draining it, or building ditches, say – only to have his lord turn him off the improved land forthwith, or else raise the rent on what was now a more desirable property. Security of tenure was something that eluded the Irish peasantry over the centuries and its lack was a deep-rooted, pernicious ill.

Even where cereal-growing was practised, the unfamiliar methods used by the Irish were liable to disturb the English officials. The custom of separating the grain from the stalk by burning was remarked on by Fynes Moryson in his *Description of Ireland* in 1617, and forbidden by statute in 1634. The Irish found the practice of burning the sheaves extremely handy. Sometimes in harvest time, the corn could be reaped, the grain dried and ground into meal and the bread kneaded, baked and eaten all on the same day – from ear to mouth, you might say. This was most often true in the case of oats. The threshing, winnowing and drying were all accomplished at a stroke by burning the sheaf of oats. The husks and stalks burned away, leaving the grain behind, and the heat of the fire dried the corn, leaving it ready for grinding in the quern. The authorities frowned on this 'burning in the sheaf' as wasteful since the usable straw was burned away, and they passed several laws against the practice.

Despite discouragements, however, crop growing never completely died out even in the disadvantaged areas of the west and north-west, and was extensive in the more fertile lands in the midlands and along the stretches of the south and east coasts.

In times of plenty, meal was handed over to the women and they would make batches of bread, kneading the dough in a wooden trough, a losset, set aside for that purpose. But at other times, bread was scarce. In 1533 the King's Council in Ireland comments that the Irishry 'can live hardily without bread or other good victuals'.

Bread in the Oven

The larger monastic settlements were more like small villages, and it was a law of charity in the early Christian monasteries that no visitor or petitioner who came to their gates would be turned away hungry. The kitchens were equipped with impressive wall ovens – holes were let into the thick stone walls and a fire was lit inside of turf, timber and gorse bushes. So as to get the greatest heat possible, they were sealed with a heavy metal door, then as the fire began to die down, the coals and ashes were raked out and the bread put inside on the end of a long-handled spade. These wall ovens were capable of taking large quantities of bread, and the monks were always ready to feed an unknown number of travellers or beggars. Since a good many of the monasteries contained hospices for the care of the sick and dying, these people, too, needed wholesome food.

The early Christian brothers were undoubtedly devout and ascetic. None would resemble the twelfth-century English bishop and scholar, Robert Grosseteste, whose belly was so large that a half-moon had to be cut out of the refectory table at the place where he sat.

The wall oven was completely unknown in the basic Irish cabin, in part because the walls were often nothing but mud. If you wonder why the Irish never thought of building a communal oven, such as is found in rural villages elsewhere (in France or in Greece, say), one reason is that villages in the countryside in Ireland did not exist in the sense that 'village' suggests a cluster of houses centred on a church, perhaps an inn and a school. Cabins were disposed in the Irish landscape very differently, lacking a pattern that lent itself to communal activity. A townland was a more common term, denoting a strung-out group of dwellings, within reach of a church. Naturally, there were towns and cities (at one time Dublin was regarded as second only to London, as its magnificent buildings and parks testify) but the countryside was never developed in the English manner as the landlords, many of them absentees, could see no advantage in so doing.

Another reason for the lack of a communal oven, I surmise, is that even if families were poor, they had their pride and would baulk at letting neighbours know how much or how little they had to eat.

Originally, bread for the family was baked on a corner of the 'flag of the hearth', the large smooth flagstone in front of the fire that had been heated with a small fire, as hot as could be managed. (The rest of the floor was probably beaten earth.) Once the flag was judged hot enough, the coals would be moved elsewhere and the hot area dusted off to receive the cake of bread. While the loaf was cooking, the *bean an tí* (the woman of the house) would be heating another area, ready to shift the bread there as the first spot cooled down. Sometimes, a bakestone or, if it could be afforded, a flat iron griddle above a bed of hot embers was used. Griddle bread made of wheat was commoner in the south and east. (An Englishman visiting Ireland in 1620 remarked, 'If you stay half an hower you shall have a cake of meale unboulted and mingled with butter, baked on an yron called a girdle.') Always before putting the dough to cook the bread maker would cut a deep cross into it. You may think of this as testimony to the deeply religious spirit of the people, or you may think that it was handy to divide the bread into four pointers or farls, or both. (People still say 'farl' in Ulster and potato farls are, as visitors to any B&B will tell you, an essential part of the Ulster Fry.) The breads were sometimes baked directly on the turf embers, protected by a leaf such as a cabbage leaf, and this is a method I have tested myself with great success.

During the nineteenth century, the pot oven was introduced. This round cast-iron pot had a tight-fitting lid and a high slim handle which swivelled from two lugs on either side at the top. It was also known as a bastable, the word being a corruption of Barnstaple, the town in Devon where the iron cooking pots were made. No *bean an tí* would consider cooking a stew in her bread-making bastable: the pot was reserved for dry baking only, and another pot used for anything liquid. When I decided to have a day cooking in the old style with my pal Jane Hansell, we set out to bake a loaf of soda bread, some oatcakes, some potatoes and onions and to cook an entire salmon in two different wrappings. More of that below and in the chapter on fish, shellfish and seaweed. But we did not have a second bastable, so plans for a stew had to be postponed, rather than spoil a dry pot oven by making a wet meal in it.

An old Irish adage, '*Nua gacha bidh agus sean gacha dighe*', can be translated as 'The newest of food and the oldest of drink'. Irish women who baked bread daily were ashamed if an unexpected visit meant yesterday's bread had to be put out. Often, bread was baked just before a meal and eaten while warm. In more recent times, home-baked bread began to be seen as inferior to shop-bought baker's bread, especially white wheaten bread, and the *bean an tí* would be sure to buy it in if the priest were coming, which led to it becoming known as 'priests' bread'. Robert Lynd, writing of his travels in the west in 1909, records that he often received profuse apologies if there was only home-baked bread in the house.

An Instant Food

In Ireland, buttermilk is to be found in every shop. You can drink it – it's particularly good in hot weather – but it's seldom bought other than for baking. And no one thinks twice about whipping up a cake[1] of bread at short notice because no yeast is involved. No proving, no kneading, no rising. No fuss. The essence of making Irish brown bread or soda bread is that you can make it in a jiffy – indeed, you daren't hang around once you have mixed the bicarb with the buttermilk, because you have created a chemical reaction that will alter within a short time.

Many breads rely on the interaction of yeast with gluten during kneading, but to make Irish brown bread two of the oldest foods in

[1]   This use of the word 'cake' rather than 'loaf' is striking. When speaking English, Irish people differentiate between a cake (bread) and 'sweet cake', and since the Old Scandinavian word for a flattish round of bread (made from any cereal, leavened or not) is kaak, we may assume a connection.

Ireland, wheat flour and buttermilk, are leavened with bicarbonate of soda (often called bread soda). It mixes with acids in the buttermilk or sour milk and acts as the raising agent. If you can't get buttermilk, you can sour milk quite easily by adding two teaspoonfuls of lemon juice to each 225 ml of milk and leaving it for half an hour to thoroughly curdle. You can, if you must, use fresh milk, but this requires you to use baking powder (a mix of bicarbonate of soda and cream of tartar) instead and this can affect the taste.

My aunt, the late Mary-Kate Slattery, began to make soda bread (with a mixture of strong white and brown flours) when she was a girl, and until she reached ninety-five she was still baking every other day. I used to find it a lesson in itself to watch her stoop to the oven in the turf-fired range and pull out the cake of bread, tap it on the bottom and apply eighty-odd years of experience in deciding whether or not it needed a few more minutes. Her children, grandchildren and great-grandchildren all knew what was hidden beneath the clean tea towel beside the sink, where she always set the bread on its wire grid to cool, and the smell in the kitchen announced to all comers *This is a house where bread is still baked.*

Here is one recipe for making brown bread the Irish way: there is no single true recipe. Do not feel you have to stick religiously to the quantities listed here; if your dough is soft after adding only some of the buttermilk, don't feel obliged to use it all up. These instructions assume your bread is to be baked in a conventional oven. The older tradition was to bake it in an iron pot oven or bastable.

Irish Brown Bread

Makes one large cake or loaf.

450 g wholewheat flour (can also be called wholemeal)
175 g plain white flour
1 heaped tsp bicarbonate of soda
1 heaped tsp salt
450 ml buttermilk, added little by little

In addition, you may add any or all of the following:

A handful of pinhead oatmeal
A scatter of wheatgerm
A scatter of bran

Pre-heat your oven to 200°C/400°F/Gas Mark 6. Have all necessary materials to hand – this should be a swift operation.

Mix the flours, bicarbonate of soda and salt in a large mixing bowl. Add enough of the buttermilk to make a soft dough, then flour your hands and work the dough quickly and lightly until it is smooth. (Don't bash it as if you were working a yeast dough.)

Shape into a circle 4–5 cm thick, take a sharp knife and cut a deep cross into the surface. (Flouring the blade means it won't stick in the dough.) Place on a floured baking tray and bake for 40–45 minutes. You will know if it is fully cooked by tapping the bottom with the tips of your fingers. If it sounds hollow, it is cooked; otherwise, give it a couple of minutes more. Put the cake of bread on a rack to cool, covered in a clean tea towel to prevent the crust from becoming too hard.

To these basic recipes you can add your own touches. Some may add seeds, such as sesame or poppy. Traditionally, caraway seeds were added to give the bread a distinctive flavour. Some cooks swear by adding a little butter, rubbed into the flour at the beginning. Others add a beaten egg. Yet more add sugar or honey. I have even come across a recipe that recommends golden syrup and malt vinegar. It is up to you to create your own special brown bread. In place of the buttermilk, you may use sour milk or experiment with sheep's or goat's milk. (Bread made with goat's milk was called 'goaty bread'.)

Of course, bicarbonate of soda is a brash newcomer on the scene, certainly no older than the first half of the nineteenth century. Before that, bread was baked, but either no attempt was made to raise the bread (as in oatcakes) or else a different raising agent was used.

A popular raising agent was barm, the froth that forms on top of fermenting ale and a form of yeast. Since the purity of drinking water could not be taken for granted, and small or weak beer was often a safer option, every well-set-up household (monasteries included) brewed beer, and accordingly the supply of barm was plentiful. However, we are principally concerned not with the doings of the more affluent Irish, but with those of the vast majority of the people, for whom water, milk and buttermilk were the daily drink. A much more common form of leaven for them was a little bit of the previous dough (the principle behind all sourdough breads), or potato juice, made by grating potatoes and allowing the potato water to sour, or else sowans – of which more below.

Hannah Glasse, author of *The Art of Cookery Made Plain and Easy*, written in the mid-eighteenth century, claims to have learned about the sourdough method from the Dublin Society, who published this advice in 1747: 'Two pounds of dough from the last baking is kept in a wooden vessel covered well with flour. This is the leaven. The night before the next baking, this was worked with a peck of flour and warm water and kept warm. By morning this dough will have risen and is enough to mix two or three bushels of flour worked up with warm water and salt. The fresher the leaven, the less sour the bread.'

Sowans. (What a word! Can't you hear it in the mouths of Chaucer's pilgrims?) Sowans refers to a drink made by soaking the inner husks of oats or the unsifted, milled grains in water, and letting them stand uncovered, until the natural yeasts that float around in the air settle and start to ferment it to produce a sourish drink.

Although I had read that the sowans were sometimes left for as long as three weeks, from my own experiment I saw that after only two days the oat bran put steeping in cold water had separated into a thin, clear liquid below, with a whitey-grey, slightly thicker film floating on top. Perhaps I am more adventurous than most, but I found the taste of the thin liquid sharp and not unpleasing, certainly thirst-quenching.

By skimming off the top whitish liquid, you get what is known as bull's milk, and this could be used for bread-making, or as a substitute for milk in your tea. It was part of the prescribed diet of the monks of certain strict orders and on days of 'black fast', Spy Wednesday and Good Friday, it was used by everyone. One report from the Glens of Antrim about the magical and romantic properties of sowans had it that 'If you stirred it a certain way and then gave the liquid to your boy to drink, you had him hooked.'

Should you choose not to leaven your bread with barm, nor potato juice, nor yet sowans, there is still the chance that buttermilk alone will raise your bread, but you mustn't count on it.

Porridge and Stirabout

In earlier centuries, long before bread soda came along to aerate and raise them, cakes of bread were usually flattish and heavy, and alternative ways of eating cereal were common. Freshly ground oatmeal mixed with butter was often served as iron rations to soldiers on active service, a mixture sometimes referred to as *meanadhach*, the same name also given, confusingly, to a watery gruel. The first mention we have of it is in a record of the diet given to the monks at Culdee, who lived according to the ninth-century Rule of Tallaght. Centuries later,

Edmund Campion in his *History of Ireland*, 1571, notes that 'Oatmeal and butter they crame together.'

Cereals were also likely to be eaten in various semi-liquid states: in gruels and porridges and preparations resembling today's muesli. For the toothless, or those with bad teeth, porridge was a boon, as it required no chewing and any extra nourishment that came along – perhaps a sup of milk, a knob of butter, an egg or a slice of apple – could be stirred in.

The very thinnest porridge was no more than an oatmeal water: *brothchan* or *meanadhach*, similar to today's barley water. (Remember when lemon barley water refreshed Wimbledon players?) A later version of this oatmeal water, much loved by travelling pedlars, was *porter meala* which they made by pouring a measure of porter (stout or ale) over some dried meal and letting it steep a while before they drank it.

Thicker porridges were taken for breakfast and supper alike. In the 'Vision' or 'Aisling' of Mac Con Glinne, the poet drools about 'fair white porridge made of sheep's milk' and 'porridge, the treasure that is smoothest and sweetest of all'. And then there was stirabout. The Brehon laws laid down that 'children of the inferior grade are fed to a bare sufficiency on stirabout made of oatmeal on buttermilk or water, and it is taken with stale butter. The sons of chieftain grades are fed to satiety on stirabout made of barley meal upon new milk taken with fresh butter. The sons of kings are fed upon stirabout made of wheaten meal upon new milk taken with honey.' (Even among porridges, wheatmeal was the most highly regarded.)

Stirabout was a thicker mixture, a porridge as we know it today, made by trickling the husked and split grains, what we call today pinhead oatmeal, into water which is kept stirred to prevent lumps forming, as in making a risotto, and cooked for about half an hour. (These days pinhead oatmeal is made of oats that have been brushed, polished and cut into three pieces.)

My daily breakfast consists of pinhead oatmeal porridge. I soak plenty overnight, cook it the next day and then I have enough for three or four days. It is rather like a risotto in texture and is wonderful with some natural yoghurt.

The porridge leftovers could be used to make *leite faoi chupóig*, cold thick porridge, which was cut into slices and wrapped in vegetable leaves, either cabbage or dock, and baked directly on the turf embers. *Praibin* was made by coarsely grinding mixed grains that had been first toasted in a dry pan over the fire and then served with milk or cream, and honey or salt.

We might also return here to sowans, made from the fine husks of oats, sometimes called sids. If the sowans was boiled, it thickened to the consistency of blancmange or thick custard, and this food was commonly found in Ireland, Scotland, the north of England and Wales. As it happens, the Welsh word for it, *llymru*, was corrupted into English as 'flummery'. (In Co Mayo, a prime insult for a stupid person was to call him or her 'as thick as flummery' and 'flummery' was also used to describe idle, unreliable talk, the same as 'blarney'.) Nevertheless, flummery was regarded as a treat for it provided a creamy but bland base, ideal for seasoning. If sugar or honey and cream were added to the oatmeal jelly, it was pronounced delicious.

A Dublin recipe dating from 1804 is vague on quantities, but for curiosity's sake I reproduce it here.

Flummery

Get some oatmeal. Put it in a broad, deep pan. Then cover it with water. Stir it together and let it stand 12 hours. Then pour off the water clear and put on a good deal of fresh water. Shift it again in 12 hours and so on in 12 more. Then pour off the water clear and strain the oatmeal through a coarse hair sieve, and pour into a saucepan, keeping it stirring all the time with a pot-stick till it boils and is very thick. Then pour into dishes. When cold, turn it onto plates and eat with what you please, either wine and sugar, or beer and sugar, or milk. It eats very pretty with cider and sugar.

Irish Crispbread

Irish oatcakes are baked very thin without leaven. A seventeenth-century traveller in Ireland wrote, 'Their general food is a thin oatcake which they bake upon a broad flat stone made hot, a little sheep's milk cheese or goat's milk, boiled leeks and some roots.' Writing in 1681, Thomas Dinley gave the diet of the vulgar Irish as potatoes, new milk, whey, curds and a large oatcake a foot and a half in breadth, baked before an open fire. He adds, 'They use wheat or rye for great days.'

Irish oatcakes, much as Scottish ones, consist of coarse oatmeal, salt and water, the water being added hot to help make a paste that will hold. The north of Ireland is the richest source of baking lore and variety, with soda farls and boxty being particularly northern. The plantation of Ulster centuries ago by Scots immigrants established a permanent influence on its culinary traditions and the Scots are, of course, famous bakers of the plain persuasion.

The heavy griddle, usually some 45 cm across, was the essential piece of kitchen equipment. It was most often laid flat on a little three-legged trivet standing over hot coals and heated ready to receive the oatcakes. The art of successful oatcake making is to roll the dough out thinly, scattering pinhead oatmeal onto the work surface to be picked up by the dough. The Irish tradition is to cook one side of these little flat cakes on a griddle until they begin to curl, then set them to harden beside the fire on an iron three-legged stand. This little stand, called in northern Ireland a hardening or harnen stand, was usually made by the blacksmith and could be quite fancy. The poorest of the poor put their oaten cake before the fire supported by a three-pronged stick and a three-legged stool against which to prop it, or some would have a smooth flat stone that they warmed to serve the same purpose. Originally only oatmeal was used in making oatcakes, but a firmer oatcake results if a little flour is added.

Easy Oatcakes

This recipe makes at least a dozen oatcakes, depending on thickness.

225 g medium oatmeal, plus a little in reserve

100 g sifted flour

50 ml boiling water

2 good tbs melted butter or lard or even bacon fat

1 tsp baking powder

1 tsp salt

Mix the oatmeal and flour together, then pour boiling water into a measuring jug and stir in the fat. Add the baking powder and salt to the water and pour it into the flour and oatmeal mixture. Knead quickly and lightly into a ball to make a firm dough, then sprinkle a board with more oatmeal and press the dough into a flattish circle. Roll this out lightly and fairly thin, then slide it onto a warm baking tray that has been lightly greased and cut it into eight farls, or triangles with rounded edges.

Bake at 180°C/350°F/Gas Mark 4 for about 25 minutes, then allow to cool and keep in an airtight tin.

Although people ate oatcakes fresh, many an emigrant carried a bag of oatcakes or oaten bread across the Atlantic.

On the day set aside for old-style cooking, Jane Hansell and I were in my kitchen, where I had made a good fire in the giant fireplace with turf cut in my own bog. We made the bread first, using the first recipe listed above, setting the loaf (or cake, as it is often called) into the pre-heated iron bastable or pot oven and then putting on the lid upside down, so as to hold some hot turf embers, thus making sure of a more even spread of heat. We set this bastable squarely in the fire, then, while it was cooking, we suspended an iron flat griddle from the crane that we'd swung out right over the fire. If you haven't experienced a turf fire, you might be expecting flames, but in fact turf doesn't need a draught underneath it, nor does it burn with a lively flame, like coal or wood. We had a job keeping the oatcakes from crumbling, in their uncooked state, but once they'd been over the fire a little while, they kept their consistency and we were able to prop them up in an improvised harnen stand, a bit like a toast rack. The thing with oatcakes is to leave them to dry a good while, and then while they are hardening (surely the etymology of harnen) you can get on with the next thing. In our case, this was putting washed whole potatoes and onions still in their skins into the bastable once the bread was done. This was then set back on the fire while we prepared the salmon. See Chapter Six for an account of our further adventures!

Oats are still used extensively in Ireland today, for soups and broths and for grinding to make the finer textured oatmeals used in baking. Coarse ground oatmeal is used to make porridge and oatcakes and for coating fish and meat before frying or grilling, as well as in stuffings. Fine ground oatmeal, sometimes called oat flour, is a good baby food and can be used in bread, cakes and pastry. In these days of growing health consciousness, the bran or outer skin of the oats and the inner germ of the grains are often separated from the oats during processing and sold separately, the bran as a source of fibre and the germ as a vitamin and mineral supplement.

Now that the old mills have virtually disappeared, you have a job to find stoneground oats, as what are commonly sold as porridge oats, rolled oats and flaked oats (all more or less the same thing) are oats softened by steam and put through heavy rollers, a process which partly cooks the oats and makes them quicker to cook than pinhead. For my part, I think pinhead oatmeal makes a porridge superior to that made with any of the other oatmeals, a porridge that is nutty in flavour with a lovely, nubby texture. Always cook it with a little salt and then, while purists may salt it a little more, hedonists will add cream and moist dark muscovado sugar, maple syrup or honey.

Cheese and Biscuits

Aside from the various non-yeast breads, Ireland has also given the world two other baker's delights – water biscuits and cream crackers.

Water biscuits, those thin little biscuits that go so well with cheese, were first made in 1851 in Waterford by William Beale Jacob and his brother, both Quakers who had come to live in Ireland in the 1670s, their name first being recorded as Yego or Igoe. The influence of the Quakers in Ireland in many fields of activity is out of all proportion to their numbers. To single out but a few in the food world, there are the Jacobs family (who were also responsible for inventing cream crackers), the Bewley family, who were behind the coffee houses that were for so long a Dublin institution, and the dynasty of Allens, sprung from Myrtle and Ivan Allen of Ballymaloe.

To make water biscuits, you need very little:

Water Biscuits

450 g plain white flour	**150 ml milk**
Pinch of salt	**2 heaped tbs butter**

Sift the flour and salt together, then heat the milk and melt the butter in it. Add the flour and mix well to make a smooth dough. Roll out thinly on a floured surface and cut into 5 cm or 7 cm circles. I used the rim of a wine glass to stamp the circles out. Place on lightly greased baking sheets, making sure they do not touch, prick all over with a fork and bake at 200°C/440°F/Gas Mark 6 for about 10 minutes or until the biscuits are pale brown. They retain their crispness well.

Sweet Delights

Thus far, we have considered types of savoury bread, but now and again the sweet tooth was given something to sink into. Saffron is one of the most expensive foodstuffs on the planet, because of the immense amount of labour required to produce even a small amount of it. The stamens of a certain type of crocus are picked by hand and then dried – a very labour-intensive operation. However, saffron was grown in Ireland in the eighteenth century and since labour was to be had for little or for free, it was less precious than it is today. Saffron 'cake' bread was made with warm water in which saffron stamens were steeped and this was mixed into a yeast-risen dough. The cakes were sometimes, not always, sweetened with honey or sugar, and their colour was especially pleasing.

In poorer homes, it did not take much ingenuity to transform white soda bread into a fruit loaf. Here is a recipe for what was variously called Curranty Cake, Fruit Soda or Fruit Bannock (in the north-east).

Fruit Soda

450 g plain flour	50 g butter
1 heaped tsp bicarbonate of soda	100 g dried fruit – sultanas
1 tsp salt	for preference
50 g caster sugar	450 ml buttermilk

Sieve the dry ingredients into a large mixing bowl and rub in the butter until the mixture resembles fine breadcrumbs. Now stir in the dried fruit and make a well in the centre. Pour the buttermilk into the well and mix to form a softish dough.

Lightly grease a shallow 20 cm cake tin and turn the dough into it. Sprinkle the surface with a little plain flour and bake in a pre-heated fairly hot oven, 220°C/425°F/Gas Mark 7, for 10 minutes, then reduce the heat to 200°C/400°F/Gas Mark 6, and cook for 40–45 minutes more until the bread is risen and brown. To test the cake, if in doubt, insert a skewer into an inconspicuous part, perhaps where there is a crack; if it comes out clean, the cake is baked.

Remove it from the oven and cover with a tea towel. When it is cool enough to handle, lift it out of the tin, wrap it in the cloth and when it is cold, slice thinly and spread with butter and jam or honey.

Continuing the bicarbonate of soda motif that runs through so much Irish baking, another variation on a theme is the fruit scone made with buttermilk.

This recipe should make a dozen scones, which should be light and spongy in texture. Speed of working and having the oven pre-heated are the two secrets of a light scone.

Buttermilk Fruit Scones

225 g plain flour
1 tsp bicarbonate of soda
1 tsp cream of tartar
¼ tsp salt
25 g butter or margarine
25 g caster sugar

25 g dried fruit (this was sufficient fruit in hard times, but nowadays we might like to increase the quantity a little)
Scant 200 ml buttermilk (or sour milk)

Pre-heat the oven to 220°C/425°F/Gas Mark 7.

Sieve the flour, bicarbonate of soda and cream of tartar together into a large mixing bowl, stir in the salt and rub in the butter or margarine until the mixture resembles fine breadcrumbs. Stir in the sugar and fruit, making sure it is well distributed. Make a well in the centre and pour in the buttermilk, stirring it in swiftly to make a soft dough. Turn out onto a floured work surface and roll out to a thickish circle. Cut into scones and place on a hot, lightly floured baking sheet. If you like, at this point you can brush the surface of each scone with beaten egg or a little milk to give them an appetising glaze when cooked.

Bake in the pre-heated oven for 15 minutes or more until they are risen and golden in colour.

Ideally, they should be eaten directly from the oven, with butter and jam, or cream and jam. If you must leave them until the next day, toast them. A variant of the above recipe can be made by adding one or two tablespoons of treacle, blended with the buttermilk.

Cakes and Ale

In the Pale of Dublin and the Anglo-Norman strongholds of the east, servants used to bake a rich plum cake decorated with almond paste – a simnel cake, which they took home on Mothering Sunday, the Sunday before Lent. In *Ulysses*, Joyce describes a funeral scene with hawkers selling simnel cakes outside Glasnevin cemetery. This, however, is a tradition imported from England, and not native to Ireland. Talking of English imports, my friend Mary-Jo Dermody told me that another name for Spotted Dick cake (a version of the English pudding) was Railway Cake because in most cases there was only the odd currant strung out here and there, like stations on a railway line.

More peculiarly Irish is the cake dance. This was held on Easter Sunday or Whit Sunday, occasionally on a 'pattern day' or other festive occasion, when friends and neighbours would gather for a welcome break from their hardworking lives. Often it was a fund-raising dance, the participants being invited to pay their way in, and the proceeds going to some local good cause. The eponymous cake could be a griddle, barley or oaten bannock, but if the times permitted, it might be a currant loaf or even a barm brack. (This latter is a sweet cake made of yeast dough and speckled with dried fruit and spices, of which more below.)

The cake was prominently displayed on a fine white cloth spread over a milk churn or butter dash, for the dance usually took place in a shed or barn. Neighbours would assemble, and musicians would strike up to signal the start of the evening. It was a poor parish that could not raise a fiddler or two, with perhaps someone to play the flute or the pipes. The winners were the pair judged to have been lightest on their feet or those who never sat down, or the couple who had just announced their plan to marry. Whichever of them took the cake usually divided it there and then among their friends. (The expression 'That takes the biscuit!' or 'That takes the cake!' is derived from this.)

This tradition of the cake dance was sometimes formalised. Readers of the *Dublin Evening Post* of 1 October 1734 were informed: 'On Thursday next Mary Kelly at the Queen's Head in Glasnevin near this city will have a fine plum cake to be danced for by the young men and maidens of the country who are generously invited by her, no doubting but they will be as pleased with her ale as they are with her cake.'

Another cake of old lineage is seed cake. In 1600 an English traveller noted, 'In cities they have such bread as ours but of a sharp flavour and some mingled with aniseeds and baked like a cake, and that only in houses of the better sort.' From the sixteenth century on, caraway seeds were much in vogue, and were often used in seed cake. This plain sweet cake seems to have fallen out of favour, but for a time it lingered on in convent kitchens, and it would be good to see a revival of it. On no account be tempted to add spices or dried fruit – you will ruin its elegant, subtle flavour.

Seed Cake, also called Carvie Cake

225 g caster sugar
225 g butter
4 eggs, whisked to a froth
250 g self-raising flour

½ tsp baking powder
1 heaped tbs caraway seeds
3–4 tbs milk

Cream the sugar and butter well, and beat in the eggs a little at a time, adding a small handful of the sifted flour with each. Then fold in the remaining flour, the baking powder and the caraway seeds. Add the milk to make a soft mixture. Put into a greased and lined 20 cm cake tin and bake in a pre-heated oven at 160°C/325°F/Gas Mark 3 for 1½ to 1¾ hours. Leave in the tin for 10 minutes, then cool on a wire rack.

Three more cakes cannot be overlooked, as they are regular features of the Irish tea table: the tea brack, the boiled fruit loaf and the porter cake.

Tea brack makes use of what has been freely available in every Irish kitchen from the latter part of the nineteenth century: tea. In fact, the Irish are the world's greatest tea drinkers – perhaps because, contrary to the stereotype, many an Irish person is a teetotaller. The cake is moist, dark in colour and rich in fruit and has a glossy shine on top, just inviting you to cut into it.

Tea Brack

You need to start this cake well in advance of baking it – the first step should ideally be taken the night before.

225 g sultanas	350 g plain flour
225 g raisins	2 tsp baking powder
50 g mixed candied peel	1 tsp ground nutmeg
225 g soft dark brown sugar	1 tsp cinnamon
(organic sugar is incomparably	2 eggs
the best)	1 tbs runny honey or a thick
375 ml strong hot black tea	sugar and water mix

Into a large mixing bowl put the fruit, peel and sugar and pour the hot tea over them. Stir well to dissolve the sugar and let it all soak overnight to plump out the fruit. (Do not skip this stage.)

Next day, sieve the flour, baking powder and spices together and then little by little mix first the beaten eggs, then the flour into the fruit mixture until all is incorporated. Line the bottom and sides of a 20 cm x 7.5 cm cake tin with greaseproof paper and brush with a little melted butter. Pour the mixture into the cake tin, smooth the top with the flat of a knife and bake in an oven pre-heated to 160°C/325°F/Gas Mark 3 for roughly 1½ hours.

Ten minutes before the baking time is up, heat the honey in a small pan and brush onto the surface of the tea brack. Pop it back into the oven to finish. Remove and allow to cool in the tin for 15 minutes, then turn onto a wire rack. This will keep for a week or so in an airtight tin. Some people slice it and butter it, but I think that is gilding the lily.

This next cake is made in an economical way, but it rivals the more expensive rich fruit cake for flavour.

Boiled Fruit Cake

300 ml water
100 g butter or margarine
225 g soft brown sugar (organic
   for preference)
225 g currants

225 g sultanas
3 tsp mixed spice
350 g plain flour
1 tsp bicarbonate of soda
1 egg, beaten

Line the bottom and sides of a 20 cm round, deep cake tin and brush with melted butter or oil. Put the water, butter or margarine, sugar, fruit and spice into a large saucepan. Bring gradually to boiling point point and simmer for 20 minutes. Set to one side to go cold.

Sieve the flour and bicarbonate of soda together and stir into the fruit mixture together with the beaten egg. Turn the whole thing into the cake tin, smooth the top and bake in a pre-heated oven at 180°C/350°F/Gas Mark 4 for 10 to 15 minutes, then reduce the heat to 160°C/325°F/Gas Mark 3 for another hour and 15 minutes. If in doubt that the cake is cooked, insert a fine skewer into the centre. If it comes out clean, remove the tin, allow the cake to cool for 10 minutes, then turn it out onto a wire rack. To keep, wrap well in greaseproof paper or foil and store in an airtight tin.

Porter cake is a classic Irish cake, which would originally have called for porter, alas no longer available; instead, we have to use stout, a stronger version of porter. It takes willpower to leave the cake to mature, but it is important to do so.

Porter Cake

450 g plain flour
1 tsp mixed spice
1 tsp cinnamon
1 tsp ground nutmeg
½ tsp ground cloves
150 g raisins
150 g sultanas
100 g mixed chopped peel
Grated rind of 1 lemon

300 g soft brown sugar (organic
   for preference)
4 eggs, beaten
1 tsp bicarbonate of soda
150 ml stout (Guinness,
   Beamish, Murphy's, etc.)
A little melted butter or oil to
   grease the tin

Line the bottom and sides of a large cake tin (23 cm x 9 cm) and brush with melted butter or oil. Sieve the flour and spices into a large bowl, then rub the butter into the dry ingredients until it resembles fine breadcrumbs. Next, stir in the fruit, peel, lemon rind and sugar, then add the beaten eggs. Dissolve the bicarbonate of soda in the stout and add to the mixture. Mix everything together well and pour into the cake tin.

Bake in a pre-heated oven at 160°C/325°F/Gas Mark 3 for 1 hour, then reduce the temperature to 150°C/300°F/Gas Mark 2. Cover the top of the cake loosely with a sheet of greaseproof paper and bake for a further 1½ to 2 hours.

At the end, the kitchen should be fabulously fragrant and the cake a deep brown colour. Leave in the tin until completely cold, then remove the paper and store in an airtight tin.

Unlike most cakes and breads in the traditional Irish baking repertoire, barm brack requires yeast of the type that is usually bought from the baker.

Barm brack is strongly associated with Hallowe'en and by tradition a ring is wrapped in a scrap of paper and poked into the dough. Supposedly whoever gets the ring in their slice is to be married the following spring. When a small coin is found, its lucky finder is on the way to riches.

During the run-up to the 2008 presidential election in the United States, it was thrilling for the Irish to discover Obama's mother had links to the village of Moneygall, on the Tipperary–Offaly border. The election took place that November and the local baker had the wit to produce a Hallowe'en cake that he called the Barm Barack!

CHAPTER FOUR

ON THE HOOF

This conversation, overheard in my local butcher's, sums up with poetic concision attitudes that people have towards meat nowadays.

> *Male customer*: I want a joint for the weekend.
> *Butcher*: Yes, what will I give you?
> *Male customer*: A piece of meat.
> *Butcher, his hand hovering over the array*: Pork? Lamb? Beef?
> *Male customer*: Well, you know what they say. Fish is fish and pork is pig, but only beef is meat.

There you have it in a nutshell. Forget about Irish stew being the national dish – it most definitely isn't. A good case could be made for bacon and cabbage as the national dish – especially in rural areas. But given the choice, most Irish people opt for beef.

Beef sold in Ireland can be among the best found anywhere. My local butcher, Gene McEntee, knows where his animals come from, slaughters them himself, hangs the meat for a set number of days and swears he would rather die than release it before time. 'Nowadays I let my beef mature for fourteen days. By the time a person gets it, it could even be seventeen days, which is perfect to me. If someone comes to me and says, "Have you any rib roast left?" I'll say, "No." It's not that I haven't any left – I've loads of it, but I just won't sell it. Not till it's ready.'

Exceptional, you say? Yes, admirable, but I could walk into my local supermarket and buy very decent beef, too. And I have never seen in Ireland the pale pink mounds that are labelled 'Economy mince' in some British supermarkets. Irish people are very particular about certain foods, and beef is one of them.

If the history of food in Ireland is also to some extent the history of its agriculture, the importance of the pastoral tradition cannot be overestimated. Meat and milk were the rewards of owning cattle, and for centuries wealth and influence were counted not by how much money you had but by how many head of cattle. The old poem that begins 'Oh woman of three cows' exhorts her not to be haughty or proud just because she is so rich.

Cattle: Cornerstones of the Irish Economy

If there is a country in Europe less sympathetic than Ireland to the vegetarian principle, I am not sure which it is. Irish people, having been so long deprived of meat, now can't get enough of it. If you start the day in an Irish hotel or B&B the 'full Irish breakfast' contains four meaty elements: smoked or unsmoked rashers of bacon, white pudding, black pudding and sausages. The novelist Kate O'Brien detested 'the big fry'. 'That fearful meal, of which the whole hotel reeks between the hours of six and seven-thirty . . . the crowded platter of fried meats, the dull triangles of toast always of the same bread and cut the same way, the strong tea (which is the best of the awful spread) and the truly scandalous, cheap jam.'

Because Ireland escaped from grinding poverty comparatively recently, the old ways of shopping and cooking are still largely in place, especially outside the cities. There are, however, some distinct improvements. Dorothy Hartley, writing in the 1930s, protested, 'An awful thing in an Irish town is a butcher's shop . . . Calves, sheep and pigs hang out, whole, their bloody heads and severed feet dripping to the pavement. Tongues are skewered onto boards and split skulls arranged in pyramids. Hearts and windpipes sway gruesomely and drip to the pavement from outthrust iron hooks . . . I have seen garlands round the slitted throats and bunches of flowers, red spotted, thrust into the gaping mouths.'

Nowadays, Irish butchers (or victuallers – a gorgeously Chaucerean word) are knowledgeable and hygienic. Their little sprigs of plastic parsley are perky, and their trade is usually in the more sightly parts of animals. Most importantly, they are still around, for in most of Britain the local butcher is becoming as obsolete as the candlestick-maker. They scarcely exist in the USA, I believe.

Early Days

The very earliest settlers we know of in Ireland were hunter-gatherers whose entire lives were taken up in a battle for survival. Apart from picking wild fruits, raiding beehives and storing up hazelnuts, they fished, hunted and trapped game and wildfowl, every kill a victory snatched, as it were, from the jaws of other predators – the wolf, the hawk, the fox and the otter. But man is wily, capable of setting snares, digging pits and wielding weapons, so he was able to fell wild boars and the native red deer, to trap hares (rabbits had not yet come to Ireland) and snare native fowl such as pigeon, duck and red grouse. In all probability, these early people made fires and skewered small pieces of meat above them or simply ate the food raw.

A second wave of settlers was less nomadic, building settlements consisting of wood and mud houses with hearths. We know from excavations that they kept seed grain in storage pits, for they had discovered the benefits of growing grain – a godsend, particularly in the harsh winter season. We have found the polished stone axes they used to make clearings in the forest, and similar blades used to break up the soil.

Nevertheless, the amount of tillage was not enormous. This is hardly surprising, for the vast amount of energy expended on making the land productive must have nearly outweighed the returns. Without metal blades to cut the soil (let alone the sophisticated piece of engineering that is the plough), the business of preparing land for crops was clearly backbreaking. Of course, much of Ireland was covered by forest and the amount of open land for grazing was finite, so the principal purpose of the land clearances may have been to create more land for animals to graze.

Searching through piles of rubbish is one of the most profitable occupations that archaeologists engage in, for the refuse from those early dwelling places was disposed of in large middens located in the immediate vicinity, and refuse is a prime source of information. Thanks to detective work, we know that three-quarters of the cattle bones found at a crannóg (a settlement built on stilts in a lake, accessible only by a causeway) at Moynagh, Co Meath, are from animals under three years of age and the bones are broken in a way that shows marrow has been extracted. The sagas of the Ulster cycle tell us that marrow was believed to have healing properties and was used as a poultice to cure the wounds of warriors.

The huge numbers of cattle bones excavated from primitive sites point to a pastoral way of farming rather than one based on tillage, and the rearing of cattle was at the heart of it. For the mass of the Irish, this cattle culture was to survive the coming of the Vikings, Christianity, the Normans, even Cromwell; it was only at the beginning of the eighteenth century that circumstances forced the peasant into eating the potato and little else. At the time of writing the country is once again full of cattle, although how much longer this will continue is questionable – small farmers are becoming an endangered species.

Celtic Cattle

With its highly sophisticated knowledge of genealogy, astronomy, architecture and civil engineering, early Celtic society was anything but primitive – a look at the stupendous structures at Newgrange, Co Meath, will dispel for ever that idea. Key figures in the society were the druids, whose rites and interventions were respected by all and the major feasts over which they presided had a special significance for the agricultural year.

The early Celtic feast of Imbolg, held on the first day of February, and later Christianised as St Brigid's Day, marked the date that ewes would come into milk for the coming season. The word derives from the early language of the Irish and means 'sheep's milk'.

Bealtaine, held at the start of May, marked the beginning of summer, a time when cattle could once again be driven out to open grazing. To symbolise this, two great bonfires were lit and cattle were driven between them to ensure that they remained healthy and safe from disease, the purification rites supervised by chanting druids.

Lughnasa came to be celebrated on the last Sunday in July. The feast of the god Lugh, it was essentially a harvest festival, with games and ceremonial garlands. It became Christianised and is the traditional day for the Croagh Patrick pilgrimage in Co Mayo.

The feast of Samhain, when the main dish seems to have been the *banb samna* – the piglet of Samhain – was held at the other end of the year, on the last day of October, and marked the end of the free grazing season when the herds were brought together. Only the best animals, fit for breeding, were spared from slaughter, for there was not enough food to see the whole herd through the winter. This time of mass butchery gave the whole extended family, or tuath, an occasion to eat their fill and feast for days on end, setting themselves up for the hard times to come.

For the farmer, the festivals were important because a young animal rose in value at these times. A female calf worth two scruples at birth became worth three at its first Samhain, four at the following Bealtaine and so on until it reached its maximum value of twenty-four scruples.

In Celtic Ireland, from about 200 BC onwards, lawyers, or *brehons*, laid down the rights and social position of everyone. Under this dispensation, a man's wealth and social position were judged by the number of cattle he possessed. Ownership of land was not yet a yardstick; indeed, land was measured in terms of the number of cows it could sustain. Cattle were the cornerstones of the economy: the basic unit of value was a cow – the price of a bondsman or slave, for example, was four cows. Legal compensations were measured in cattle. (There were no prisons under the Brehon laws; instead, anyone who committed a crime had to pay compensation to his victim or victim's family.)

Guarding the herd was one of the most important jobs in those times. Cattle raids were rife, not only because the rustlers wanted to appropriate wealth for themselves, but also because a king without cattle could be usurped: cattle-raiding was a recognised form of warfare. Moreover, when the country was full of young men bursting with testosterone, cattle-raiding was a fine adventure. Young nobles took part, and a successful foray into another king's territory was part of a prince's coming of age.

The most famous cattle raid of all is that of Cooley, immortalised in the great saga known as the *Táin Bó Cúailnge*. The story goes that Queen Méabh of Connacht makes a tally of her possessions and those of her husband, Ailill, and becomes furious at discovering that Ailill has one bull more than she does. Nothing will satisfy her other than besting him, so setting her sights on a famous bull of Ulster, the Donn of Cooley, Méabh sends her soldiers with orders to carry it off to Connacht, which they do. However, the brown bull of Cooley kills one of Ailill's bulls, thus equalising the herds of the two rulers. After the warriors of Ulster recover from a curse they have been under, they go in search of the Donn, manage to retrieve it, and are on their way back home with it when the bull's mighty heart bursts and it dies.

If the old sagas are to be believed, overlords and kings went in for conspicuous consumption, throwing lavish feasts, at which meat a-plenty was served, while their bondsmen and clients were lucky to get the occasional piece of offal. Despite these almost competitive meatfests, cattle were kept principally not for their flesh but for milk and milk products. Cattle were, as we shall see, also useful as draught animals. In addition, they gave manure for the ground, provided hides for garments and vessels made of leather (treated leather was the skin of the currach, the native small rowing boat), plus horn, a tough material from which to make kitchen utensils, spoons and the like. They even provided much-needed protein in times of severe need, when the hungry would open a vein in the necks of the cattle and bleed them. The blood was either drunk or left to coagulate and then made into a kind of pudding. Bleeding was also, in early times, a rite with sacrificial significance.

Skilled stockmen, the Irish depended on cattle, sheep and pigs for their livelihood. Ireland long ago was reported to be a green island, ideal for grazing cattle. Giraldus Cambrensis claims that 'the grass is green in the fields in winter, just the same as in summer. Consequently, the meadows are not cut for fodder, nor do they ever build stalls for the beasts.'

As usual, Giraldus is inaccurate. Ireland in those days knew some long, cold winters and there are several reports of cattle being famished to death, resulting in want, famine and disease. In AD 961 the *Annals of Clonmacnoise* state, 'there was a great dearth of cattle this year and many diseases reigned over Ireland by reason of the great frosts and snow which procured the intemperature of the air'. The period when animals are most vulnerable to cold and lack of food is at the end of winter and in 1107 a heavy snowfall on 13 March, lasting a day and a night, was responsible for widespread loss of cattle when the limited amount of winter fodder was exhausted. Later on, farmers built shelters: a pigsty, a calfpen, a sheep pen and a cowhouse, or *botheg*. (The origin of the word 'bothy', commonly used in Scotland and Ulster, becomes evident.)

Anglo-Norman Attitudes

Although the Irish never welcomed invaders, the coming of the Anglo-Normans improved life for many, inasmuch as there was more food available. The bondsman did not better his lot, but merely changed his name and became a serf; the client found he had now to pay his food rent and other dues to the lord of the manor. But the Normans were good at managing and moreover they introduced new sources of food.

The old way of the native Irish was something of a hand-to-mouth existence, which suited a national genius that is uncomfortable with too much organisation. Fynes Moryson, the Tudor commentator, observed that when the Irish kill a cow 'they distribute to all to be devoured at the same time'. (This is not so careless. Meat perishes quickly.)

Tending cattle and letting them roam to graze, moving them from one pasture to another was the norm and this freedom was disapproved of by those who came to Ireland to impose their ways. The Normans chose land as their principal value system, and the Irish were obliged to recognise this. Attachment to the land did indeed take root – so much so that every inch of land has, since that time, been fiercely defended. John B. Keane's *The Field* is eloquent on this.

The attitude to life that prevailed in Ireland contrasted sharply with the methodical organisation of the Norman incomers. The Irish did engage in trade, because we know that a very healthy amount of wine was imported – much of it claret – but the Normans saw great potential in growing crops to sell. Counting their wealth in terms of acres, they saw good land undeveloped and crying out to be exploited.

The Normans wanted to be assured of reliable sources of food, particularly for the uncertain winter months, and accordingly brought with them freshwater fish to be kept in ponds, rabbits to breed in managed warrens and doves (pigeons) to breed in dovecotes. In addition, they introduced the common hare to course alongside the native hare and brought in fallow deer to roam the woods along with the native red deer. Hawking, coursing hares, hunting deer and wild boar were all sports practised with gusto. Other foods the Normans brought in were peas and beans (which could be ground to make meal in times of hardship) and flax for linen.

The market place for cattle was called the shambles and was always kept separate from the markets for other goods. Merchants of the British persuasion disliked the shopkeepers of the Irish sector, who settled on the outskirts of towns, charged less and constituted a threat. To deal with this, regulations were imposed: meat had to be served by butchers wearing spotless aprons and no horns were to be kept anywhere near meat exposed for sale. These seem perfectly reasonable rules of hygiene, but were principally designed to quash competition from the native traders. (The famous covered food market in Cork, the English Market, derives its name from the fact that only those who passed as English were allowed to trade there.)

In post-Norman times, the wandering Irish and their herds of cattle posed a persistent threat to the settled farmers within the Pale and were the constant target of legislation. A statute of 1430 forbids certain classes of Irish to graze their livestock on the borders of the colonised lands, for at the time it was a common Irish practice to encourage herds of livestock to roam where they could find good grass, and the herdsmen were not too particular whose grass was grazed. The long acre, that unclaimed strip of grass that runs the length of hundreds of miles of country roads all over Ireland, was always seen as free grazing and harks back to those old free-wheeling attitudes.

By the mid-seventeenth century much of Ireland was once again under pasture, the better to rear vast quantities of red meat for export to England and elsewhere in Europe. Care of the bullock ousted all other activities and much of the village desertion in rural Ireland may have occurred during this period, with pastoral expansion eroding old tillage-based villages in Roscommon, Westmeath, Tipperary, east Galway, east Limerick and north Cork.

Ireland was (and remains) a great place to rear cattle. The country abounded in fair pasture on a healthy limestone base. An ancient tradition could be tapped into, with all its skills and knowledge, the people would work hard for virtually no wages, the climate was relatively mild and they could often get away with not building winter housing. Other countries, troubled by wars and less advantaged in terms of climate, could not compete.

The merchants of Irish ports grew wealthy selling butter, salted beef, barrel staves, fish, wool and hides. In Cork, in a single year, 1688, 10,000 bullocks were slaughtered, causing the Earl of Orrery to call it the ox-slaying city.

So many goods were exported in the seventeenth century, however, that British farmers became angry. In order to protect their own trade, they put pressure on Parliament so that heavy import duties were levied on Irish goods. The first of the Cattle Acts passed in London in 1663 imposed hefty tariffs on the exportation of cattle from Ireland, while three years later an all-out embargo was placed on the exporting of cattle, sheep, pigs, beef, pork and bacon from Ireland to Britain.

Faced with such protectionist measures, the landlords and large estate owners in Ireland turned abruptly to the development of the provision trade, with unprocessed primary products being turned into processed farm produce in the form of salted beef, salted butter and bacon. (This is but an early example of the value-added principle.)

From the 1690s onward, dairying took over from extensive sheep and bullock fattening. In Munster, especially in the valleys of the rivers Lee and Blackwater, the new system began to dominate. This revolved around a great dairy master who could own as many as 1,000 cattle, hence the name *fear mile bo*, man of a thousand cattle. The dairy master leased up to forty cows to a dairyman in return for rent payable in barrels of butter. He never leased more to a single family as they couldn't feasibly milk any more. In addition, he supplied a room for storing the milk plus the necessary utensils for milking and butter-making. It was up to the man leasing the cows to dispose of unwanted calves and he could keep the buttermilk left over from the butter-making, plus he was given a cabin in which to raise his family and a small patch of land for growing potatoes.

From having had a booming trade not just in meat but also in wool, the Irish merchants saw their markets contract and as the situation in the country took a downturn, the peasant, hungry and miserably housed even in relatively good times, felt the pinch acutely. The poor had to restrict their diet severely and depend more and more on the potato. Even those engaged in butter-making in the lusher counties hardly ever had the luxury of eating the butter themselves, for all of it was needed to make sure the rent was paid and the dairy master was satisfied with the return on his loan.

To compound the worrisome conditions of the native Irish, land in Ireland was confiscated on three occasions and given to so-called 'planters'. In 1587 a vast tract of land, some 192,000 hectares (480,000 acres) in Munster was seized and given to selected planters, of whom the best known are Sir Walter Raleigh and Edmund Spenser, both of whom settled in Cork. The land was granted to planters on condition that they brought over English farmers and estate managers, English breeds of cattle and English equipment. In Ulster in 1609, 1.6 million hectares (4 million acres) were confiscated and divided between

English and Scottish gentlemen and officials, planters who were also known as 'undertakers' because they undertook to bring in tenants to run the farms, and 'servitors' because they had served King James.

Cromwell was even more generous with land that was not his. He inaugurated a new wave of immigrant plantation in the 1650s, with about 2.6 million hectares (6.5 million acres) of good land being given to those who had been loyal to him and otherwise ingratiated themselves.

Finally, when William of Orange defeated King James in 1691, a further 0.4 million hectares (1 million acres), mostly in the north of the country, were divided among William's supporters. The peasantry were allowed to stay on, being needed to work the estates.

Tending cattle and other livestock was the principal employment on the land, but although cattle needed open grazing, most of the open land was being fenced in. Even the annual migration of people and their livestock to the summer hill pastures caused trouble. In Edmund Spenser's *A View of the Present State of Ireland*, 1595, he allows his main character Irenaeus to express the opinion that 'this keeping of cows is of itself a very idle life and a fit nursery for a thief'. In particular, Irenaeus dislikes the 'Irish manner of keeping boolies in the summer upon the mountains and living after that savage sort'. Spenser also refers disparagingly to the Irish custom of using the blood of living cattle for food, and similarly Edmund Campion wrote in 1571, '[From] their kyne they let blood, which growen to a jelly they bake and overspread with butter and so eat it in lumps.'

Highly Prized Beef

An early triad asserts: 'the three best hands in the world: the hand of a good carpenter, the hand of a good smith, the hoof of a good ox.' Certainly, the ox was very highly prized. The strongest and most docile of a group of castrated calves would be selected to be the draught ox, the equivalent of today's tractor. The rest would be led to slaughter in their first or second year. The modern notion of fattening cattle to slaughtering weight in eighteen months to three years was unheard of in Ireland until recently. Cattle used to be slaughtered at anything up to seven years, when they were beyond milk production. Native Irish cattle were small and it is only from the eighteenth century that larger breeds came in. The Vikings actually introduced their own red cattle to interbreed with the native Irish stock and these 'red polls' were still a distinctive breed near Crayabbey, Co Down, up to 1934, after which they died out.

Cattle, left to their own devices, eat grasses and herbs and also like the leaves of trees, especially the elm. Iulius Solinus wrote in the third century that Ireland is 'so rich in pastures as to endanger the cattle unless they are now and then removed from their feeding grounds'. (Today, a farmer will not let cattle out into lush pastures too soon or for too long.)

Farmers beside the sea used seaweed to help feed their cattle, thereby providing salt, iodine and other nutrients. Because the modern scheme for feeding silage and hay to cattle in winter was not then practised, there used to be a category of land called 'preserved grassland'. Fields of grass were used for grazing in the spring before the cattle were let off to hill, moorland or woodland pasture for the summer. This gave the grass a chance to grow back again so that come the autumn and winter, the cattle could be led back to the farm and would find fields of fresh grass waiting for them. Cattle were also put to graze on the stubble of cereal crops after harvesting.

When grazing was sparse, the branches of holly and ivy were also cut for winter foddering. The fourteenth-century pilgrim, Count John de Perilhos, says 'the beasts eat only grass instead of oats and the leaves of the holly, which they roast a little on account of the prickles which are on the leaves'. In Co Kerry until quite recent times, they fed cattle the upper (relatively unprickly) leaves of holly.

When circumstances allowed, yearlings were fed a diet high in milk and good grain to impart succulence and flavour to the meat. For the feast of a nobleman named Bricriu, a calf was given special treatment to ensure that its flesh would be of the first grade: ' . . . a fine beeve . . . from when it was a little calf neither heather nor *foigdech* [some undesirable plant] entered its mouth, but full new milk and . . . green grass and corn.'

As we have seen, Irish cattle were exported in vast numbers on the hoof, and yet more left the country as salt beef, or corned beef. Cattle from the west were bought up cheaply by dealers, driven to the rich grasslands of Co Meath to be fattened up and then sold on for home consumption and to be shipped abroad. Similarly, cattle from south Limerick, Clare and Kerry were driven down to Cork.

The animals that were slaughtered young were eaten as veal, defined strictly as meat that comes from two-to-three-month-old calves. There are eight cuts of veal: cutlets, loin, shoulder, breast, middle neck, knuckle, scrag end and fillet. According to the food writer Monica Sheridan, 'Veal is not as good as well-matured beef. That the French give it such prominence in their cuisine is due to the fact that they do not have enough beef to go round. Except in Normandy and part of Brittany they have not the lush pasturelands that are essential for fattening beef-cattle.'

Leaving aside Ms Sheridan's tart assessment of veal, it has never been much liked by the Irish, perhaps due to the notion that only sick calves were killed. Much more to the native taste is corned beef, also known as salt beef. (Perhaps I should write 'was', for it is seldom enough that you see it nowadays, although it is still available in the English Market in Cork city. Saltpetre, which imparts a fine red colour to the meat, is no longer allowed in commercial butchery, which may be part of the problem.)

To make corned beef, the cook uses either the brisket, which is fat and lean in layers, or silverside, or the tail end, which is all lean with just a small rim of fat. (Pork can also be treated in the same fashion.) Corned beef boiled and served with green cabbage and floury potatoes was considered a feast of a dish, to be served at the important feastdays of the year, Hallowe'en, Christmas and St Patrick's Day, and good enough to be eaten at weddings and wakes. In *The Vision of Mac Con Glinne*, the poet sings, 'Corned Beef, my son, whose mantle shines over a big tail. Beef-lard, my steed, an excellent stallion.'

Not so far removed from corned beef is spiced beef, a dish that is particularly associated with Christmas. In the later medieval period, an incredible range of spices were brought into the country – candied ginger and powdered cloves, galingale and mace, cinnamon and peppercorns – and in 'The Land of Cokaygne', a poem preserved in a fourteenth-century manuscript, spiced beef is mentioned.

> The meat is spiced, the drink is clear,
> No raisin-wine or dull slops there!

Cold spiced beef, cut thin, is one of the Irish kitchen's epicurean treats.

A much more mainstream dish is pot roast of beef. The pot-oven or bastable used for this pot roast was, as we have seen elsewhere, a flat-bottomed pot standing on three legs, with a flattish lid.

Pot Roast of Beef

This recipe supposes you are using a modern-day hob. To cook a pot roast, you need to buy a fairly lean piece of beef from the top rib, known in Ireland as the 'housekeeper's cut' and tie it with string.

Heat a little fat (dripping would be ideal, otherwise good quality oil will do) and brown the joint on all sides to seal in the juices. Now put it into a large saucepan or oven-top casserole with a bay leaf, a few cloves, some whole allspice, 2 large or 3 medium carrots, sliced, and 1 large thinly sliced onion. It is not traditional, but I like to cut some slivers of garlic and insert them into little slits in the beef – you can use as many or as few as you like. Season well, add about 500 ml of good beef stock and bring it to the boil. Please note that a cheap stock cube will not produce the same results as a good home-made stock. (It's not so difficult.) Reduce the heat to a simmer, put on the lid and keep over a low heat for 30 minutes to the pound (450 g) or longer, until the beef is tender. Add stock if it runs dry, but only a very little.

Irish beef is generally of such high quality that if you buy one of the prime cuts, you should cook it simply to let the flavour emerge uncloaked.

To conclude this section on beef, I must pass on this observation from Irish cookery writer Monica Sheridan: 'Passing through a fair, in, say, Mullingar, you will see four-year-old Irish bullocks in the very pink of condition. They have the roving eyes and the debonair looks of first-year medical students.' According to her, there will never be a better time for them to meet their maker.

The Little Gentleman Who Pays the Rent
Winston Churchill once said, 'A cat looks down on you, a dog looks up to you, but a pig looks you straight in the eye.'

For millennia, Irish farming has centred on cattle, yet while the tenders of cattle could herd them, breed them, feed them, guard them, even slaughter them, it was not their lot to actually eat them. Goats and sheep were reared, deer and wild boar were hunted and other smaller types of furred game and wild creatures provided the odd taste of meat, but these were of lesser importance. For the peasant, it was another meat that counted – the meat that came from an animal with a curly tail.

It is impossible to overestimate the importance of the pig in Ireland. For centuries he sustained the poor in their cabins, and he acquired the semi-affectionate nickname 'the little gentleman who pays the rent'. From time to time the unlanded class ate a piece of salted pig on high days and holidays. Jack Spratt would not have been well served by the Irish pig, because although they were unfettered and free to exercise, the meat was fatty.

Right from the start, the pig was central to the Irish diet. The pig (*mucc* in Old Irish) features prominently in the earliest literature of Ireland, and was at that time a small, long-legged and bristly animal. (The pig we are used to has been bred into existence by crossing with quick-fattening oriental breeds.) Long before the Normans came, pigs were raised in large numbers and fed on the mast freely available in the extensive Irish woodlands. This mast, the fruit of native trees such as beech, oak, chestnut and whitethorn, was their food and it was said to give the flesh of the swine a most delicious flavour. It is reported in the early annals that a certain oak wood had mast and 'no mast was ever like its mast for size and for fragrance. When the wind would blow over it, the odour thereof would be smelt throughout Erin, to what point soever the wind would carry the scent so that it was a heartbreak to the swine of Ireland when it reached them.'

There are plenty of references to the mast crop in the annals, evidence of its immense importance to the rural economy. In 1038 the *Annals of Clonmacnoise* state that in that year there was such an abundance of mast that even the runts of the litters got a share. In such times of plenty, it was possible to trade surpluses, and in 1031 and again in 1097 mast was sold for silver in the monastic cities.

Ireland long ago was very heavily wooded, which made it ideal for rearing pigs. Their natural instincts to root and to break up the ground with their powerful snouts made pigs invaluable to the Neolithic farmers. The wild pig was domesticated very early on in the history of mankind. In Ireland, bones from the domestic pig have been found at Neolithic sites such as Ringneill Quay in Co Down and Tankardstown South in Co Limerick. When archaeologists examined early Christian sites, they found that almost a third of the animal bones came from the pig.

Sows seem to have been considered past their best in breeding terms after producing two or three litters, and so they were despatched, to provide both fresh meat and meat for preserving to see the people through the hard winters. As many as half the scapulas of pigs found at a crannog in Moynagh, Co Meath, had holes in them, and we must surmise that these holes were bored so that a hook could be passed through to let the carcase be hung up for curing.

Pigs were sometimes killed as sucklings, perhaps for a special feast, but they were more commonly fattened up for slaughter. A *lupait*, a female pig of six to eight months, was traditionally killed at Martinmas, 11 November, but mostly pigs were slaughtered at some point between their second August and the following spring.

The pig played its part in the early mythology of Ireland, and the swineherd himself was a significant figure.

The early Celtic sagas rely on exaggeration to fit the heroic mode, and in the ninth-century tale *Scela Mucce meic Datho*, Mac Datho's pig is supposed to have been fed on the milk of sixty cows for seven years, culminating in a bulk so huge that forty oxen are needed to drag its carcase into the feasting hall and nine men are required to hold up its belly. There were no fewer than seven cauldrons in his hall and 'each cauldron contained beef and salted pork, and as each man passed by he thrust the flesh-fork into the cauldron and what he brought up is what he ate; if he brought up nothing on the first try, he got no second chance.'

In the Fenian tale *The Pursuit of Diarmuid and Gráinne*, it was a magic pig that killed Diarmuid on top of Ben Bulben. And the legend of Bricriu's pigs relates how they could be eaten only to come alive again.

Hunting the boar is associated particularly with tales of the Fianna and their leader Finn MacCool. It is told of Finn that he had hunted a wild boar on many occasions but failed to capture it, only to see it finally killed by a peasant working at a drying kiln at Drumlea, Co Tyrone. Finn felt the ignominy and chastised himself:

> It is not well that we fed our hounds,
> It is not well that we rode our horses,
> Since a little peasant from a kiln
> Has killed the boar of Druimm Leithe.

A triad from the ninth century refers to the death of a fat pig as among 'the three deaths that are better than life'. An early eighth-century triad refers to the 'boar that removes dishonour at every season' – in other words, it provides a feast for high-ranking guests whenever they visit. (The early Irish were positively Japanese in their dread of losing face.)

When the early Irish went after wild boar, they hunted them with dogs, but were equally happy to trap them or down them with an arrow because the purpose was to bring home the carcase for meat. All that changed when the Normans arrived. Their passion for hunting, hawking, chasing and every other outdoor sport meant that the pursuit of wild pig was conducted for pleasure first and the meat was a side issue.

Giraldus Cambrensis, who first came to Ireland in 1183, sent by Henry II, mentions an abundance of wild swine in Ireland but they did not long survive the Norman invasion, and the wild boar became extinct through a combination of over-hunting and the destruction of the oak woods that provided them with food. Thereafter, it was the domesticated pig that became such an inextricable part of the Irish food scene. (The very word 'pork' has its root in the French word for the pig, *porc*, and the same applies to mutton, from *mouton*, and beef, from *boeuf*.)

Pork fresh and pork salted as bacon were favourite foods mentioned in the sagas and lives of the saints, and *The Vision of Mac Con Glinne* confirms its status as a highly desired food wherein even the 'rich juicy lard of a well-fed choice boar' is praised and the poet sees a living embodiment of pig-man. 'Fair was the shape of that man and his name was Bacon-lad, with his smooth sandals of old bacon and leggings of potmeat encircling his shins.'

Prior to the Great Famine, pigs were present in vast numbers throughout Ireland. Arthur Young, the English agriculturist, travelling through the country in the 1770s, was struck by their ubiquity. 'Hogs are kept in such numbers that the little towns and villages swarm with them', he wrote, and of Mitchelstown, Co Cork, he declares 'I believe there are more pigs than human beings.'

For the most part, what poor people ate, when they ate meat at all, was salt meat.

Not everyone had such sparse diets. Andrew J. Kettle, a gentleman farmer who owned a substantial farm at St Margaret's in north Co Dublin, describes the unusually generous amount of food distributed there to the labourers in the years preceding the Great Famine.

> The food was nearly all home-made; wholemeal bread, oaten meal flour, ground on the farm, made into stir-about, potatoes all floury, first quality butter, bacon raised, killed and cured on the premises, milk unadulterated ad libitum for everyone and everything, and honey bees in almost every garden ... I often held the scale for my grandmother to weight a pound of bacon for each workman's dinner, three days a week with a quarter of fresh mutton and four duck eggs on the other days. No tea, not much butcher's meat, unless at Christmas and Easter, but plenty of pork steaks at the pig killing periods and the best of pigs' puddings and sausages.

The one time when fresh meat was abundant was when the pig was killed. On that extremely important day, some of the neighbours would gather to give a hand. The man most experienced at killing (the butcher) would be in charge of the operation, making sure the pig was hamstrung and held down before its throat was slit. Thereafter, it was hung up and bled, cleaned and its carcase split from neck to fork. While this was going on, the women would be frantically busy, drawing water (heavy pail after pail, often from a distant well, pump or even stream) and heating it. Not only did they have to work quickly to make sure that all the perishables were dealt with before they could begin to spoil, but they had to keep things clean and hygienic, and on top of that they would be expected to feed the company, which was much larger than normal.

Thereafter, the serious business of making puddings and salting the flesh would begin. Each neighbour used to bring a handful of salt and scrupulous care was taken to scald out the barrel in which the meat was to be salted. Any carelessness could result in a barrel of putrefaction, so it was crucial to watch out at every stage of the proceeding – the lining with clean straw, the salting and the tamping down. It was judged best to cure the hams and bacon in the smoke of green wood.

Black puddings were made straight after the pig was killed, to use up the blood. White puddings, made mostly of toasted oatmeal, onions boiled and chopped finely and chopped lard, pepper and salt, also featured in the performance, for although they contained not much meat, they needed the casings that were prepared then.

My friend and neighbour Veronica Halloran described to me the meat she and her family ate when she was growing up in the first half of the twentieth century.

> We used to eat cow's head, pig's head, crubeens, heart and liver. I couldn't stand pig's head or crubeens. My mother used to boil the pig's head with onions and the rest would have it. We used to make puddings out of the pig. First cold water, then hot water. Water and salt we used. It was cold on your hands, of a winter's evening coming up to Christmas. You'd be washing them [the pig's intestines] and washing them, and when you'd think you'd have them clean enough, you'd steep them in

a basin of cold water and salt. You'd keep them there for three days and three nights, keep changing the water. And on the fourth day, you'd make the puddings with the blood . . . We'd eat the liver and the heart. Fry the liver and the heart. There was enough for a meal from the heart; you sliced it down and flavoured it. And the liver was a good big piece. Griskins [pork steak] was a treat for the neighbours. You shared it, but then your neighbours were so close to you in those times – you shared everything.

It is not so easy to get your hands on meat from truly free-range pigs. Alfie McCaffrey and Margaret O'Farrell, from near Lorrha, Co Offaly, are among the few whose pigs rootle around at will and get extra snacks of vegetables considered too ugly for an easy sale. The meat they offer would forever put you off buying pork from intensively reared pigs. Aside from knowing these porkers have lived well, the flavour is nonpareil.

Bacon and Ham

In Ireland only the leg of the pig is called ham – all the rest is bacon – and hams were often treated separately for curing. The ham being a prime cut, it was reserved for the well-off. (In fact, some families were so wealthy they could afford to roast the joint – a very profligate way of cooking it.) Hams were usually smoked, and for centuries Irish ham was renowned, especially Limerick ham. By the nineteenth century there were three important bacon factories in Limerick, one of which opened a factory in Russia in 1891 and had offices in Romania and London, and Limerick ham and bacon were found all over the British Empire.

Why Limerick? Originally it was because the ham got its characteristic flavour by being smoked over branches of juniper, a shrub widespread all over the county. Oak shavings were often used as we see in this eighteenth-century recipe: 'Hang [the ham] in a chimney and make a fire of oak shavings and lay over it horse litter and one pound of juniper berries. Keep the fire smothered down for 2 or 3 days and then hang them to dry.'

The brilliant food writer Marwood Yeatman was present when an old abandoned house was demolished, and as the chimney started to sunder, a ham was discovered hanging from a hook halfway up. Blackened as it was, it was taken home, cut into and declared perfect in every way.

What remained after the removal of the ham was the flitch for curing. It was usually dry cured, by rubbing it with a mixture of salt, sugar and saltpetre, after which it was dried and smoked. Most bacon today is wet-cured in brine and 'smoked' chemically. Both ham and bacon that have been cured need to be soaked before cooking.

With the diminished stocks of mast from the forest floor, once available to the domestic pig, other food had to be found. By and large, this consisted of kitchen scraps and root vegetables, potato peelings in particular after the late sixteenth century.

At this point we must look at the dish that is universally associated with Ireland. If there is a national dish, it is surely not the muttony Irish stew, but cabbage and bacon, the meat of the pig. The writer John B. Keane in his book on Irish food, *Strong Tea*, rhapsodises about bacon. 'Lest the wrong impression be given, let me say at once that the type of bacon I have in mind is homecured. It has been hanging from the ceiling for months, and when you cut a chunk from it, there is the faintest of golden tinges about its attractive shapeliness. When this type of bacon is boiling with its old colleague, white cabbage, there is a gurgle from the pot that would tear the heart out of a hungry man.'

Its popularity is undiminished, in rural areas at least. My local butcher Gene McEntee explains, 'As time moved on there was a problem with the bacon. At that time it was always very salty and the next generation found it too salty. I'd say between 1975 and 1988 – that period – the bacon trade really died because the rasher was too salty, even coming from the factories. Hey, people's tastes are changing. Then they started the mild curing and over the next ten years that trade came right back up again. We must be one of the biggest bacon eaters in the world.'

The usual cuts for making this dish are the shoulder, the collar or else a thick piece of streaky bacon cut from the flitch. Unless you are buying from a butcher you trust, you are probably getting factory-cured bacon and this can be very salty. Ideally, you are advised to soak the meat for several hours, changing the water a few times; you may wish to bring the piece to the boil for 5 minutes, then discard the water.

Bacon and Cabbage

This recipe will feed however many you wish. All you have to do is adjust up or down the size of your cut of bacon.

Put a piece of bacon in a pot of fresh water, together with an onion. If you wish, you can also add some carrots, a bay leaf or two, some chopped celery, a handful of parsley stalks, some juniper berries, a tablespoon of brown sugar and a dash of vinegar – cider vinegar for preference.

Bring your pot to the boil then reduce to a bare simmer, allowing 25–30 minutes to the pound (450 g). Traditionally the trimmed cabbage is sliced and put into the pot along with the bacon. Those of you who don't believe in boiling the life out of cabbage will just have to trust me on this one – if you cook the cabbage lightly at the last minute, you will ruin the whole thing. The nutritional value of the cabbage will be diminished, I grant you, but the cabbage should be extremely soft and much reduced in volume. It will also taste very creamy. Lightly boiled or steamed cabbage is marvellous, but to be had on another occasion!

When you reckon the meat is cooked, lift it from the pan and put it on a warmed plate. It is important to drain the cabbage extremely thoroughly. If you save the liquid, you have a well-flavoured (if rather salty) stock for making soup. If you don't eat the whole piece of meat at one sitting, leave on the skin and put it back in the cooking liquid to cool slowly. It will form a semi-jellied stock around itself.

Mutton and Lamb

Sheep are integral to the story of food in Ireland even if they lack the high prestige of cattle or the affection that belongs to the pig. Dogs came first, but then sheep and goats are thought to have been the next animals to be domesticated, around 8000 BC. Originally they were kept for their meat, but as the early shepherds learned to breed long-fleeced sheep, their wool became prized for its warmth. (And as it is naturally oily, wool left unwashed and unbleached is also mildly water-repellent.)

In *The Vision of Mac Con Glinne*, the poet considers that boiled 'full-fleshed wether' (a wether is a castrated sheep older than one year) is no mean food, and a ninth-century text instructs the reader: 'do not dress elegantly unless you possess sheep . . . for elegant dress without sheep is a crime in the gatherings of the world'. In those times sheep were mainly the responsibility of women and we know that some were left out of doors, even in dead of winter, for losses of sheep due to snow and frost are recorded in the annals. But others were housed in folds during the worst months and there are occasional references to them being fed in stalls. Irish sheep, according to Giraldus Cambrensis, were mainly black, although white were considered superior. Among contemporary Anglo-Norman breeds, there was a high proportion of white-fleeced sheep, which were two or three times more valuable than the black-fleeced stock of the Irish, so it is likely that larger, white-fleeced breeds of sheep were imported by the colonists.

Sheep played an immensely important part in the Norman

economy, for they manured the land, supplied wool as a cash crop, provided milk to make cheese and at the end of their days became mutton or lamb. The Normans hugely expanded the keeping of sheep and introduced new breeds. Wool was a commodity of vast economic importance in the medieval period. (Even today, in the British Houses of Parliament, the woolsack is retained as a symbol of trade and wealth.) From 1300 on, goods on sale in most Irish cities included skins of various livestock and wild animals.

But our interest is in the milk they give and their flesh. In *The Vision of Mac Con Glinne* the poet refers with obvious relish to 'fair white porridge made with pure sheep's milk'. In fact, we know that sheep were regularly milked, as they were all over the rest of Europe, especially on the Atlantic coasts. In general, though, sheep's milk was not highly prized and was judged inferior to that of the goat, let alone the cow. In a prophetic poem, one of the signs of the End of the World is 'the grey goat will have the milk-yield of a sheep' – in other words, the milk-yield of goats will become reduced in both quantity and quality.

In the early seventeenth century, Fynes Moryson remarked that the people ate great quantities of unsalted beef and pork but seldom ate mutton. Around the same period, the English-born judge Luke Gernon was given a fattened wether when he arrived at a castle of the old aristocracy. Treated to great hospitality, plied with beer, whiskey, sack and old ale, he made a selection from the various meat dishes set before him. 'The dish which I make choice of is the swelled mutton, and it is prepared thus. They take a principal wether, and before they kill him, it is fit that he be shorn. Being killed, they singe him in his woolly skin like a bacon and roast him by joints with the skin on, and so serve it to table. They say that it makes the flesh more firm and preserves the fat. I make choice of it to avoid uncleanly dressing.' Note that sting in the tail!

Sheep meat was always valued. According to an Old Irish passage on clientship, the food rent that a client must give his lord included a wether, together with its fleece – one in summer and another in autumn. A reference in the epic poem *The Lament of the Old Woman of Beare* makes it clear that wethers were killed for a wedding feast and over the centuries mutton was valued as a great celebration food.

Testimony to the festive roast mutton was given by Mme de Bovet, a highly critical French traveller to Ireland in the late nineteenth century, who remarked after a party where the guests were served a baron of mutton, that the delicious gravy was 'the only triumph of Irish cookery'.

A century earlier, the Englishwoman Mrs Delany wrote of a curious mutton dish she was given during an elaborate picnic at Patrick Down, near Killalla on 4 July 1732. 'For our feast there was prepared what here they call a "swilled mouton", that is, a sheep roasted whole in its skin, scorched like a hog. I never ate anything better; we sat on the grass, had a rock for our table; and though there was a great variety of good cheer, nothing was touched but the mouton.'

In *The Farm on Lough Gur*, a charming story of life in a Limerick now long disappeared, the narrator tells of the excitement when chance delivered an occasion to dine on lamb: 'there's roast lamb for our dinner . . . the crayther! fallin' from the rocks the way it did to break its neck, and it neither a lamb nor a sheep. "With mint sauce it is lamb," I said firmly. "Make a good fire and have it on the spit in plenty of time . . . and then run to the eel-stream for a double-handful of mint."'

Nowadays, we are led to believe that lamb alone is worth eating (lamb being an animal younger than between fifteen and eighteen months). Most mutton comes from sheep three or four years old and its full flavour is one we are no longer accustomed to.

At one time in Ireland there were travelling kitchens, housed in a kind of tent in which two fires were on the go. Wherever there was a throng of people, these tents were set up, and the main dish was ladled from large pots of spoileen – a boiled mutton stew. These spoileen tents would be found at fairgrounds and other gatherings across Ireland up to the mid-nineteenth century.

A very ancient way of eating mutton was devised by peasant ingenuity. It uses the lesser cuts to make a warming and sustaining meal out of very little. This is the classic Irish stew. In some ways it is not so far removed from the equally classic Lancashire hotpot – a one-pot meal that is made using scraps of meat and the vegetables easily available and made unctuous by long, slow cooking.

Samuel Beckett, in *Molloy*, pays it some attention: 'I peered into the pots. Irish stew. A nourishing and economical dish, if a little indigestible. All honour to the land it has brought before the world.'

The cardinal rule for making an Irish stew is to avoid making it runny. Purists insist on nothing but potatoes, onions and the meat, together with herbs and seasonings. Other recipes call for carrots and several include barley. I am of the view that carrots add a welcome touch of colour. In this updated version, I recommend you use stock, but in the old days they would have made the stew with water.

Irish Stew

In place of the best end of neck chops you might use shoulder, gigot chops or even trimmed breast of lamb/mutton. Serves four.

1½ kg best end of neck chops
450 g onions, sliced into
    thick rings
300 g carrots, sliced into
    thick rings
900 g floury potatoes, peeled
    and cut into very large chunks

2 tbs parsley, chopped, plus
    another 1 tbs kept back till
    the end
2 tsp thyme
Salt and pepper
2 cups lamb stock (or vegetable
    stock will just about do)

Trim off any gristle from the meat, but leave at least some of the fat (it will melt into the potatoes) and leave the meat on the bone. This doesn't look so good when serving, but the flavour compensates for that, and the meat falls straight off the bone, in any case.

Starting with the onions and ending with the potatoes, layer the meat and the vegetables in a deep casserole dish, seasoning each layer well with the parsley, thyme, salt and pepper. Pour in the stock and cover with a piece of buttered foil, then the lid, to make it as tight a fit as possible, and bake in a slow oven, 150°C/330°F/Gas Mark 2 for about 2 hours. If you prefer, you can cook it on top of the stove on a very low heat, ideally over a diffuser mat, shaking it now and again to prevent sticking. Add a very little more liquid if you suspect it is drying out towards the end. The potatoes should have almost melted away, leaving a velvety finish to the stew. Some people put a few whole potatoes on the top layer so that they keep their shape.

Sprinkle with the final amount of chopped parsley as a garnish.

Some contend that the traditional Irish stew was made not from mutton but from kid, claiming that sheep were too valuable to put in the pot for the poor man's family dinner. This may be true, although the lesser pieces of mutton might well have come the way of a poor family without them having had to kill a sheep. In some parts of the country, a thick paste of flour and water was laid over the top of the pot oven to seal in the steam before the lid was firmly fixed in place. When the stew was about to be served to the family, this flour crust was cut away and flung out to the hens.

Mutton Pies

Mutton pies, known as Dingle pies, come from Kerry. These pies were made for special occasions: for Lady Day in September, for Holy Thursday before Easter and for All Saints at the beginning of November. On fair-days, when nobody had time to sit down to a proper meal, the pie sellers were thronged. According to Myrtle Allen of Ballymaloe House in east Cork, the local children used to chant a little rhyme:

> Make a pie, make a pie, make a pie.
> Roll a pie, roll a pie, roll a pie.
> Pinch a pie, pinch a pie, pinch a pie.

For farmers and for fishermen, they provided a snack, and they were very economical to make, using up scraps of mutton or the meat of a sheep's head, for Dingle is in mountainous sheep country. Several recipes for mutton pies are circulated in and about Dingle, some calling for the pastry to be shortened with dripping, others for rendered mutton fat. All agree that the pastry should be rolled out and cut with a saucer, then the meat seasoned and heaped in the middle before being capped by a smaller circle of pastry, cut with a glass or an old teacup. The pastry base was traditionally brought up to fit over the top circle, its edges pleated to fit neatly, then the edges were moistened and pinched on or secured by pressing with the tines of a fork.

The pie was baked in a slow to moderate oven for about an hour. Fishermen brought them to sea in a can and heated them over a fire made in a tin box, at the bottom of the boat. (Not as dangerous as it sounds, I hope!) A cold baked pie was better for the farmer's pocket.

It is not difficult to see parallels with the Cornish pasty. It *is* difficult to see why the savoury pie never caught on outside Dingle. I was brought up in the north of England and pork pies were ubiquitous, as were meat and potato pies, too. My pal Clarissa Webb makes steak pies, chicken and ham pies and confit of duck pies – all delectable. Her pork pies, made with puff pastry rather than the traditional hot water crust, are top notch. Her output is small and I'm lucky to know her!

Game

For a land so rich in wildlife, it is strange that game does not figure more strongly in the story of food in Ireland because game was used as food by all classes of society. It is inconceivable that the early settlers failed to exploit the beasts of the forest, but as land became enclosed and proprietorial rights were claimed, the ancient freedoms were lost, and catching game, both feathered and furred, turned into poaching.

The noblest beast of the forest is the deer. The red deer, the only native species, seems not to have been eaten to any great extent. In crannógs in Ballinderry, Co Westmeath and also in Moynagh, Co Meath, the middens gave up only very small numbers of deer bones as compared with bones of other animals, mostly cattle. In Old Irish sagas, venison is very little mentioned and although deer were hunted with hounds they were also caught by guile. A ninth-century stone cross in Banagher, Co Offaly, shows a representation of a stag with two of its legs caught in a trap.

After the arrival of the Anglo-Normans, deer hunting became a major sport, and bringing home a carcase was of secondary importance.

William the Conqueror designated red deer, roe deer, imported fallow deer and wild boar as 'beasts of the forest' and the meat of all four was called venison. He reserved their meat for himself, allowing others to hunt the rest: wolves, wild cats, badgers, foxes, pine martens, otters, hares, rabbits and squirrels.

Giraldus Cambrensis contends that the stags of Ireland were so fat they could not escape their hunters! Be that as it may, sustained hunting in the seventeenth and eighteenth centuries had reduced the wild red deer to remnant populations scattered in the remote mountains of the south-west, the west and the north-west of the country. By the mid-nineteenth century all the indigenous Irish red deer were shot to extinction with the single exception of those in the Killarney area. (Red deer were reintroduced to Donegal and Wicklow in the nineteenth century with stock brought in from Scotland.)

The Tudor Fynes Moryson alludes to game in his *Itinerary* written in 1605. 'Ireland hath great plenty of Pheasants, as I have known sixtie served at one feast, and abound much more with Rayles: but Partridges are somewhat rare . . .' He also wrote, 'There be very many Eagles and a great plenty of Hares, Conies . . . And of Venison . . . yet in many woods they have many red Deare.'

The Normans first introduced the fallow deer, *fia buí*, in the twelfth century. The common name for this species is derived from the Old English *fealu*, meaning yellowish-brown, and the Irish name means the yellow (*buí*) deer (*fia*). Nowadays they predominate. The Phoenix Park in Dublin, the largest enclosed park in Europe, is home to a 600-strong herd and throughout the country their numbers are growing. Twice a year Portumna Forest Park, near where I live, is closed while a cull is on.

My father, Jim Hickey, remembers how things were in the 1920s in the forested areas of his part of south-east Galway: 'Most people had a shotgun, men of course, had one for shooting. They'd go up the bogs. That time there were geese, snipe and there was plenty of pheasants knocking about. Another bird called a partridge – they were in wild ground. Then there was the deer as well. Sometimes a farmer would shoot a deer. It was not allowed to do it . . . they'd have to get rid of the evidence. Have to be divided up amongst the farmers, you know. I never tried it, venison. I believe it is strong. There's plenty of deer now in th'ould forest. I suppose they cull them sometimes to keep the numbers down. At that time the demesne was a guarded place.' The demesne he referred to was the estate of the Earl of Clanricarde, who was an absentee landlord.

Nowadays, trade in venison is strictly licensed and a taste for the meat is (slowly) gathering support outside the restaurant trade. Its reputation for being dry militates against it, but my pal Roman Duell, who is an excellent cook, has served me butter-soft venison full of flavour. It is, incidentally, lower in cholesterol than beef or pork.

Urban Eating

Aside from a relatively small number of people who are true Dubliners born and bred (perhaps the same might go for Belfast), no one in Ireland, even today, is more than a couple of removes from the land. For that reason, I have concentrated mostly on rural affairs, but it is only proper to recognise that Dublin was once a hugely important city under the British monarchy. Dublin was a city of great elegance and great poverty – in parts of the city, the living conditions were exceedingly squalid for the very poor and cooking facilities were almost non-existent.

At the turn of the nineteenth century thirty cattle dealers were engaged in exporting 15,000 cattle, sheep and pigs every week and some 600 dairies supplied Dublin. A visiting Frenchwoman, Mme de Bovet, looked at the permanent market street of St Patrick's in the capital with disgust, finding that 'shops with overhanging roofs expose for sale sides of rancid bacon, jars of treacle, greens, cauliflowers and musty turnips, flat baskets are spread with cow's feet, overkept sheep's head, flabby pink veal, skins and fat of every animal and at every three doors a tavern.'

By the second half of the nineteenth century, the staple diet of the urban poor was black tea and bread, with the occasional addition of herrings, dripping, sheep's head and pig's cheek.

In Brendan Behan's story *The Confirmation Suit*, he tells of how, as a young boy, he and his granny were at home together in the northside Dublin tenement where they lived and all they had to eat was a sheep's head. It was put on to boil and the two of them endured the stench of the wretched thing simmering away until Brendan got up and looked into the hellish brew 'in fear and trembling', where an eyeball was staring back at him and some wicked teeth were clenched in anger. At his grandmother's request, he grabbed the saucepan and flung the whole lot out of the window, not caring where it landed. 'My grandmother had to drink a Baby Power whiskey, for she wasn't the better of herself.'

Although sheep's head was well known to the urban poor in Belfast, Limerick, Cork, Galway and other cities, it has a particular resonance for Dubliners. Another dish that has been a firm favourite since the eighteenth century and is said to have been well liked by Dean Swift is Dublin Coddle, *codal Duibhlinneach*. Some say that the Vikings were the first to cook up something along these lines but I wonder . . .

It was especially liked as a Saturday night supper. Always made with streaky smoked bacon cut in cubes, pork sausages and Spanish onions, the mixture is covered with water, brought to the boil and cooked in a heavy saucepan over a low heat. Sometimes sliced raw potatoes are added but most Dubliners prefer bread to mop up the gravy, then wash it down with strong tea.

Dublin Coddle

450 g bacon bits

450 g good sausages

3 large onions

Handful of chopped parsley

1½–2 kg floury potatoes

Bacon bits are off-cuts – they could be skin and fat and meat all mixed and odd shapes. If you can't get hold of them, you can use streaky bacon but the slices are usually very thin, and not so satisfactory for this dish. Getting hold of belly bacon in a piece and cutting it up is better – it will be thicker than rashers and carry more flavour. Leave on the rind. Finding good quality sausages is not easy, but get the best you can – butchers' own tend to be a good bet.

Peel and chop the onions roughly and chop the parsley. Peel the potatoes as thinly as possible, and if large, cut them into two or three pieces, otherwise, leave whole. Choose a heavy pan with a tight-fitting lid and put a layer of onions in the bottom, layer the other ingredients, and finally add no more than 2 cups (16 fl oz/440 ml) of water. Bring the pan to the boil then cover, reduce the heat to a bare simmer for a minimum of 2 hours. It won't matter if you leave it longer – up to 5 hours, although you might check that it isn't drying out too much.

Actually, although it was usually cooked on top of the stove, the ideal would be to cook it in a heavy casserole in a very low oven, 120°C/250°F/Gas Mark ½, and the longer and slower the cooking, the better it will be.

Peter Somerville-Large was born into a family that was comfortably off, and he spent much of his childhood in a house in the heart of Georgian Dublin. He recalls, 'Outside purchases from Finlater's and the butcher in Dundrum, carefully recorded in Miss Moore's book, were turned into rissoles, minced beef, minced turkey, cauliflower cheese, macaroni cheese, boiled bacon and cabbage and braised liver.

"Corned Brisket 3s 8d. 2 Ox-tails. 5½ pounds tail end 4s 7d. 2 rabbits no charge.'"

He has clear recollections, too, of another house and Sunday meals after church. As he stepped into the hall, 'the lines of stuffed animal heads on the walls seemed to be sniffing up the smell of roasting barons of beef and legs of lamb. After grace came the carving ceremony . . . I remember Uncle Paddy's horror when he was old and saw the younger generation carving up meat with electric carving knives; the result was nothing like the slices of beef he used to distribute, thin as paper. The beef was never rare, no one liked that, it was always brown through and through . . . It was a pity about the accompanying boiled carrots in cornflour sauce and the chocolate brown gravy – the Bisto Kids were already at work.'

Nose to Tail Eating

Offal was once the frequent food of the poor. In the late eighteenth century, butchers who started selling the entrails of cattle abroad caused a riot among the poor of the city who depended on this offal for their food. Labourers in Cork slaughterhouses, aside from their wages, brought home bread, beef and beer and their fringe benefits included 3 kg (7 lb) of offal a week for their families.

But offal was not only for the poor. Certain types of offal were highly thought of, often being supposed to be health-giving. The hero of *Ulysses* is the world's most famous lover of offal. 'Mr Leopold Bloom ate with relish the inner organs of beasts and fowls. He liked thick giblet soup, nutty gizzards, stuffed roast heart, liver slices fried with crustcrumbs, fried hencod's roes. Most of all he liked grilled mutton kidneys . . .'

Gene McEntee recalls, 'Offal was the most popular – liver, kidneys, heart and tongue. We still sell tongue, kidneys, liver and heart, but no brains – never – and no sweetbreads. I sell 1 per cent kidneys and no beef liver – only lamb's. Tripe was fairly big in Limerick. When I started, we had a sale for lambs' heads and pigs' heads. During the war sheep's head was a huge seller. All that's gone now. By the mid-seventies it had died, even the pig's head. Back then everyone was working outside – the work was physical. The fatter the bacon was, the better they liked it.'

Pig's feet are still a part of today's Irish culinary repertoire and I cherish them as a living link to the past. These trotters, also known as crubeens, from the Irish *crúibíní*, are a country dish once accompanied by brown soda bread and pints of stout. The pig's trotters are sold lightly brined and the rear feet are favoured, being thought to be meatier.

If you want, you can cook two together with a thin piece of timber slipped between them and tied with string. This should prevent them from sticking together. Crubeens are very sticky things!

The country method is to boil them in water with an onion, a carrot and some herbs and seasoning, for about 2 hours, after which they can be eaten warm from the pot or cold, taken up in the fingers and chewed, as with corn on the cob. A modern refinement is to split the foot in two after cooking, remove the bones, allow to cool, then brush with mustard, roll in beaten egg and breadcrumbs and finally fry or grill it and serve with a piquant sauce. Pierre Koffman, in his Michelin-starred London restaurant Tante Claire, used to serve Gascon-style pigs' trotters as a signature dish.

Crubeens, by the way, are particularly associated with Cork, and it was in that county that I saw a sign in the butcher's window propped against a tray. 'Pig's trotters. Very low mileage.' Again, Cork is one of the last places you can get hold of skirts and bodices without having to call into an old-fashioned draper's emporium. A skirt is the diaphragm of the pig (or beef or lamb) and is rarely sold today, being minced up for sausage filling instead. Bodices is a fanciful name for bacon ribs.

And while on the subject of Cork, now is the time to introduce the particular blood sausage called a drisheen. Blood puddings are probably one of the oldest foods made with meat. They exist all over the western world, particularly in Celtic countries, and I often ate *boudin antillais*, a soft Caribbean black pudding, when I worked in Paris. Where nowadays pig's blood is more usual, traditionally drisheens were made with sheep's blood. In Cork city they do not put the drisheen into a skin at all but cook it in a bowl. Its basic ingredients are blood, fat, milk or cream and some kind of cereal, herb or spice, and seasoning.

H. V. Morton, in his book *In Search of Ireland*, muses about them.

> When I asked in the hotel for 'drisheen' they thought that I was trying to be funny. They treated me to that snobbish amusement which the Ritz would bestow on a man who was honest enough to demand a black pudding or a pound of tripe . . . This drisheen, which looks like a large and poisonous snake, is a native of Cork . . . Superior Dubliners pretend that it bites . . . But drisheen is above such low comment: one might call it the caviare of Cork.
>
> They brought me the drisheen boiled on a plate. When cut, it looked like a firm chocolate blancmange. In a moment of mistaken enthusiasm they poured melted butter on it, but I felt instinctively that drisheen lovers employ a less sickly garnish. It is a peculiar, subtle dish, pleasant and ladylike. I believe that I would like it better fried.

Tripe is the stomach tissue of cud-chewing animals, especially beef, sometimes veal and occasionally pork. Sold by butchers as dressed tripe, it is cleaned and given long cooking to tenderise it. The honeycomb tripe of the second stomach is said to be more tender than the flat or ridged tripe, but I don't agree.

H. V. Morton makes mention of tripe and onions and this was a firm Irish favourite and a famous Saturday night dish, the most common method being to slice the tripe and cook it in milk with a lot of sliced onions, salt and pepper and a pinch of nutmeg or mace.

Just before serving, it was the practice to thicken the sauce with a tablespoon of either flour or cornflour.

In Oliver St John Gogarty's *Tumbling in the Hay* (the Hay being the name of the Hay Hotel, Dublin) he relates, 'It was the long table (at the end of a long passage) full of boiling coffee, hot tripe and onions, skate (on Fridays) and crubeens that attracted the weary nightfarer.' One nightfarer fares badly. 'The tall lady fell backwards among the plates of tripe. "Two coffees and a collared head!" Maria announced emerging from the kitchen before she saw the long drawn-out sweetness on the tripe. "The tripe and onions is off!"'

All those of us who happily order *fromage de tête* from a French restaurant menu or buy it from a *traiteur* ought to start a movement to reinstate brawn, which was an ancient food of Ireland and the rest of these islands for centuries. It is passing hard to get hold of brawn these days, and yet it can be delectable.

Traditionally it was made from the head, shoulders and trotters of wild boar, but it was not uncommon for brawn (head cheese) to be made from calves' heads, sheep's heads or a mixture of several meats.

Usually brawn-making took place around pig-killing time. The jobs of cleaning the head and feet were not the most popular. In some households the brains were taken out to be blanched and put by for the following day, when they would be parboiled, then dipped in batter and fried. In other households, more squeamish, the brains were given to the dogs. When I lived in France I saw a dish of uncooked pigs' ears for sale on a market stall in Coulommiers and, to my shame, passed them by. But in Ireland the ears were put to use for making the brawn. Once the head and feet had been thoroughly cleaned, they were rubbed with a mixture of salt and saltpetre and put in a big pickling crock for 24 hours. The next day, the contents would be slow cooked along with pepper and onions and spices until they were almost melted away to jelly. After this the meat would be lifted from the bones, and as soon as it was cool enough to handle, chopped small and packed with a few spoonfuls of the cooking juices into bowls to set firm. Over each bowl would be put a plate weighted down with a flat iron or other heavy object. When it was cold and set, it was sliced up, jellied, pink and piquant.

At one time black and white puddings were lowly items of food, to be enjoyed by the family but not worthy of being offered to guests. Myrtle Allen of Ballymaloe House changed all that, putting them on the menu at her country house hotel, following the logic that if she and her family enjoyed them, so might her visitors.

Days of Feasting

Let us consider the importance of feasting in the history of food in Ireland. The word, of course, calls up its opposite. The Great Famine of 1845 and beyond looms over any discussion of food in Ireland. But despite the centuries of struggle against want and famine, feasting played its part in Irish life. The rare day of feasting was hoarded up in the memories of the very poor, to be returned to now and again as a source of comfort and courage. For those whose wealth lay in little more than their muscles and a willingness to make the best of a bad lot, there was much misery and uncertainty.

Yet there is an Irish genius that wrests the very best out of a bad situation. Ireland endured hardship for centuries, often meeting it with laughter, dance and song. Many of the songs were sad, much of the laughter defiant, but that refusal to succumb to misery is a leitmotif throughout Irish history.

An instance of a day of feasting that shone like a beacon in the darkness, was the great banquet that Brian na Murtha O Ruarc, Prince of Breffni, held in the great hall of his castle at Dromahair, Co Leitrim, at Christmas 1591. The occasion was later celebrated in the folk song '*Plearácha na Ruarchach*' ('O'Rourke's Feast'). Here is the first section, translated from the Irish.

The feast of O'Rourke is remembered by many
Who came or are gone or who never were there.

Seven gallons of whiskey and casks full of vino
From dawn of the morning such rat a tat tat
Your pipe it was broken, my pocket was opened,
Your breeches were stolen. Well, who burned me hat?

Sure, I lost me ould cloak and me shirt and me garters
My handkerchief, too, but we'll let that one pass,
Let us sing, let us dance, come along with the snuff box
And come on sweet Annie, and fill up me glass.
Ten score pigs, sides of beef and fresh mutton
Were killed for the gluttons and nothing left spare.

Still later it was immortalised by Dean Swift who wrote these lyrics
to be sung to the music of the blind harper and master composer,
O'Carolan.

O'Rourke's noble fare will ne'er be forgot
By those who were there and those who were not.
His revels to keep, we sup and we dine,
On seven score sheep, fat bullock and swine.
Usquebaugh to our feast in pails was brought up,
A hundred at least, and a madder our cup.
Oh there is the sport, we rise with the light,
In disorderly sort from snoring all night.

It was no chance that the feast was held at Christmas time.
Midwinter was always a focus for feasting and jollity to banish the
cold and hunger of winter and shorten the dark nights. Among
'strong' farmers, it was a practice to kill a beast at this time and share
it out. The divisions were traditionally as follows: 'To the smith the
head, tongue and feet; to the tailor the small ribs that go with the
hindquarters; to the physician the kidneys; to the harper the udder;
to the carpenter the liver; the marrowbone to the strong man; the

heart to the cowherd; a choice piece to the midwife, another to the stableman; black puddings and sausages to the ploughman and sweetbreads for the mother.' In addition, the tallow was used to make candles and the hide traded for wine and whiskey. The beast in question was the pig.

Writers usually chronicle events more entertainingly than social historians and sometimes more accurately, too. These next accounts tell of a country beginning to recover from the devastation of the Great Famine.

In the Big House the feasts were of very varying quality. In *Some Experiences of an Irish RM*, Somerville and Ross give an account that I can recognise as being no exaggeration.

'Detestable soup in a splendid old silver tureen that was nearly as dark in hue as Robinson Crusoe's thumb; a perfect salmon, perfectly cooked, on a chipped kitchen dish; such cut glass as is not easy to find nowadays; stew that, as Flurry subsequently remarked, would burn the shell off an egg; and a bottle of port, draped in immemorial cobwebs, wan with age, and probably priceless.'

James Joyce, despite living in exile, recalled in minute detail the social world of Dublin at the turn of the century. In his short story *The Dead*, the sumptuous Christmas table of the Misses Morkan is described, with a fat brown goose presiding over one end and a cooked ham and a round of spiced beef at the other. 'Between these rival ends ran parallel lines of side-dishes . . . ' The combination of sweet and savoury dishes all presented at the same time is what strikes the modern reader. Jellies, blancmanges and jam, a vase containing some tall celery stalks, figs, 'a pyramid' of oranges and apples, raisins and almonds, and a dish of custard sprinkled with a fine dusting of nutmeg – such might have featured at a medieval banquet.

Cooking Methods

Barnaby Rich in *A New Description of Ireland*, 1610, wrote, 'God sends meat and the devil sends cooks': a sentiment that finds an echo in one of the early Irish sayings, 'There is no torture without marriage and no feast without roasting.'

Roasting there was, but the trouble with roasting over an open fire, as any amateur barbecue chef will tell you, is that if the item to be cooked is of any appreciable size, it will char on the outside while the inside is still raw. Skewering small birds, squirrels and the like on straight sticks and cooking them over hot embers is one thing, but it is not the ideal way to cook a deer.

It was the travelling Bronze Age people, from 1800 BC onwards, who resolved this dilemma. How to boil or bake large pieces of meat while on the move? The answer to that question was the *fulachta fiadh* and this method lasted until the Middle Ages. Having made a kill and prepared the animal for cooking, groups of hunters would dig a pit or trough in the ground and fill it with water. Choosing to dig in clay close to a stream made it easy to stop the water soaking away, and sometimes they lined the trough with stones or wood. (A cooking pit could have held up to 200 gallons of water.) A fire was lit nearby and large stones rolled into it to heat up. Once they were sufficiently hot, the stones were manoeuvred into the trough, which caused the water to boil. Meanwhile, large joints of meat had been wrapped in straw and these were lowered into the pit.

Now, the stress on red-hot stones flung into cold water was such that they sometimes split. These fractured stones were then thrown in a pile on the far side of the cooking pit and many of these ancient *fulachta fiadh* were found because the discarded stones made a distinctive horseshoe shape below the ground and invited archaeologists to dig at that spot.

At Craggaunowen, Co Limerick, you can see a working example, and after one experiment in reproducing the technique exactly, they say that the meat cooked at 20 minutes to the pound (450 g), the same as you would expect today.

A later method of cooking was to take the fresh carcase, skin it, cut it up and boil the meat in its own skin over a fire. Derricke's *Image of*

Irelande published in 1581 shows meat being cooked in this way. You might think that the skin would burn and burst, but this was not the case, all the heat being transferred to the liquid inside.

When we reach less primitive times, most cooking takes place indoors. A large cauldron (*coire*) was regarded as an essential piece of equipment in any prosperous household. The highest grade of *bóaire*, cattle owner, should have a bronze cauldron big enough to cook a boar while a high-ranking lord should have one capacious enough to fit the flesh of a cow as well as a flitch of bacon.

The protocols surrounding food and feasting vary widely from one society to another, but are never absent – there are always rules governing this prime human activity. Some early Irish texts specify that when a lord gave a banquet the different ranks must sit in their appointed places and eat the cut of meat appropriate to that rank.

One early book shows a bard with a poetic staff and above him the cooking spit. The main dish is evidently pork. The most important guests get the haunch or tenderloin steak, those of lower status get the shank, or the *leschruachait* (probably the centre-cut loin steak). Low-ranking persons get the belly, the chine or the shoulder fat.

Carving meat was a matter of ceremony. Quarrels flared up when a warrior was not given the portion he thought due to him. A Middle Irish tale tells of a magic cauldron, the *coire ansic*, in which pork and beef was cooked. Each guest who plunged a fleshfork into the cauldron pulled out the cut of meat appropriate to his or her status, so to a king would go a haunch, a queen would get the loin and so on. This fleshfork was a sturdy, long-handled fork used to lift pieces of meat out of the steaming cauldron. Brehon laws make it clear that the cook is not responsible for splashing hot broth on anyone in the kitchen, if he gives warning in a loud voice, 'Look out! Here goes the fork into the cauldron!'

In *The Vision of Mac Con Glinne*, this is well illustrated.

Seven strings of tripe, dangling
About each neck.

Swathed in a mantle of beefy fat
Beside his well-proportioned wife
I glimpsed the Chief;
Before the mighty cauldron's mouth
Crouched the Dispenser, his flesh fork
Upon his back.

Sometimes meat was boiled to make a broth but if so, this broth would still count as meat. St Mael Ruain's ascetic rule stated that a monk who is on a vegetable diet must refrain from broth made of meat as well as from meat itself.

In *The Yellow Book of Deichen*, preserved in Trinity College Library in Dublin, there is an illustration of the spit of Deichen, a legendary blacksmith of Tara. On the right is seen a handle for turning. In the picture, the spit is made of iron but there are many references to wooden spits. In *The Vision of Mac Con Glinne*, pieces of beef, mutton and ham are roasted on four straight spits of whitebeam. The cook (Mac Con Glinne himself) in a clean linen cap and apron was cooking for the king of Munster. In the story, the hero, in an attempt to coax the demon of gluttony out of the king's belly, orders Pichan, a wealthy chieftain, to provide him with 'juicy old bacon', tender corned beef, a side of mutton, a comb of honey, English salt on a silver dish and four perfectly straight hazel spits to carry the joints. Lighting a fire of clean ash wood, he sets up the loaded spits over it and as the meat cooks, he runs about the fire rubbing salt and honey into the pieces and turning the spit so deftly that not one drop of juice falls into the fire and all the flavour stays in the meat.

In the cabins of the poor, the fire was not usually raised in a grate, but made directly on the flat of the hearth. You could use the fire flexibly, splitting it up, so there were in effect three or four different fires.

Water would be boiling on one, the bastable with its cake of bread would occupy another, a small fire would be heating a flatiron and maybe a pot staying hot on another.

Most food was boiled, but you could bake a fowl in the bastable and in some farmhouses there were spits for holding meat. Old-time dressers have slots where they were stored when not in use. These spits consisted of a slim iron bar, bent into a crank at one end and tapered at the other. The pointed end was stuck through the fowl or joint and the spit supported at each end by a metal stand. A pan was set on the ground beneath the meat to catch the juices, and usually an old person or child was asked to turn the crank to ensure even roasting.

The thoughts of George Bernard Shaw conclude this chapter. He was a carnivore until the age of seventy, after which he became a committed vegetarian and lived a further twenty-four years as a lean and healthy one. The story goes that Alfred Hitchcock, portly and teasing, said to Shaw that just by looking at him he knew there was still famine in Ireland. Shaw replied, 'One look at you, Mr Hitchcock, and I know who caused it.'

But although Shaw believed that 'if we do not kill animals they will kill us' and he urged humane killing, he felt his own conscience was clear. 'My will contains directions for my funeral, which will be followed not by mourning coaches, but by herds of oxen, sheep, swine, flocks of poultry and a small travelling aquarium of live fish, all wearing white scarves in honour of the man who perished rather than eat his fellow-creatures. It will be, with the exception of the procession into Noah's Ark, the most remarkable thing of the kind ever seen.'

CHAPTER FIVE

POULTRY AND FEATHERED FOWL

Easter Sunday and Christmas Day are the two best days for eating. Today I had chicken and smoked ham for my dinner.
Amhlaoibh O Suilleabhain's diary, Easter Sunday, 6 April 1828

Poultry has always been popular with Irish people; if, over the centuries, the pig and the cow were essential farmyard animals, so, too, were the hens, ducks, geese and, eventually, turkeys. When they were choosing the images to put on the first coinage of the newly created Irish republic, a representation of a hen and her chicks was among those chosen, for they were an indisputable part of Irish rural life.

Until quite recently for most households in Ireland, chicken formed the centrepiece of a rather special meal, and often the bird was boiled, a method seen as less wasteful than roasting, as it gives not just meat but valuable stock, too. Young people nowadays laugh if you tell them that chicken was ever special, yet I can remember when a chicken was a once-a-month Sunday treat and a capon was a feast. That once-a-month chicken was not to be despised, because it was a bird that had pecked around in the fresh air and was chockful of flavour and nourishment. If you take the trouble to source a bird that has been reared in the old-fashioned way, its beak and claws intact and its day governed by the passage of the sun, you will discover that chicken has a flavour all of its own and there is no need to smother it with sauces and coatings to compensate for the texture and taste of intensively farmed chicken. A better life for the bird, too!

Arthur Young, an English agriculturist travelling in Ireland towards the end of the eighteenth century, notices that 'poultry in many parts of the kingdom, especially Leinster, are in such quantities as amazed me . . . this owing probably to three circumstances; first, to the plenty of the potatoes with which they are fed; secondly, to the warmth of the cabbins [sic]; and thirdly to the great quantity of spontaneous white clover (*Trifolium repens*) in almost all the fields.'

The Irish have kept fowl since time began. Even the poorest people managed to keep a few birds, feeding them on potato skins and household scraps, for hens and cocks gave a rich return for the small amount of food and labour expended on them – they produced eggs, feathers and, when their laying days were over, they were put in the pot, sometimes with a young rabbit or bit of bacon.

Even in rural towns, families kept the odd few so as to have eggs for the table, and maybe ducks, too. It was once commonplace for certain farm animals to wander in and out of the house (and to sleep in it, too). Tomás O Crohan explained, 'We had a post bed in the corner, and two beds at the bottom of the house. There used to be two cows in the house, the hens and their eggs, an ass and the rest of us.'

Inevitably, the hen entered into the general consciousness. An elderly friend, Austin O'Toole, described to me how lively his sister (a nun) was, despite her advanced years. 'She's full of pep. She's like a hen pecking oats.' And there is an old saying which is translated from the Irish as 'The three sharpest things on earth: a hen's eye after grain, a blacksmith's eye after a nail and an old woman's eye after her son's wife.'

Hens and cocks were so imbued into the fabric of daily life in Ireland that they were chosen as the standard from which early measurements were taken. The egg of a full-grown hen was taken to be four inches in circumference and five inches around the long axis and, halved, was used to measure liquids. The distance within which a cock-crow could be heard was used to measure area.

In the early Celtic period, a laying hen was valued at two bushels of grain, whereas a sexually active cock was worth only one. Once the hen stopped laying and the cock could no longer serve the birds in his flock, neither of them had a value of more than half a bushel – they were only fit for the pot. This system meant that only fairly old and stringy birds were eaten, so stewing and braising were the chosen methods of cooking – it was the rare cock, capon or hen that ended up being roasted, at least in the homes of the poor.

Keeping poultry was not entirely without its troubles. An early law text gives details of the various trespasses hens might perpetrate: snatching away, wasting and spilling. A fine could be imposed on their keepers if it could be proved that they had trespassed on someone else's property, and in fact, if the birds could not be made to stay inside their enclosure, they were required to be fitted with shoes made of rags, so they could only hobble around.

Keeping an eye on the laying or 'clocking' hen was the job of the woman of the house and the children. The half door that you see on many old Irish houses served several purposes – it let light in, it let smoke out, it kept a draught from cutting you about the ankles, and it kept the hens and their chicks in. The *bean an tí* often kept her laying hens in the house, because in the warmth of the kitchen they knew nothing of the seasons and continued to lay throughout the year. Arthur Young remarks that a family sitting down to a meal of potatoes was joined by 'the cocks, hens, turkeys, geese, the cur, the cat and perhaps the cow'. Chickens were not always given a place in the house, however – sometimes they were put into a wickerwork hencoop that could be kept in an outhouse or even up a tree to keep it safe from the attentions of Mr Fox.

It was not just the peasantry that kept fowl, either. The writer Peter Somerville-Large recalls a house in the country where he spent some of his boyhood: 'Illaunslea – my mother was creating a garden there . . . I enjoyed my own gaudy brood of bantams, little bright coloured cocks with their eunuch's crow, and the ridiculous Polish bantams, their eyes covered like miniature Bruins. But my mother's hens hated me and only by lifting up their rears with the end of a spade could I retrieve an egg without being savagely pecked.'

With the sizeable flocks of hens kept by the larger households someone could run out into the yard, grab a bird, wring its neck, pluck and singe its feathers and plunge it into the pot or skewer it on the spit at a moment's notice. The monastic settlements in particular, with their commitment to feeding all who came to their gates, were well stocked with poultry of various classes, so that they were as familiar around the place as a cat or a dog. Pictures of ducks and geese can be found doodled by the brothers in the margins of various manuscripts they were working on, and in the *Book of Kells* fantastical birds are painted in exquisite detail.

It is told that St Moling had tamed a fox, but that it reverted to its true nature one day and stole a hen from the monastery and ate it. (An old Irish adage maintains that 'breeding will break out in the eyes of a cat'.) When his master confronted the fox with his crime, the fox skulked away to a nearby convent, where he stole the abbess's hen in order to replace the one he'd killed. Carrying the substitute back alive, he laid it at the saint's feet, but the saint was not mollified and ordered him to take it back whence it came and admonished the fox, saying,

'From this day on live without stealing, as other animals do.' According to the legend, the fox obeyed and never stole again.

In 1926 Tomás O Crohan wrote, 'We lived in a cramped little house, roofed with rushes from the hill. Often the hens would nest in the thatch and lay a dozen eggs there.' He goes on to relate how the hens would nest so deep in the thatch that the women often lost them, for a hen wouldn't even answer the call to food when she was broody.

He recalls a story that happened in one of the 'big houses' (three to four metres wide and six to eight metres long). The man of the house was sitting at the head of the table, with his family gathered around for supper. He was startled when something fell into his wooden mug full of milk. 'He looked down and there was a lump of something drowning in the milk. They had to fetch the tongs to get it out, and not a one of them had the faintest idea what it was.'

The woman of the house identified it as a young chicken, whereupon her husband accused her of losing her wits and all looked set for a row, when another chicken fell down into the potatoes.

'"For God's sake, where are they coming from?" said the woman of the house. "Can't you see that they're not coming from hell, anyhow," said the man of the house. "It's some consolation that they're falling from above".' Then one of the children looked up at the roof and saw the wind and the sun coming through and when they went to the hole to close it, they found ten other chickens and the hen.

Eggs

Eggs have long been close to the heart of the Irishwoman, for by selling them she was able to bring a little money into the house, and since it was usually the job of the children to go looking for eggs laid under hedges and in other out-of-the-way places, they grew up familiar with hens and chicks, too.

In *The Vision of Mac Con Glinne* the poet describes them as 'pearls of the household', and in all of nature there is nothing more perfectly achieved and poetic in its simplicity than the egg. A new-laid egg is a treat, its shell hard to crack, its white viscous, its yolk a deep gold and its flavour deep and satisfying. The watery whites and pale yolks of battery eggs, along with a faint hint of fishiness in the taste, make them unappetising, and certainly not good enough for mayonnaise or soufflés.

Eggs have been beloved of the Irish for millennia – they were especially seen as food for the weak and sick, but they also served as a source of protein in the meatless diets of the ascetic orders. The clerical penitent was used to eating only bread, gruel, milk, vegetables and herbs from the garden, so the addition of eggs was greatly valued. On great religious holidays, the monks of Culdee were allowed eggs (hard-cooked) with curds and cheese or apples. On lesser feast days they might have eggs and lard and the flesh of deer and wild boar.

From the early legal commentaries, we learn that a hen was expected to lay up to fifty eggs a year, and we think the size was more or less that of a small pullet or bantam egg. In the wild, red junglefowl tend to lay a clutch of five or six eggs twice a year, but over the centuries broodiness has been bred to a minimum and we can now expect to get up to three hundred eggs a year. (If you keep taking eggs from a nest, birds will continue to lay, and it has been shown that you can take up to thirty eggs in one season from a pair of gulls without causing them to abandon their nest.)

One of the most famous stories in the early literature of Ireland is *The Banquet of Dun na nGedh*. King Donall, descendant of the legendary Niall of the Nine Hostages, desired some goose eggs – as great a luxury as caviar today – for a banquet he was to hold to show off his power and wealth in his new seven-rampart fort in the Boyne Valley. His servants went from place to place gathering enforced tribute for the feast but when it came to goose eggs, the men drew a blank. Dreading to return without them, they redoubled their efforts and finally heard of a hermit, Earc of Slane in Co Meath, who would wade out into the River Boyne up to his armpits and spend the day in prayer, returning at night for a meagre supper of a goose egg and a half, plus three sprigs of watercress. While he was at prayer, the servants found the cache of eggs and rushed them back to King Donall, but the hermit placed a curse on whomsoever would eat the stolen eggs, so when the first goose egg was placed on a silver platter and set before the king's foster son, Conghall, the platter turned to wood and the goose egg became a hen's egg. This was too great an insult to be borne by the men of Ulster, who took Conghall's part, and a battle was fought. The storyteller concludes, 'What is the difference at all between the egg of the red feathered hen and the egg of the white winged goose? Alas for him who destroyed all Erin for a dispute over an egg.'

Highly symbolic as they are, it was not surprising that eggs were often attended by ritual. Since the beginning of Christianity, eggs have been associated with Easter. In Ireland, eggs laid on a Good Friday were marked with a cross to be eaten on Easter Sunday, and eggs set to hatch on this day were said to produce healthy birds. Celebration eggs were coloured with natural dyestuffs – onion skins, spinach leaves and the like – and children made their own feasts, roasting eggs and potatoes on a fire outside, a custom called the *cludog*. The eggshells left at the end of the feast were kept to decorate the May bush. On a more sinister note, a common belief was that you could bring bad luck on your enemy by burying eggshells in his fields on the sly, so that his crops came to nothing.

The trouble with hens reared non-intensively is that they have never learned a consistency of production. A few eggs in the winter suddenly turn into a glut during March and April, so that family meals at that time are devoted to eggs – fried, poached, scrambled, boiled and even curried eggs in the more adventurous households.

When eggs were not always easy to get hold of in wintertime, methods of preserving eggs were devised, the main ones using waterglass, lard and butter. For the crocked eggs, people would buy a tin and follow the instructions printed on it. Waterglass might sound as if it came out of the Ark, but it was used within the last forty years, and eggs thus preserved were said to have a curious taste, but were all right for cakes and the sort of cooking where the egg itself is not prominent. Another method that kept eggs fresh for up to six months consisted of rubbing lard combined with borax (there to stop the lard from going rancid) into the eggs, but could not be used on any that were less than twenty-four hours old, otherwise the taste of the lard would penetrate the shell. The best method of all, and one still on the go in Co Cork, is hot-buttering the eggs. The idea is to gather eggs fresh from the nest, then smear your warm hands with unsalted butter and envelop the shell in a film of it. The hot butter soaks into the shell and when it cools it forms an airtight barrier, keeping the egg fresh for a minimum of six weeks. (Some people claim up to a year!)

Another old-fashioned way with eggs was to roast them in the ashes under a turf fire. The eggs were first pierced with a pin to prevent them from exploding and to let the sulphur fumes escape, then left in the warm ashes for half an hour or so until they were hard baked. I have tried this and can report that the yolk remains creamy and its taste is different from that of a normal hard-boiled egg.

The Irish love of poultry and eggs is attested by the English traveller, John Carr, writing in 1805, 'After a refreshing repose in clean beds, we rose to renew our rambles. At our breakfast we had excellent honey and eggs; the latter the Irish have certainly the merit of having introduced to the English tables . . . So much do the Irish consider their own eggs to be superior for sweetness and flavour, that some Irishmen will not allow that an English hen can lay a fresh egg.'

Another English traveller, Dorothy Hartley, reports from a cottage in Joyce's country in the 1930s, 'We all had tea together, new fresh soda bread, cream butter from the churn, and turkey eggs, herself looking after us . . . It was a lovely spacious sort of meal that replenished the teapot twice and politely lost count of eggs.' And she is struck by the sight that met her eyes on market day in Galway. 'Dozens of real jaunting cars. Early in the morning the country people come pouring in, donkeys, ponies and horses down the road . . . Donkeys trot in, bulky with panniers full of carrageen and dillisk, and by truck, lorry, bus and cart come eggs, eggs, eggs, hundreds of eggs in big, deep baskets.'

It was the housewives of Ireland who were the most intimately concerned with eggs, for eggs were their currency. In return for eggs they could get tea or sugar or tobacco from the local grocer – any commodity in which the farm was not self-sufficient. And on days like Galway market day, they might take in their surpluses to sell for actual cash. For the *bean an tí*, the goose really did lay a golden egg.

In Patrick Kavanagh's semi-autobiographical novel *Tarry Flynn*, the eponymous Tarry is a young man still living on the family farm, but dreaming of more. He finds an egg in a manger and eats it. 'It was not that he liked raw eggs but he believed that raw eggs produced great virility. Stallions got a dozen raw eggs in a bucket of new milk every day during the season.' And in *The Green Fool*, Kavanagh recalls an Easter picnic he and a friend managed to get together. 'We had our feast . . . with jam and syrup, three kinds of currant bread and three kinds of eggs. Mrs Gorman supplied the eggs – goose egg, hen eggs, and green duck eggs.'

Patrick Mackenzie, a former High Court Judge, told me how as a young man just starting out in the world of barristers, back in the early 1940s, he went down for the day to Wicklow Courthouse, part of the Eastern Circuit.

It was a pleasant start to my first day out of the Law Library and as we adjourned for lunch, I had a good appetite. I asked the young lady what there was on the menu. 'Eggs,' she replied. Thinking of fluffy scrambled eggs, omelettes, or even eggs Florentine, I asked her what way they were done. 'Hard boiled, medium boiled or soft boiled,' she said. And that was the fare. We all sat around one big table. Gus Cullen, the State Solicitor, presided, slopping out cups of tea from a huge tin teapot. We waited and waited until the girl came in with thick rounds of toast and a pot of marmalade. Eventually the eggs arrived in a bowl. 'Which are these?' asked Gus. 'These are the hard boiled,' said she. Five minutes later the medium arrived and the soft boiled last of all. I could never get to the bottom of why they invariably arrived in that order.

Molly Keane, in *Good Behaviour*, paints an unforgettably dry and clear-eyed portrait of the Anglo-Irish Big House during the 1920s. Someone arrives from the kitchen: "'It's Teresa's night out, so I brought ye a hunting tea – poor Mrs Lennon's poached eggs and rashers." The eggs were perfect, swelling primly on large slices of buttered toast, the lightened dust of cayenne blown over their well-matched pearls.'

Geese

While the cock and the hen were the most ubiquitous of farmyard poultry, the goose was not far behind. The Irish goose was a domesticated form of the greylag, and it was widely kept, for in the early law texts it was laid down that the grazing of two geese is the rough equivalent of the grazing required for one sheep.

Geese were seen as a luxury food. The poem, *The Land of Cokaygne*, found in a fourteenth-century manuscript, lists the delights to be found in Cokaygne, a land more sensual and more gratifying than heaven, with geese prominent.

Throstle, thrush and nightingale,
Woodlark and golden oriole,
Never stint their might,
Singing merrily day and night.
Fat geese roasted on the spit
Fly, God knows, to that abbey
And 'geese, all hot' they cry,
Carrying garlic in great plenty,
The best garnished man might see.
The larks, plump and couth,
Settle into man's mouth,
Stewed until they taste well,
Stuffed with gillyflower, caramel.
No one speaks of lacking liquor
But fills up without a care . . .

(Version by John Montague from Middle English)

One of the traditional days for serving goose in Ireland was for dinner at Little Christmas or the Women's Christmas – the Feast of the Epiphany, 6 January. It was also eaten on Michaelmas Day, 29 September, on St Martin's Eve, 11 November, and was the chosen dish for Christmas dinner. An old saying held that if you eat goose at Michaelmas (29 September) you will have good fortune all the year round, and that was the day when the goose fair was held. From Norman times a hiring or a rent day also took place on that date in some parts of the country. In Carlow in 1315, a landlord would accept as his rent either twenty old pence or its value in the form of a goose. In later times Michaelmas became one of the days of the year on which well-to-do farmers killed an animal and gave the food to their poorer neighbours – very often a goose or two from the flocks kept by the farmers' wives. In the apple-growing areas of Ireland, Munster and south Ulster, this was the day on which the apple harvest began, a time to make cider and serve it with a goose and baked apples or apple sauce.

Geese hatched out in the spring were put out to grass and were known as 'green' geese and regarded as something of a delicacy, as they were killed young. Folk wisdom has it that the best goose is less than a year old, with yellow feet. Most geese were kept until the grain was harvested after which they were put into the field to feed on the fallen grains – the so-called 'stubble geese'.

The signs to watch out for in a good goose are enumerated by Swift in his *The Progress of Poetry*.

> The farmer's goose, who in the stubble,
> Has fed without restraint or trouble,
> Grown fat with corn and sitting still,
> Can scarce get o'er the barn door sill;
> And hardly waddles forth to cool
> Her belly in the neighbouring pool:
> Nor loudly cackles at the door;
> For cackling shows the goose is poor.

The goose was usually cooked in the pot oven, stuffed. In the northern parts of the country, they would parboil the goose to draw off some of the copious fat then, when the broth was strong enough, they stuffed the goose and roasted it in the pot oven over or before the fire. In humbler homes, they would put the goose into a pot along with cold water and hang it from the crane over the turf fire until the water boiled. At this point it was removed and placed on a stand next to the fire with hot embers under it and left to simmer for an hour or more. At the end of that time, the bird was basted, and if there were any parsnips in the house they were slid in next to the bird and more coals were heaped on the lid. Finally, the lid was removed, the bird basted and a few rashers were draped over the breast. The fire was then stepped up to give a lively blaze and after a while the bird was cooked, with a golden brown skin and good broth in the pot.

Roast goose was an extravagance, but no stranger to the kitchens of the better off. Roasting was a cooking technique reserved for special occasions – a wedding or anniversary or when a match was made – as no one wanted to kill off birds that were still providing eggs. In medieval times the roast goose was served with apple sauce or garlic sauce and was stuffed with fruit and herbs. Later it was stuffed with mashed potatoes, breadcrumbs, bacon, onions and herbs. A side benefit of roasting was that pints of fat could be drained off the bird, and this fat was carefully put aside to serve as an all-purpose lubricant, from frying to easing machinery, and was commonly used as an embrocation to be rubbed into bad chests.

A rhyme dated 1709 goes as follows:

Question
Yet my wife would persuade me (as I am a sinner)
To have a fat goose on St Michael for dinner;
And then all year round, I pray you to mind it,
I shall not want money – oh, grant I may find it!
Now several there are that believe this is true.
Yet the reason of this is desired from you.
Answer
We think you're so far from having more
That the price of the goose you have less than before.
The custom came up with the tenants presenting
The landlords with geese, to incline their relenting
On following payments.

Up to fifty years ago, a common winter's pastime for country people was to gather at someone's house and spend the evening playing cards to win a goose. The prize was one worth having, and a dozen or more would try for it.

In some parts of Ireland, the details of finance and the dowry, discussed before a wedding, were known as 'plucking the gander', and Tommy Hanley told me a story of a house sale, where the vendor's solicitor sent a message over to the solicitor engaged by the buyers. Unfortunately for him, it was intercepted and inside the envelope they found a note saying, 'Here are two fat geese ripe for the plucking!'

Duck

Duck was another favourite bird, and Whitsuntide was a traditional time to eat it. At one time every farmyard had a few waddling around and duck eggs were much prized for boiling and baking. Anyone who has ever had a beautiful green duck egg will know that there is a lot of yolk and not too much white, and the flavour is rich and dense. When Josephine Lynch's ducks are laying, I feast on a boiled duck egg each morning. In some families, it was daddy that got the duck egg or even the goose egg, and mammy and the children took the hen's eggs, as being lighter and sweeter. The duck most commonly seen around the pond is a domesticated form of the mallard, native to most of the northern hemisphere. The wild duck was hunted, but it was only of minor importance.

Boiling seems to have been the common way of cooking duck. In the Middle Ages, duck was usually boiled with turnips or parsley and sweet herbs and in some places it was cooked with juniper berries and occasionally roasted with sage and onion stuffing.

The greatest complaint made about ducks is that they were greedy. One old lady in this parish used to say, 'Look at the ducks – the shovels on them! Ye'd never keep the food coming to them.' And another woman who kept them told me, 'Ducks would eat and eat and the neck swelling on them and they'd lay down and get up and eat again! You couldn't fill them.'

Saint Colman lived by a holy well near Templeshanbo, Co Wexford, and some ducks swam on a pool fed from it. St Colman tamed them so they would feed from his hand and they were as sensitive as the miner's canary – at the least disrespect offered to the clergy or the church they would fly off and return only when the sinner had done penance. One day a thief stole one of the ducks and put it in a pot of water to boil. But no matter how great the fire under it, the water stayed cold and the duck swam around on the surface of the water, so that in the end the hapless thief became frightened, and took the duck back.

Turkey

The turkey came into Ireland with the Tudors and Stuarts but has only been associated with Christmas dinner since the twentieth century. Sara Power's receipt book of 1746 gives a recipe for soused turkey.

> Get a fat Turkey Cock of a year old, kill and hang him up for two or three days, then take out the bones, and get four nutmegs and the like quantity of Mace, some beaten pepper, Cinnamon, and Salt enough to season it. Put all these in the body of the Turkey and a good piece of butter; boyl in half a pint of White Wine, and half a pint of Water, with the rind of the lemon.

They were not found on most mixed farms, and turkeys were not as easy to rear as other birds – they had a tendency to get sore eyes and the young would often sicken and die unexpectedly. The most common breed of turkey used to be the bronze, which is large and has a distinctive flavour, but a new breed of turkey, the small white turkey that came over from America, is very widespread now. The carcase is small in proportion to the weight of the meat and it looks impressive with its broad breast and pale flesh. Connoisseurs continue to favour the bronze.

The English writer Thackeray was drawn to Ireland, using it as a setting for one of his novels, *The Luck of Barry Lyndon*. In his *Irish Sketch Book* he relates how he once ended up at Kilroy's Hotel in Galway, along with four other travellers, and saw with incredulity that two turkeys were being brought to the table! Thackeray volunteered to carve. 'There are, as it is generally known, to two turkeys four wings. Of the four passengers, one ate no turkey, one had a pinion, another the remaining part of the wing, and the fourth gentleman took the other three wings for his share. Does everyone in Galway eat three wings when there are two turkeys for dinner?'

Feathered Game

While medieval monasteries in Britain and on the continent had a columbarium or dovecote, where pigeons were reared for the eating, there is no record of the equivalent in early Irish monasteries, although Saint Columba (Columb Cille) took his name from the dove, a symbol of peace, and Saint Patrick is described as 'a dove for gentleness and simplicity'.

The Anglo-Normans wrought many changes and built elaborate dovecotes, housing hundreds of birds. (This was still relatively small scale, for in medieval England at Willington, Bedfordshire, nesting boxes were provided for 1,500 pigeons in dovecotes.) Many of the smaller farmsteads within the Pale had dovecotes that held a dozen or so birds. There may not be a deal of meat on a pigeon apart from the breast, but they were a marvellously available source of food, particularly during the winter months.

Giraldus Cambrensis wrongly claimed that neither partridges nor pheasants could be found in Ireland, while we know that the pheasant was introduced by the Normans, and the partridge may well be native. Giraldus goes on to write that quail are plentiful, and his references to 'wild peacock' in the woods may well be a mistaken identification of the capercaillie, because the male's glossy blue-green breast is somewhat similar to that of the peacock. The capercaillie was common in Ireland and Scotland until the eighteenth century when it was hunted to extinction.

Under the Norman dispensation, the swan was categorised as a bird of the forest and reserved for the king, although the meat is said to be tough. In Old Irish sagas, warriors went out hunting the *geis*, a bird thought to be a swan, and it is thought that they also hunted wild geese that overwintered along the Irish coasts.

Puffins were not deemed to be meat and could therefore be eaten with a clear conscience at times of abstinence. They were part of the fish feast held for the enthronement of the Archbishop of Canterbury in March 1504.

Robin Flower in *The Western Island*, his account of life on the Great Blasket, tells of how, in the Great Famine times, some fishermen were returning home with no catch, when they spotted a lot of birds – guillemots, puffins and others – on the cliffs at Inishvillicane. One of the fishermen attempted the climb, reached the mouth of the hole in the cliff and drove the birds in, then went after them, throttled them and threw down the carcases to his fellows. Some ten dozen birds he sent fluttering down and they floated on the water and were picked up by men in curraghs. They called to him to come down, but he could not and he bade them goodbye. 'Home with you now in God's name, for I think these are the last birds I shall ever catch.' But the next morning at daybreak the fisherman's son went after his father and once the father reached level ground his welcome was mighty.

Giraldus notes that the Irish loathed heron flesh. While being entertained by the Irish kings in Dublin, Henry II attempted to persuade them to taste heron meat but it met with their displeasure. Actually, it is difficult in Ireland to be sure which bird is meant, the crane or the grey heron, for both tend to be called heron. The heron feeds on fish, insects and rodents, while the crane is mostly vegetarian in its diet. Moreover, the heron is difficult to domesticate (even from an egg) while the crane easily bonds with humans and in the laws of the sixth-century Franks there are references to the domesticated crane.

The young of the gannet are called *corrai* and, when they are in season, they are all fat. Many of the islanders along the coasts of Ireland at one time were eager to catch them because a young bird could weigh as much as a fat goose.

In Norman castles, blackbirds appeared on the table (four and twenty perhaps, but not, in Ireland, baked in a pie) and the usage did gain a certain currency; up to the early part of the twentieth century people would eat blackbirds and thrushes caught in snares. My father, Jim Hickey, recalls his childhood activities: 'In winter, we'd make cribs to catch birds. With twigs we'd make a beehive with a filed stick to hold it up. It'd be propped up in the snow. A filed stick just resting on something, very shaky. If a blackbird came – you'd put berries down, or bread – if a blackbird came and seen that, he'd disturb the stick and the cage would fall down on him. They called them cribs. Aye, we were cruel little bastards.'

At the beginning of the last century hunting was a major sport of the landed classes. Peter Somerville-Large remembers, 'Occasionally the menu might have been livened by birds shot by my Uncle Paddy. They were retrieved by Cicely, the springer spaniel named after a cousin who lived in Mayo. Her family was so poor that her brothers could not afford retrievers or hunting dogs, so Cousin Cicely used to put on her black bathing suit and plunge into the bog after the shot birds.'

In earlier times, snipe, woodcock, pheasants, partridges and plover were usually roasted on a spit or rolled in clay, feathers, beak and all, and baked in a hot fire. When it was judged that the bird was cooked, the lump of clay was raked out and broken apart over a plate, whereupon it was found that the feathers came away and the meat inside was cooked.

Native red grouse are very rare in Ireland today. But if you get your hands on one, the old way of stuffing grouse, with a lump of butter inside along with some wild bilberries or *fraughans* is hard to beat.

CHAPTER SIX

FRESH FROM THE SEA

According to *Larousse Gastronomique*, the following recipe makes a typical traditional Irish dish: 'Take a salt herring, open it out and remove the bone. Pour poteen over it and set it alight. When the flame dies down the herring is ready to eat.' Some innocent researcher was surely unaware of the equally traditional Irish delight in pulling someone's leg.

If the Irish now avoid rabbit and most other game, feathered or furred, and won't eat offal, their coldest shoulder is reserved for fish and shellfish. For a great many Irish people, especially in rural areas, sea urchins, mussels and oysters are seen not as luxury items but as objects of revulsion.

In fact, throughout the centuries, the knack of enjoying fish is one that few Irish people ever really acquired. The historian Roy Foster points out that in the early seventeenth century, 'English observers were surprised that the rich and various resources of fish and wildfowl were not tapped by the natives: fishing, for instance, tended to be monopolised by foreigners. During the Desmond wars, an English soldier found Burrishoole on Clew Bay in Co Mayo "the best fishing place for herring and salmon in Ireland; where a ship of 500 tons could ride close to the shore and frequented annually by fifty Devonshire fishing smacks, the owners of which paid tribute to the O'Malleys".'

Naturally, the bounty of the sea, the shore, the river and the lake were not totally ignored. Far from it. In ancient times hunters and fishermen relied greatly on fish, shellfish and seaweeds. Eels were an essential part of the diet of the early inhabitants of the island and continued to be so until very recent times. Seabirds were valued not only for their meat but also for the eggs in their nests, the gathering of which was often a perilous occupation, as anyone can well imagine who has stood shivering on the edge of the towering cliffs that ring the coast of Ireland.

Nevertheless, that intense love of seafood that one finds in Spain, for example, or in Japan, has never lodged itself into the Irish heart. The salmon and the trout may figure in the mythology and poetry of Ireland, but are essentially loved only by poets and game fishermen. It is ironic that one of the songs associated with Ireland worldwide is 'Molly Malone', for cockles and mussels are more eagerly sought out by immigrants to the country than by the Irish themselves. Molly may have wheeled her barrow through its streets, broad and narrow, but Dublin's true native dishes are Dublin Coddle, and sheep's head – both meaty treats for poor people until recent prosperity turned us all squeamish.

Some of the Irish lack of enthusiasm for fish is doubtless based on grim experience. Such cries as 'Fresh herrings, large Dublin Bay Herrings alive here – Here's a large fresh cod alive, here's large sole or plaices alive, or fine Boyne salmon' were woefully misleading. Even in Dublin, beside the sea, the fish were not actually *alive* and before transport was mechanised, the horse and cart carrying fish to such inland places as Athlone or Portlaoise could take days to reach its destination. In even mild, let alone hot, weather the fish soon started to stink, so it was little wonder that it was not viewed with favour. Dean Swift writes bitterly of the duplicitousness of fish-hawkers in Dublin:

> The Affirmation solemnly made in the cry of Herrings, is directly against all Truth and Probability, Herrings alive, alive here . . . And, pray how is it possible that a Herring . . . should bear a Voyage in open Boats from Howth to Dublin, be tossed into twenty Hands, and preserve its Life in Sieves for several Hours? . . . But this is not the worst. What can we think of those impious Wretches, who dare in the Face of the Sun, vouch the very same affirmative of their Salmon, and cry Salmon alive, alive; whereas, if you call the Woman who cryes it, she is not asham'd to turn back her Mantle and show you this individual Salmon cut into a dozen Pieces.

It is striking that in *The Vision of Mac Con Glinne*, wherein the poet catalogues all the delectable foodstuffs that might constitute a feast, it is cream, butter, cheese and milk that are given most prominence, with fish figuring very little. When the twentieth-century food writer Theodora Fitzgibbon admits, 'Generally speaking, methods of cooking fish in Ireland are not elaborate or unusual; often it is cooked simply with plenty of good butter and cream', one cannot help thinking that the butter and cream are more welcome than the fish itself.

There are, of course, instances of someone relishing the pleasures of fresh fish, simply cooked. A sportsman wrote in his diary in 1897:

> Here I will describe a morning repast. First a large iron pot slung by three sticks over a good clear

turf fire; well washed but not skinned potatoes, a perch, split and well-seasoned and a crimped trout [crimped means slits cut across the sides], of eleven pounds, hot even unto burning; plenty of lake water clear as crystal; and finally an infusion of the best Cork whiskey.

The sportsman, however, was English.

Another English writer on a visit to Ireland was bewildered by the native lack of interest in matters piscine. The admirable Jane Grigson spent a week or more in a Donegal village but although the fishermen were constantly plying their trade with lobster pots, not one lobster was ever spoken of, let alone put on the table, and she came away wondering if the only thing the Irish ever ate was boiled bacon, cabbage and potatoes.

I can add to this catalogue of evidence from my own experience. I once lived near Paris and ate out a great deal. A favourite restaurant, the Brasserie Flo, was located in a mildly seamy part of the city and access to it was up an alleyway. Outside the doors stood men in rubber boots and aprons, engaged in the Sisyphean task of opening oysters for the diners inside.

A great friend, Denis Cahalane from Dublin, was visiting Paris, so I decided to take him out for a lavish lunch, and as a treat ordered the full *plateau de fruits de mer*, which duly arrived. The huge oval metal tray with its bed of seaweed was set on a stand in the middle of the table. Oysters on the half shell rubbed shoulders with lobster, clams, sea urchins, crab claws, prawns, shrimps and whelks. Denis took one horror-stricken look at this and exclaimed, 'Jasus, there's stuff there I'd be afraid to walk over, never mind eat!'

And when I first arrived in Ireland, before I knew any better, I took my second cousin Anne Costello to Moran's seafood house near Kilcolgan on the Galway coast, and watched as she desperately scoured the menu for something edible among all the horrid fishy things, settling finally, with great relief, on the last item on the list, a ham salad, surely put there as an act of charity.

A Penitential Dish

I think that the basis of dislike lies in part in dreary methods of preparing and cooking fish. Boiled fish is unlikely to raise much enthusiasm, and fish well supplied with bones is even less appetising cooked that way. Peter Somerville-Large remembers 'Huge bland pollock, which always tasted of tissue paper and pins'. Many of the varieties of fish commonly found in Ireland are perfectly good, but a tendency to boil all fish has done less than justice to them. Perhaps because they could not afford to squander fat, the Irish poor seldom fried fish, although they did cook them on the griddle from time to time.

On the other hand, Thackeray wrote lyrically of some trout he ate in Ireland on a sporting holiday.

> Marcus, the boatman, commenced forthwith to gut the fish, and taking down some charred turf-ashes from the blazing fire, on which about a hundredweight of potatoes were boiling, he – Marcus – proceeded to grill on the floor some of the trout, which afterwards we ate with immeasurable satisfaction. They were such trouts as, when once tasted, remain for ever in the recollection of a commonly grateful mind – rich, flaky, creamy, full of flavour. A Parisian gourmand would have paid ten francs each for the smallest cooleen among them . . . they were red or salmon trouts – none of your white-fleshed brown-skinned river fellows.

It is often proposed that fish became associated in the minds of Irish Catholics with penance and self-punishment. Since Fridays and holy days of obligation were days of fasting and abstinence whereby meat was forbidden, the main meal of the day was often based around fish, but I must demolish the notion that Catholics were obliged to eat fish on Fridays and other fast days – they were not.

The catching of sea fish was always a fraught business, especially on the wild western coast, where the Atlantic rolls in over thousands of miles until it hits Ireland, the first landmass to check its force. The boats in which sailors ventured out were frail and Synge's *Riders to the Sea* perfectly articulates the fatalistic acceptance of the Aran Islanders that the ocean must claim some of them from time to time.

Cecil Woodham-Smith, in her classic work *The Great Hunger*, picks up on this vulnerability as a partial explanation of why fish did not play a bigger part in the diet of the people at a time when they were starving.

The national boat of Ireland is the 'curragh', a frail craft made of wickerwork, covered originally with stretched hides and latterly with tarred canvas. It was not suitable for the use of nets in deep-sea fishing. Since most of the deep-sea fish lay several miles out to sea in forty fathoms of water, a vessel of at least fifty tons would be needed to go out there. If a gale blew from the east, the nearest port of refuge was Halifax, Nova Scotia. Besides, when the potato failed, fishermen had pawned their equipment to get a little money to buy meal. There were hardly any full-time fishermen – most had to grow potatoes for their families, because the chances of going to sea were so precarious. The seas might be teeming with fish, but if they had not the equipment or if the weather was severe, the fish were inaccessible to them. In fact, there seems never to have been a time when Irish fishermen had a suitable fleet.

A Fishing History

From archaeological evidence, particularly kitchen middens, it seems the very early inhabitants of Ireland moved from one site to another according to the season of the year. In the early spring they foraged along the coastline, picking shellfish from the rocks – limpets, cockles, periwinkles and mussels – and digging for sand eels. Fish such as ling, mackerel and sole might, with a bit of luck, be found in the river estuaries. Seabirds nesting along the cliffs – puffins, gulls and auks – constituted a twofold source of food, not just meat but also eggs. In spring, too, hunters were on the lookout for the first run of salmon, even then considered a kingly fish, and later on these hunter-gatherers followed the salmon upriver to the inland loughs. Here in the summer they caught other fish, including eels, rich in protein and a good, oily fish, although they were easiest to catch when they shoaled and began to move downstream in the autumn.

Later on, new settlers arrived, equipped with better tools, including tridentine fish spears, a well-preserved example of which was found at Strokestown, Co Roscommon. It has been suggested that these people knew how to smoke fish, eels especially, and since they were driven by the necessity of laying up food for the bleak months of winter, this seems probable. In the kitchen middens all around the coast are shells of limpets, mussels, oysters and periwinkles, and bones from cod and wrasse have been found in early Christian sites, although in general the Irish concentrated on freshwater fish, for the simple reason that deepwater fish lay several miles out to sea and the flimsy craft of the time were not up to venturing that far.

Old texts refer to catching fish in a net, presumably one made of linen thread tied in meshes. A *Life* of Saint Mo Ling refers to a miraculous catch in which there was a salmon in every third mesh in the net. Net fishing was forbidden from vespers on Saturday to tierce on Monday. Anyone discovered disobeying this rule by putting out nets was dealt with severely. In addition, 'sea-picking', which meant hunting for crabs, shrimps, limpets and edible seaweed, was not allowed on a Sunday.

Especially in summertime, the porpoise (its Irish name translates as 'the pig of the sea', perhaps because of its blubbery flesh) is found in waters around Ireland and may travel far up rivers. As we learn from the *Annals of Ulster*, a great slaughter of porpoises is recorded for the year AD 828 in Co Louth, carried out by Norsemen who had sailed across the Irish Sea to the east coast. Since literacy belonged to the monks, who hated the Norsemen, and took every opportunity to portray them as barbarian invaders, we should treat their testimony with some scepticism. However, this taking of the sea mammals was especially worth commenting on because salmon, seals and porpoises were supposed to belong to kings living by the sea.

There is no evidence that the early Irish hunted whales, but stranded whales were fair game. In 1246 the *Annals of Connacht* record a whale stranded at Drumcliffe in Co Sligo, whose arrival brought 'great relief and joy to the whole territory'. As a rule, the Church proscribed the eating of carrion, but it was permissible to eat the flesh of a stranded whale, provided that it had not begun to rot. Of course, no whale automatically belonged to the people and the head of the kin group had to petition the king, who would then allow the people to keep the whale or order it to be kept for his own use. Professor Fergus Kelly speculates 'The king's entitlement to a stranded whale is perhaps linked with the idea that such windfalls are a direct result of his virtues as a ruler.'

It was believed that a good king brought fertility and abundance to the land he ruled; it was written, 'it is through the justice of the ruler that many creatures and many animals from the deep and great seas are cast up on lawful shores', and again, 'it is through the justice of the ruler that abundance of fish swims in streams'.

At the beginning of the sixth century fishing rights were more or less open to all freemen, but as the population grew, the old freedoms were restricted and the following two centuries saw more and more land being enclosed. By the end of the eighth century it is doubtful if any land of economic value remained unappropriated, and fisheries, both inland and in tidal waters and estuaries, became private property. When food was in short supply, fishing and gathering rights could be a matter of life and death and were therefore strictly regulated, not just by the kings and lords but also by the early Church. Fishing rights were given to those who owned the riverbanks, and these riparian owners were legally entitled to erect a fish-weir extending to one-sixth of the breadth of the river. Naturally, if the same person owned banks on both sides this added up to one-third, a valuable right to have, and severe penalties were laid down in law for poaching or interfering with weirs.

Since the Stone Age, man has been used to catching fish, by spearing, gaffing, tickling, netting, hooking with rod and line, poisoning and other methods. Mostly, the Old Irish sources refer to catching fish by governing the flow of rivers or estuaries by means of weirs made of stones, or stakes and wattling, or some combination of these; often the weirs fulfilled a dual purpose of trapping fish and driving the watermill.

Weirs are most effective for catching migratory fish, such as salmon and eels. One technique used by the Irish weir builders was to force the fish into a channel so that they might be easily speared, hooked or netted, and another was to set wickerwork baskets in gaps let into the weir, so that fish swimming in were unable to get out.

A gruesome image is recorded in the *Annals of Connacht*. In the year 1225, the people of Cul Cearnadha were fleeing for their lives from a rival lord and a band of Normans and many of them were driven into the water at Ballycong, Co Mayo. The annals relate that the baskets of the weir were full of drowned children.

A Land of Plenty

In the early days of Celtic Christianity, saints and beasts often engaged in conversation, if you believe the early texts. It is St Columb Cille (St Columba) that we have to blame for the look of a flounder. He was out in a boat one day and noticed a shoal of flounder passing by.

'Is this a removal, flounder?'[2] he asked. 'Yes it is, crooked legs,' replied the flounder, saucily. 'If I have crooked legs,' swore the saint, 'may you have a crooked mouth.' And so its mouth has had a twist to it from that day forth.

Early monks and scholars were familiar with the inland waters of Ireland. A ninth-century *Life* of St Ciaran of Clonmacnoise describes the Shannon as 'very rich in different varieties of fish', and the teeming fisheries of the Corrib in Galway are explained by the miracle of St Enna, who blessed the lake and 'asked God that there should be a plenitude of fish there'. St Patrick is said to have blessed the Sligo river 'so that it is the milch cow of the waters of Ireland, for in it fish is caught every quarter of the year'. The eel-fisheries of the Shannon are significant enough to be mentioned in the early text *The Colloquy of Ancients* and they also attracted the attention of our old friend Giraldus Cambrensis. He claimed knowledge of Ireland:'This Ireland is also specially remarkable for a great number of beautiful lakes abounding in fish and surpassing in size those of any other countries I have visited. The rivers and lakes are also plentifully stored with the sorts of fish peculiar to these waters, and especially three species, salmon and trout, muddy eels and oily shad.' He goes on to report that the fishermen of Lough Neagh complain 'not of a scarcity of fish, but of too great catches and the breaking of their nets'. However, he is not entirely admiring, remarking that the Shannon abounds in lamprey, 'a dangerous delicacy'. (Henry II is said to have died of a surfeit of them.)

According to Giraldus, Ireland 'does not produce some fishes found in other countries such as pike, perch, roach, barbell and gudgeon. Locks are also very rare but then,' he admits magnanimously, 'every country is deficient in some particular

[2]   A removal is what happens when a dead body is taken to church, prior to a funeral mass or is waked at home. In both cases, large numbers of people arrive to pay their respects.

product. In Great Britain there are no tortoises or scorpeans and neither Italy nor Palestine have salmon.' He concedes, however, 'On the other hand, the lakes of this country contain three species of fish which are found nowhere else . . . These three species of fish make their appearance in summer only and are not seen in winter.' He further reports that 'in Ulster, not long before the English came over, a fish was found at Carlenford of immense size – which had three gold teeth of 50 lb weight.'

Edmund Spenser who, from his home in Co Cork, wrote *The Faerie Queene* in the second half of the sixteenth century, makes mention of 'the pleasant Boyne, the fishy, fruitfull Ban', but in *The Chronicles of Ireland*, 1587, his near-contemporary John Hooker, a virulent anti-Catholic and what is known in Ireland as a chancer, reports the following less than pleasant tale:

> Likewise in the bay of Smerwick, or Saint Marie Wick, the place which was first seasoned with this rebellion, there happened a ship to be there, lost through foul weather, and all the men being drowned were there cast on land. The common people who had a long time lived on limpets, orewads [seaweed] and such shellfish as they could find, they took them up and most greedily did eat and devour them. And not long after, death and famine did eat and consume them.

Fynes Moryson was an Elizabeth Englishman, writing about Ireland as a master in a colonised land. In *An Itinerary*, begun in 1606, he remarks:

> Ireland hath in all parts pleasant rivers, safe and long havens, and no less frequent lakes of great circuit, yielding great plenty of fish. And the sea on all sides yields like plenty of excellent fish, as salmon, oysters

(which are preferred before the English) and shellfish with all other kinds of sea fish. So as the Irish might in all parts have abundance of excellent sea and freshwater fish, if the fishermen were not so possessed with the natural fault of slothfulness [that] no hope of gain [and] scarcely any fear of authority can in many places make them come out of their houses and put to sea.

A rosier picture is painted by Dr Massari, who was the secretary of Archbishop Rinuccini, Nuncio Extraordinary to the Confederation of Kilkenny in 1645. In a letter home, he reported that people were well nourished and the price of fish was noteworthy. 'Butter is used abundantly. There is plenty of fruit: apples, pears, plums and artichokes. All foodstuffs are cheap. A fat bullock costs 16 shillings, a sheep one and three pence, a pair of fowls five pence, eggs four for a penny. A good-sized fish costs a penny. We bought a thousand pilchards or oysters for a shilling.'

The poor people fared more simply. Sir William Petty, a pioneer of the school of political economy, writing around this time states 'Their food is bread in cakes, whereof a penny serves a week for each; potatoes from August till May, mussels, cockles and oysters near the sea, eggs and butter made very rancid by keeping it in bogs. As for flesh, they seldom eat it . . .'

Fish and Famine

The Claddagh is an ancient village touching Galway city but always regarded as independent of it. The famous Claddagh gold ring, with its symbol of a heart clasped between two hands, surmounted by a crown, has circled the globe, and the people of the Claddagh even today are fiercely proud of coming from this tight-knit community. Fishing was the main activity of the men of the Claddagh and at one time there was a famous market there where you could find 'cods, lings, hawkfish, turbets, plaises, hadogs, whitings, gurnanes, mackerel, herrings, pilchards, a liberall of oyster, scallops, cokles, musles, razures . . . plentie of lobsters, crabs and shromps' and even 'great whales, grampuss and porcupisses and thunies . . .'

An English visitor to the Claddagh, Francis B. Head, a former Lieutenant Governor of Upper Canada, was confident that he could capture the character of the country in the first week of his visit, leaving the second free to collect statistical data, and he published his findings in 1852 in the honestly named *A Fortnight in Ireland*.

Since his visit was made during the years of the Great Famine, an emigrant ship was lying at anchor in Galway Bay, some mile and a half out and, curious to see it, he engaged two young lads to take him out there in their boat. In reply to his enquiry as to what sort of emigrants were on board the ship, the boy replied, 'They're all from this neighbourhood.' After pausing a few seconds, he added, 'They're distroyed out of this land, and must go to Ameriky!'

The elder of the two boys volunteered that they had been fishermen 'since we were four years awake' and were often out in the boat for a week at a time, wet through and with only the stone ballast for a bed. Their conversation continued thus.

'What do you subsist on while you are out?' I enquired.

'We ate bread and cook mackerel with turf, and we arlways carry two kegs of warter with us.'

'But,' said I, 'will the fish you catch for sale keep for five days?'

'Oh yes, yere Arn'r,' he replied; 'we take the goots and liver out o' um, and then they'll keep a week.'

Tomás O Crohan, born on the Great Blasket Island in 1856, when the effects of the Great Famine were still being suffered, had little experience of the outside world and little formal learning, yet he wrote a small masterpiece, *The Islandman*.

And the food I got was hens' eggs, lumps of butter and bits of fish, limpets and winkles – a bit of everything going from sea or land . . . we had fish with them [potatoes] – salted scad [horse mackerel] and that's a very sweet fish. My mother had brought a dish of limpets from the strand with her . . . she was roasting the limpets and throwing them to us one by one like a hen with chickens.

Those who lived near the coast fared better when food was short, not just in remote places but near the cities, too. In recent times, Sandymount Strand was the favourite cockle ground of Dubliners until the waters of Dublin Bay became polluted. You spotted the site of the cockle by markings where the sand curled up like a worm. Fisherfolk said that you could not eat cockles until they had had three drinks of April water – that is to say that the tide had to come in three times before the season started. They were a favourite Dublin supper dish, well washed to remove the sand, then boiled. In addition there were 'bandals', a shellfish that looked like large mussels, and that had to be dug up by a spade.

Ling: the Beef of the Sea

A fish that kept many alive in Ireland through the winter months and through hard times is the ling. Writing of her *Irish Holiday* during the 1930s, Dorothy Hartley observed, 'Skerries has a bracing air, clean sands and good fishing. They were selling dried ling in the little stone and thatched shop halfway down the street and a huge complete fish was hanging up. Along the coast a lot of this good fish is eaten, most of it cured and such curing is done along the west coasts of both Scotland and Ireland and as far north as Iceland.'

Ling is the largest member of the cod family, reaching on occasion 45 kg, and it inspired the old Gaelic saying 'Ling would be the beef of the sea if it had always salt enough, butter enough and boiling enough.' Up until the 1950s, you would see dried ling, once called stockfish (from the Norwegian *stokfisk*) very commonly.

Nowadays, little stone and thatched shops are thin on the ground, and we are more likely to buy dried salt cod from an ethnic food store – the Portuguese in particular love salt cod. It can be as stiff as a board and will require long soaking to reconstitute it, but it can amply repay the effort, as anyone who has eaten the Portuguese *bacalao* and the French *brandade de morue* will know.

I have vivid memories of a fine, big piece of salt cod that my friend Mimi Roberts bought one Easter at a market stall in France, intending to serve it with aioli and spring vegetables. After having been assured that overnight was long enough, we soaked it a full day, with changes of water, but alas even that was not long enough and although it looked nice and plump, it tasted as if a whole drum of salt had been poured on it and we had to gather up the plates before we all turned into Lot's wife.

A site at Newferry, Co Antrim, provides evidence of fish being smoked as far back as 6000 BC, and we also know that from ancient times quantities of fish, particularly ling and herring, were salted and dried for use in the winter months. These salt fish undoubtedly supplied some essential protein, but it is difficult to find many instances of these foods being actively enjoyed. Amhlaoibh Ui Shuileabhain's diary entry for 2 April 1831 reads, 'I do not like salt fish, and fresh fish was not to be had, except too dear and seldom.'

Once a staple food in the west of Ireland, ling was saluted by the Kerry writer John B. Keane, who, being familiar with it in its common dehydrated state, declared that it was 'good enough to sole your boots with'. Certainly, the curing tended to toughen it – Sir William Petre's cook at Ingatestone Hall in Essex is recorded as having to use a hammer to break up the pieces.

Florence Irwin, who was known by the title of the book she wrote in 1949, *The Cookin' Woman*, recalls, 'Thirty years ago, as you approached Cape Clear Island the low hedges were covered in the month of July with what looked like white garments of even shape and size. On getting a closer view you found these were large flat fish being dried in the sun after salting. Ling, in fact. This fish was procurable in all country shops at 4d a pound and was a popular purchase for the dinner on Friday and other fast days.'

Nothing fancy was ever done with ling. Either it was soaked and then heated up in milk, or else cooked, flaked and whipped into mashed potatoes. In the poorest cottages, where cooking vessels were scarce and perhaps fuel, too, the ling was laid on top of the potatoes before they were put down to boil. There is a pleasing aesthetic in the simplicity of this, the ling being cooked in the steam from the potatoes rather than immersed in water.

King Herring

Of all the fish eaten in Ireland, perhaps the most widespread, and a mainstay of the kitchen in both town and country, was the herring. Appropriately, its name comes from the Teutonic *heer*, meaning 'army', for the herring travels in shoals like a regiment, and indeed it was an army of people who ate them. In Irish waters herrings shoal in September, hence the name 'harvest herrings'. They may be potted, pickled (although pickling is inexplicably uncommon in Ireland), salted, dried, smoked and sometimes a combination of these processes, as with the red herring (yes, it really exists) which is a herring first heavily salted and then heavily smoked. The kipper is a herring first split and then cured. Whitebait, the very small fry of the herring and sprat, were always eaten fresh.

Baked Spiced Herring

This is a simple but very effective recipe and you can adapt it for mackerel, too. Instead of the usual cold pickle, this cooks the fish, but once it has been allowed to cool in its juices, it produces a lovely jelly and tastes surprisingly sweet.

8 herring of an even size, if possible	7–8 cloves
1 large onion, very finely sliced	7–8 black peppercorns
2 bay leaves	Salt
1 blade of mace	Vinegar – malt is traditional, red wine vinegar more delicious

Fillet your herrings and cut each half of the fish lengthwise, so each herring gives you four long thin pieces. Roll the fish and either wedge them tightly together in a lightly greased flat ovenproof dish or, if the dish is too big, skewer them with a cocktail stick. Add your sliced onion, scatter the various spices over the top, plus a sprinkle of salt, and barely cover with equal quantities of vinegar and water. Bake the herrings uncovered for 1 hour in a slow oven, then remove and allow them to cool. Some cooks serve them hot, but I find them better cold in their jellified liquor, when the flavour is very sweet and mild. A dollop of sour cream, crème fraîche or even Greek yoghurt alongside the herring, plus a few cold, waxy potatoes makes a fine meal.

The glory years of the salt herring were the eighteenth and nineteenth centuries, when a basic and monotonous diet called for a tasty relish. Vast quantities were preserved by close-packing them into barrels between layers of salt for winter use, and when they were needed a few were removed and soaked overnight in water. (Ling, mackerel and eel were also salted in this way.)

The herring is one of the staples of the Scandinavian kitchen and the Norsemen encouraged herring fishing around the eastern and northern ports where they were most active. These early fishermen must have followed the bonny shoals of herring far enough from their home waters, for we read that in 1217 all the herringmen of Ireland from Waterford to Derry went to the Isle of Man, where, we learn, they committed acts of violence and were put to death. Herrings played an important part in the urban diet, too, and provided a cheap source of protein for the poor. Jonathan Swift transcribed the fisherwoman's cry when selling her Dublin Bay herrings.

> Be not sparing,
> Leave off swearing.
> Buy my herring
> Fresh from Malahide.
> Better was never tried.
> Come, eat them with pure fresh butter and mustard,
> Their bellies are soft, and as white as a custard.
> Come sixpence a dozen, to get me some bread,
> Or, like my herrings, I soon shall be dead.

A fine grasp of the language, she had, that fishwife. (Of course it was Swift himself, in his *Verses Made for The Women who Cry Apples*.)

It was not only to the poor that the herring appealed. Alfred Perceval Graves, Bishop of Limerick and grandfather of the poet Robert Graves, wrote in praise of the herring in 1846:

> Let all the fish that swim the sea,
> Salmon and turbot, cod and ling,
> Bow down the head and bend the knee,
> To herring, their King! – to herring, their King.

There is a grim irony in the timing of this paean of praise – it was written in one of the worst years of the famine, when the poor beyond the gates of the Bishop's palace were perishing from lack of food.

The pollan (*Corregonus autumnalis pollan*) sometimes goes by the name of the freshwater herring, a fish found in Lough Neagh, Lough Erne and both Lough Dergs (confusingly, there are two Lough Dergs in Ireland), having adapted to these lakes in the early post-glacial era when there were shorter links to the sea. Until the beginning of the twentieth century pollan fishing was by far the most important industry on Lough Neagh. The fishing season used to begin on St Brigid's feastday (1 February) and end at Hallowe'en (31 October) but over-fishing depleted the stocks, causing commercial exploitation to cease.

In the old days the fishmongers' cry, 'Pollan alive and kicking in the cart' would bring out the housewives, who would buy the fish for frying, although occasionally they went into the soup pot. It was customary to save some pollan for the winter by gutting and stringing them on sally (willow) rods to be wedged under the chimney canopy, where the smoke from the turf fire would dry and flavour them.

Fried Pollan and Fried Herring

Generally, both pollan and sea herring were trimmed, scaled, gutted and their heads removed before being tossed in flour or, in the Scottish fashion, in fine oatmeal. Some fat (lard, dripping or bacon fat) was then heated in the frying pan and both sides were sealed over a lively flame to make the skin crisp, before the heat was reduced or the pan moved to a cooler part of the fire and the fish fried more slowly for another 5 minutes or so.

In a meat-loving country such as Ireland, the six weeks of abstinence during Lent were hard to get through and there had to be a scapegoat. On the last Saturday before Easter, parades took place centred on 'The Whipping of the Herring', during which a bedraggled fish was tied to the end of a long pole and marched through the streets, gleefully whipped by a crowd of lads, who were often, unsurprisingly, butcher's apprentices, only too glad to be back in business after a lean period. In some towns they even drowned the herring!

In the last hundred years the fortunes of the herring have fluctuated a good deal. After the Congested Districts Board intervened at the beginning of the last century and imported special teams of Scottish curers to teach local people around the main fisheries off the Donegal coast how to process the catch properly, the resulting Donegal 'matje' (a virgin herring maturing for the first time) acquired such an excellent reputation on the German and Russian markets that Buncrana, the centre for trading, saw considerable numbers of buyers congregating each year for the spring fishing.

This happy state of affairs did not last, however. Revolution in Russia and the impoverished state of much of Europe following World War I destroyed demand from those countries and once the Scottish fleet had resumed fishing after the war, the British merchants no longer needed Irish fish. Moreover, if Russia was experiencing great upheaval in the early years of the twentieth century, so was Ireland itself, where a civil war was raging.

By the end of the decade fishermen had become so discouraged that many of them neglected their equipment and when they were unable to meet their loan repayments their boats were confiscated by the State. Things got worse during the 1930s, a grim period worldwide, with the Depression spreading despondency. Although matters did take an upswing again, thanks in large part to Franklin Roosevelt, people had lost the habit of buying herring and demand declined.

In the last few decades, the traditional cured herring has given way to the herring frozen at sea and exported to Germany and Scandinavia, where they love soused herring or rollmops. Japanese dealers are also very interested in buying herring roe, although there is an inherent danger in supplying this, as in order to get good quality roe you must catch the herrings immediately before they spawn, when the shoals are densely packed and moving slowly, leading to very high catches. Great for securing roe, not so great for the next generation of the fish.

Saltwater Staples

Mackerel are so beautiful, with their highly recognisable metallic blue-black markings, it is a pity they are dismissed, rather. They have always been found in great numbers off the coast and were once very widely eaten in Ireland, if not always enjoyed. The problem with them is that they need to be eaten ultra-fresh. Once they have been out of the sea for a while, it is best to hot-smoke them and serve them with a sharp sauce, such as gooseberry or rhubarb stewed with only a little sugar. Because they are naturally very oily, they are excellent grilled and make a great choice for a barbecue as they need no marinade.

Apart from the equally venerable expedient of boiling fish in seawater, a very old method of cooking fish, mackerel especially, is to poach or steam it over seaweed, which gives a wonderful flavour, providing the fish is spanking fresh and the seaweed well washed.

A hollow was dug in the sand or earth, and a fire lit inside it. When the flames died down, the fire was covered with seaweed, cress or sorrel and the fish laid on top. Large fish such as turbot or salmon took around 30 minutes, while smaller fish such as mackerel or trout took far less.

In Ireland the mackerel was often the mainstay of a poor family living along the coast, and scad was another fish they had recourse to, this scad being commonly called a 'horse mackerel' although it is not part of the mackerel family, lacking the distinctive markings of the true mackerel and having rather coarse, bony flesh.

Pollack, also called lythe, is a quality eating fish that has been plentiful in Ireland for centuries. Good-sized ones have large-flaked white flesh and pollack nowadays would provide a decent substitute for cod, whose stocks are seriously depleted.

The Silver Trout

Different fish have their admirers. Ewan MacColl wrote a superb modern-day folk song about hunting for 'The Shoals of Herring', sung incomparably by the late Luke Kelly. The salmon is accepted as the noblest of fish. But the most inspiring is surely the trout.

In a poem written somewhere between the eleventh and twelfth centuries, Marban, a hermit, sings gratefully of his sparse diet.

> All at evening
> the day's first meal
> since dawn's bread:
> trapped trout, sweet sloes
> and honey, haws
> beer and herbs.

A thousand years later, in Yeats's lyrical 'The Song of Wandering Aengus', the singer cuts and peels a hazel wand and uses a berry as bait.

> And when white moths were on the wing
> And moth-like stars were flickering out,
> I dropped the berry in a stream
> And caught a little, silver trout.

In more recent times, Seamus Heaney wrote about the trout in his early collection of poetry, *Death of a Naturalist*. The sharpness of his observation, the intensity of his images and the absolute precision of his words make his poem as muscular, sinuous and magical as the trout itself. Go and read it!

Although the rainbow trout (*Oncorhynchus mykiss*) can be found here, the two kinds of trout most significant in Ireland are the sea trout, sometimes called the white trout, and the brown trout. They are so similar that if sea trout are unable to escape from freshwater to the sea, they will live as brown trout. Nevertheless, given a chance, the sea trout migrates from the sea to spawn in gravel on a riverbed, while the brown trout moves upstream or else goes from lake to river. Controversy surrounds the state of sea trout in Ireland today, for many people believe the commercial salmon farms working off the west coast are having an adverse effect on the wild sea trout.

The brown trout is found in lakes and rivers all over the country, and Ireland is its westernmost reach. Its native range is to the Urals in the east, to Iceland in the north and in the south to both Greece and the Atlas Mountains of northern Africa. The Irish name *brecc* means 'speckled one', referring to its spotted sides.

Fishermen have a mental hierarchy of fish, with trout, sea trout and salmon at its pinnacle. One fledgling Irish fisherman, proud of his trout despite its modest size, wondered whether it was not just the sort of fish people had in mind when they said, 'Sure, wouldn't he be grand with a rasher!'

Trout with Sorrel and Hazelnuts

For an intimate supper party for four, this dish is hard to beat. You can serve a greater number, but the essence of the dish is to serve it straight after cooking. Should sorrel not be available, you can substitute spinach, and if the trout came from the river to your kitchen, in flavour and texture it will eclipse farmed trout. The added virtue of this recipe is that you use only one cooking vessel.

4 brown trout, all of much the
    same 1 kg size, if possible
50 g plain flour
50 g unsalted butter
150 g sorrel, well washed and
    roughly chopped
4 tbs sour cream

100 g hazelnuts, chopped
Salt
Freshly ground pepper (pink
    peppercorns for preference)
2 tbs finely chopped parsley
1 lemon, quartered

Pre-heat your oven to 180°C/350°F/Gas Mark 4. Clean and wash the trout, leaving them whole, then pat them dry. Season inside and out with salt and pepper and dust well with the flour. Put the butter into a shallow roasting tray and fry the fish in it for a minute on either side, just enough to set the flesh, then transfer the roasting dish to the oven. Baste the fish and cook for half an hour or less.

About 10 minutes before the time is up, cook your sorrel in salted water and drain it thoroughly before returning it to the pan and stirring in the sour cream. Heat through, then put a mound of the mixture on each person's warmed plate.

Taking your trout from the oven, put one on each mound of sorrel. Quickly whizz the chopped hazelnuts around in the fish juices and butter for a few moments, then drizzle a little onto each trout, sprinkle the parsley over all and give each person a wedge of lemon.

The Shannon, having made its long journey from its source in Co Cavan, widens out into Lough Derg at Portumna, Co Galway and runs down as far as Killaloe on the Clare side and Ballina on the Tipperary side, before narrowing again and continuing out to the Atlantic. I can walk down the bog road behind my house to get to the river and if it were as clean as it was when Arthur Young reported on it at the end of the 1770s, I might have a chance of catching a trout in it: 'The Shannon adds not a little to the convenience and agreeableness of a residence so near it . . . Pike swarm in it . . . I had also the pleasure of seeing a fisherman bring three trouts, weighing 14 lb, and sell them for six pence halfpenny a piece. Perch swarm; they appeared in the river for the first time about ten years ago in such plenty that the poor lived on them.'

Fishermen claim that nothing compares to a trout grilled over a wood fire on the very bank of the river where it has been landed, but if you cannot attain that absolute pinnacle of freshness, a trout only out of the river for a few hours is a handsome treat. It is usually best to soak the fish in slowly running water for an hour or so to avoid any risk of its tasting muddy.

Lough Neagh Harvest

Lough Neagh is a lake some 153 square miles in extent, and has always provided much seafood. Eels, pollan, trout and perch are all to be found in its waters, but to my delight I learned that around Lough Neagh the young of perch go by the delicious name of 'grunts'.

While grunts may be reserved for soup, once they have grown into perch they become one of the best tasting of all freshwater fish and are found quite freely in Irish lakes and slow-moving rivers. They have greeny-gold scales and superb coral-coloured fins, and although they are not often available commercially, a friendly angler ought to be able to provide you with one. The dorsal spines of the perch are rather fierce, so be careful when skinning it – immersing the fish in boiling water for a minute will loosen the skin a little. Small perch can be cooked *à la meunière* (browned butter, lemon juice and parsley) while larger (and larger fish, as a rule of thumb, always taste better than small ones) should be stuffed and baked or can be fried long and slowly in clarified butter.

Freshwater Fish

Too much handling is a sure way to make fish unpalatable, something the Normans set about remedying when they arrived. Introducing the notion of keeping fish in ponds or 'stews', a ready-made fish larder, as it were, they set the example and it was followed enthusiastically by the heads of the monasteries and by the owners of the big houses. Domestic fishponds were far from common, and for most people living inland preserved fish is what they knew best.

A freshwater fish that was once greatly favoured by the monasteries, where it was kept in fishponds, is the carp, an aristocrat of the fish world. High in Omega 3, this toothless fish with its golden-green scales can grow to enormous size and age – up to 45 kg and up to 150 years old. It is much more highly regarded in parts of Europe than it is in Ireland, and in Poland it is carp that lies at the centre of the main Christmas dinner on Christmas Eve. To cook carp, you may stuff and bake it or poach it and serve with a sorrel sauce. It is even robust enough for a horseradish sauce.

Roach is a freshwater fish of the carp family and has delicate but very bony flesh. Traditionally it was shallow-fried, most often dipped in milk then flour or, much less attractively, it was steamed, perhaps above the potatoes, in the way that ling was once cooked.

Pike is a long, slender fish, and when it is young, known at that stage as a jack, it has bold markings. An adult can reach weights of 18 kg or more and the large fish are usually cut into steaks. Sadly, most pike in Ireland were brought home and consigned to the boiling pot, and enthusiasm for them was limited, because they are full of vicious bones. In France, where they care much more for fish, they take the flesh and make featherlight fish dumplings – *quenelles de brochet* –

which are a labour of love to make and are nowadays more often found in restaurants rather than in the home.

The Versatile Eel

Eels have played an important role in the diet of Irish people, from prehistoric times, through the medieval period and up until very recently. In pre-famine times they were sold both salted and fresh.

The eel has a life cycle of baroque complexity. The European and the American eel is spawned in the Sargasso Sea, then travels up to 7,000 kilometres to find the fresh water of its ancestors, where it will spend most of its life. The perils it faces on this long journey, the predators it escapes and the obstacles it overcomes to get back to its home waters are the stuff of adventure films. Sadly, numbers of this once popular fish have declined and it is now almost impossible to get it in Ireland. Until recently, a neighbour of mine was my source for smoked eel, and fine handsome eels they were, too. However in the last few years only little eels, more like elvers, are found around this part of the Shannon.

It was not always thus. In 1832 W. H. Maxwell in *Wild Sports of the West* tells us that, 'At the particular times during the summer months when these eels run in upon the estuary, quantities sufficient to fill several barrels have been collected during a night. When dressed the fish is reckoned by the peasantry a great delicacy.' And rightly so, for eel is a marvellously versatile fish, although it must be cooked when freshly killed or else eaten smoked.

Some fifty years later, in his short story, *The Silence of the Valley*, Sean O'Faolain writes about eel-catching in the lake at Gougane Barra, Co Cork, 'To lure the eels a few random bits of guts has been thrown into the brown shallows at their feet and there swayed like seaweeds . . .' And in one of Seamus Heaney's poems, the poet often finds himself in conversation with an eel-catcher, always turning away the conversation if it begins to turn towards writing, deflecting it instead to the eel-catcher's trade.

Back a hundred years or so, people used often to gather on the strand to dig up sand-eels or sand-lances, which is a better name, as they are not eels at all. The reason for the digging was for food, of course, as sand-eels were considered a delicacy for human beings as well as good bait for fish, but it also became a social gathering, and very large crowds – up to a thousand people or more – were not uncommon on certain sandy shores in the nineteenth century. Usually these sand-eel digs took place at very low tides, especially in spring, when large expanses of sand exposed. Any surplus catch was salted and dried for use in the hungry months before the field crops were harvested.

The Leaping Salmon

Of all the fish that swim in the seas and rivers of Ireland, one can lay claim to primacy: the salmon. It has played a key part in the myth and folklore of the island, and is so much a part of Irish life that it was cast on the first coinage of the newly independent Ireland, along with a hen and her chicks, a woodcock in flight, a horse, a sow with her bonhams, a hare and a bull. At its best, wild Irish salmon is a world-beater and in the early literature it is referred to as 'the crafty one of the water' and a triad maintains, 'Three deaths better than life: a salmon, a fat pig, a robber.'

As every Irish schoolchild learns, it was from the salmon that Fionn MacCool took his supernatural powers. King Fintan escaped the Flood by being changed into a salmon and settled in a well surrounded by nine magical hazel trees. Whenever a hazelnut fell into the water, the salmon swallowed it and a red spot appeared on the fish, as a sign of the knowledge it had taken in. (From that day to this the salmon has spots on its body.) Fionn MacCool was a pupil of Finneigas, a sage who had long been searching the River Boyne for the Salmon of Knowledge. When it was finally caught, he looked forward to eating it and absorbing its magic powers, but he was called away from his fire, so told his pupil to keep an eye on the salmon, but not to eat any of it.

Conscientiously, Fionn turned the fish to cook it evenly on both sides, but he burned his thumb and instinctively put it into his mouth. From that instant the wisdom of the Salmon of Knowledge passed into him and thereafter whenever Fionn needed to know the answer to some riddle or discover some secret, he would put his thumb in his mouth for enlightenment. The magical elements of the story draw on old Irish traditions – the hazel is considered a magic tree and the salmon a noble fish of power and mystery.

In Irish waters there are two runs of salmon: the spring run of fish which may commence as early as January in some rivers, but generally speaking starts in March and April, and the summer and autumn run of smaller fish (peal or grilse) which usually starts in July. The dates for sea trout more or less coincide with those for the run of salmon. Finding a truly wild salmon today is extremely rare. What is commonly served is farmed salmon, and much controversy surrounds the conditions in which these fish are reared. Some are given more space in colder waters and thus are of a higher grade than the rest, but the proliferation of salmon farming off the west coast of Ireland has seemed to encourage the numbers of sea lice, which in turn is very bad news for sea trout. This is something that needs attention!

In a fanciful old tale of fishing on King Gartnan's island of Inis moccu Chein, we are told that fifty fishing nets were spread in the water, each with a rope trailing from it up to the windows of the king's kitchen. At the end of each of these ropes was a bell and when it rang the steward and four men hastened to haul in the salmon of first swimming.

Legend also has it that Saint Patrick ordered some fishermen to cast their nets into the main river of Sligo, the Garavogue. The men were doubtful, pointing out that salmon were never caught at that place in the winter, but they obliged the saint and were amazed when their nets became heavy with a catch of large salmon. These they gave to Patrick and he then blessed the river, so that from that day to this fish are caught in it all year round.

Since then, on St John's Day (23 June) fishermen would ask the priests and holy men to bless their boats and nets. At Port Ballintrae, Co Antrim, the salmon fishermen of the River Bush used to hold a communal 'Salmon Dinner', consisting of fish soup, freshly caught local salmon and the first digging of new potatoes with butter. An essential feature was the accompanying Bushmills whiskey.

In the earliest days the salmon was highly prized at table and was often eaten with a flavouring of honey. Surprising as this may sound to modern ears, honey used to be a regular condiment, put on the table for each diner to use as we would use bottled sauces.

A very primitive and effective way of smoking salmon used to be practised by fishermen in the west of Ireland in the far-off days before the invention of matches. Fishermen going out after salmon always brought with them in the boats a few sods of lighted turf in a three-legged pot so as to have a means of lighting their pipes.

The fishermen would bring back to the boat the first salmon they caught so as to have it for their supper. Generally, though, the fire had died down and the few smouldering embers in the bottom of the pot gave out too little heat to actually roast anything. Nothing daunted, they would gut and bone the fish, open it out flat and spear it on two sally rods, which they rested across the edge of the pot. Going off to continue their work, they left the salmon hanging over the cool smoke so that when they returned at dusk the fish was beautifully smoked and moist.

In the far-off days when everything was cooked over an open fire, more delicate foods had to be protected from the immediate heat of the turf or the timber. In some countries, a pastry crust was wrapped around the food, or perhaps a salt crust. In Ireland it was more likely to be a crust of mud. Following this method, birds such as duck or pheasant or small mammals such as hedgehogs or young rabbits were rolled in clay, thrust into the hot ashes and were deemed to have been cooked when the clay was dry.

Wrapped Salmon

The principle seemed simple enough and I wanted to develop it, so on the same day as we were baking over the turf fire, my friend Jane Hansell and I tried out two different wrapping techniques.

Taking a salmon, I cut it in half across the middle, then wrapped the head end in layers of plain wrapping paper and soaked it thoroughly in cold water. The tail end was wrapped in leaves – first, spinach leaves next to the skin, then long, floppy cauliflower leaves outside, making a neat package. If you fancy trying it, any leaves should do; sorrel would be handy, or, as Jane suggested, the big leaves from lovage. Back in time, the most commonly used leaves would be cabbage leaves, for sure.

The soaking wet paper bundle was put right into the bottom of the grate, over the hot turf ashes, and I shovelled some more hot turf embers on top. The paper simply began to dry out and we waited until it started to burn, before scooping up the bundle on a coal shovel and opening up the package with some trepidation. No need to be apprehensive. The skin peeled away along with the paper, revealing a fish that was neither raw nor dried out, but nicely pink and cooked in its own juices.

The bundle of salmon wrapped in leaves had been put in the other side of the fireplace, and when the outer leaves burst into a little flame, we reckoned that was the sign! Once we opened this, we could not decide which method was better, for this, too, was salmon cooked to a turn and looking marvellously pink and clean against the scorched and blackened cauliflower leaves. And there you have it – a whole salmon baked in the fire, with no washing-up to be done after it and a glow of satisfaction, too.

By some miracle, all the elements of that day's cooking came together. The bread had cooled sufficiently to be cut into, the oatcakes had firmed up, the potatoes and onions that we'd put into the bastable were a revelation! The unpeeled spuds had got a fairly hard crust on them by the time they were cooked, but when they were broken open the inside was fluffy and light, while the onions, once the charred skin had been discarded, were meltingly soft inside and the perfect accompaniment to the salmon. You can be sure there was some of Barbara Harding's buttercup-yellow butter, too. And then two men arrived (once all the work was done) and laughed at our smut-streaked faces and our eyes, red and watering from being so close to the smoke of the fire for such a long time. It's quite an arduous job, bending over to a fire on the ground and handling the very heavy cast-iron cooking utensils. Until of late, Irish women who had to work for a living were not particularly tall, and that's just as well! Still, the feast we had that day will stay with us all. Did we wash it down with some poteen? I can't recall. To be honest, it was probably a teapot filled to the brim with Barry's tea.

As an envoi to the king of fish, I offer you an old Irish saying, *Sláinte an bhradáin chugat*. May you be as healthy as the salmon.

Shellfish were among the foods that kept the early inhabitants of Ireland alive. As agriculture developed and farmers began to keep livestock, this resource gradually became less important, although shellfish always remained a valuable free food. The strange thing is that somewhere in the Irish psyche there has grown up a resistance to shellfish.

Oysters

Oysters were once so popular that artificial oyster beds had to be set up, some dating back to the eighteenth century. Seafood restaurants around the coast these days are thronged with diners eager for oysters, lobsters and crabs, and festivals celebrating shellfish are hugely successful. And at every St Patrick's Day celebration around the world, oysters are served with big pints of creamy stout. (You'd surely agree that a big pint is better than a small pint!) Yet for all that, huge numbers of Irish people, very conservative in their eating habits, have never touched shellfish in their lives. The Irish country kitchen that has seen an oyster or a crab is a rare one and a quare one.

This ignorance and rejection of shellfish is rare among rural communities elsewhere in Europe and is hard to fathom. Undoubtedly the experiences of the famine left a profound distaste, revulsion even, for any foods that smacked of those evil times. When the countryside was scoured for anything edible, people were driven to eating all manner of unaccustomed animals, birds and insects, and it is not difficult to sympathise with an inherited mistrust of anything that recalls those foods of desperation.

Another reason may well be that because shellfish go off quite fast, a lack of speedy transport to bring them inland meant that most of the catches had to be consumed fairly locally. If ever shellfish did make it into country places, it could hardly be of the freshest, and one bad oyster seems to put most folk off for life.

Yet even beside the sea finding lovers of shellfish is not so obvious. I spoke to one major west-coast exporter of oysters who confessed that he never ate them, nor did anyone in his family – they appealed to foreigners and the restaurant trade and that was good enough for him. The waters off the west coast of Ireland are home to some of the finest seafood in the world, yet most of the catch is sent crated up for export or professional kitchens. I spent an unforgettable day on board a boat with Alan Stoney, then head of the Clew Bay oyster fishing co-operative, fishing oysters from the clean waters of the Atlantic. I can't help but think that if other nations had oysters of the quality of those natives that come out of Clew Bay, for instance, they would market them under that name and create the sort of association with the highest calibre foods that Bayonne or Parma achieved with ham or that Modena achieved with balsamic vinegar.

I have eaten oysters in the United States that were excellent and others only fit to feed the cat. Oysters in France can be wonderful, but the native oysters from Ireland are seldom less than superb. Even the farmed oysters are good in their own class, for the Atlantic waters are cold and clean. Oysters farmed at Carlingford Lough also have a good reputation.

Things may be on the turn. Ireland's newfound prosperity has given people the opportunity to travel, thereby sampling new dishes and new flavours and widening their food horizons. Folk memories of the Great Famine are fading, especially among those who have gone to live in the towns and cities. And as more people dine out, there is more encouragement for them to be adventurous and order a dish that they would never prepare at home. Relatively bland foreign foods such as pizza could be the thin end of the wedge that will eventually open the door. Ireland may yet give a broad welcome to its native lobsters, its crabs and its oysters, providing they avoid over-fishing for export.

Stewed Oysters

Put the oysters, with their liquor and a little water or milk, into a saucepan; add a bit of butter kneaded, that is, well mixed with a tablespoonful of flour; pepper, and a little salt; stir the oysters over the fire until they have gently boiled for about 5 minutes, and then pour them into a dish containing some slices of toasted bread.

Máirín Uí Chomáin, in her book *Irish Oyster Cuisine*, relates the following tale that proves even saints can have little spurts of longing for earthly delights now and again. Local folklore has it that when in the sixth century St Kieran was on the Aran Islands he longed for oysters. There were none on Aran, so he set sail for the mainland. He survived a stormy crossing and was driven ashore at Kilkieran, where he built a church in thanksgiving. St Kieran's feast day is still commemorated on 9 September – just when the oyster season starts to roll.

Oysters were once found in great abundance and were particularly valued as a free food to be called on in the lean winter months. Dredging for oysters is nowhere near as dangerous as deep-sea fishing and can be conducted in relatively sheltered waters. And although they put up a fight, once their hinges are broken and their shells prised apart, oysters are ready to eat there and then.

As early as the mid-eighteenth century, several oyster beds, both artificial and natural, existed near Dublin. Two artificial beds were relocated from Arklow to Clontarf and Sutton, to the north of the city, while natural beds were found near Ireland's Eye, Malahide and Skerries, where oysters were reported as being 'as large as a horseshoe'.

As transport to markets improved, demand increased and overfishing took place. Harbour development destroyed the natural beds at Poolbeg, and although the Sutton and Clontarf beds survived until the early twentieth century, the oysters from them were eventually condemned as unfit for human consumption, due to pollution.

Stocks were becoming depleted elsewhere in the country, too, and at the end of the nineteenth century, the government encouraged landowners to take over oyster beds and use them for breeding as well as harvesting. Once in private hands, these oyster beds were the source of much resentment on the part of the local people, who believed the seabed belonged to everyone. Despite employing bailiffs to keep a watch against intruders, the big landowners lost hundreds of oysters to hardy poachers and at last the Irish state stepped in and bought back the oyster grounds, which are now fished by co-operatives.

A more structured system of oyster cultivation arose in the mid-twentieth century and there was also an effort to restrict fishing for the native oysters. The Clew Bay co-operative is a good example of voluntary restraint, where no member lifts a single oyster out of the water after the time limits strictly imposed, and where immature oysters are thrown back into the sea straight away. (Oysters spawn from May to the end of August, and take up to five years to grow to a size that is commercially viable.)

The first Clarinbridge Oyster Festival took place in 1954 under the sponsorship of local publican Paddy Burke, one of the first to really promote oysters and sell them in the half shell at the counter bar of his pub. The festival was also vigorously taken up by the Moran family, the walls of whose Oyster Bar at Kilcolgan are covered with photographs of visiting film stars, sporting heroes and politicians, including the odd American president or so. The Clarinbridge festival became a great hit so Galway city soon wanted to get in on the action, and the city's festival is inevitably played out on a much grander scale – these days, one festival follows the other and each has its devotees.

The non-native oyster, known variously as Gigas, rock, Pacific and Japanese, is available all the year round, and although it is large and reliable, it cannot compare with the nutty sweetness of some of the native oysters I was lucky enough to eat on board a boat out in Clew Bay, Co Mayo. They were only out of the water for moments before we were devouring them along with some fine home-made brown wheaten bread and creamery butter, and they tasted of the very essence of the sea.

Startling though it may sound, baby oysters develop as males and then slowly become females. Later, they revert to being male – that makes more than one sex change in one season. (The trigger for these changes is usually the temperature of the water.) And while we are on the subject of sex, the story about oysters being good for your sex drive is actually true – oysters have eight times as much zinc as fillet steak, and zinc is the mineral most scientists claim can improve your sexual health – not just the human libido but also potency and fertility levels.

In fact, oysters contain a combination of zinc and selenium – better yet for libido and stamina.

Mussels

Mussels are sometimes called the Poor Man's Oyster, and it is a pity that they are not greatly in fashion in these islands. You seldom find them in the home kitchen and they mostly survive in the more exclusive fish restaurants. Signor Francatelli, former Head Chef to Queen Victoria, wrote a recipe that he hoped would commend them to the working classes, and in fact, it is not beyond the beyonds that muscles, as he calls them, could make a comeback for all classes of people, for they can be utterly delicious. The small Irish mussel can be very sweet and the flesh tender.

Where once mussels were gathered in the wild, these days they are extensively farmed and (not a lot of people know this) the technique for doing this is credited to an Irishman called Walton who was shipwrecked in the Bay of Aiguillon, just north of La Rochelle, in 1235. To survive, he attached a net to a pole sunk into the mudflats, hoping to catch birds with it, but discovered instead that the pole was covered with mussel spawn and young mussels grew there in abundance. He became the world's first mussel farmer and nowadays the Bay of Aiguillon is full of stakes.

The basic technology has been modified somewhat; nowadays mussels are bred on ropes suspended from rafts, which technique keeps them out of the sand and safe from many of their natural predators. What is more, mussels grown this way can be harvested very easily – you simply pull up the rope.

An old method of cooking mussels was with milk or cream to make a soup but, under French influence, today we are more likely to cook them with garlic, parsley and wine or cider. They are also very good stuffed on the half shell; simply spoon a dot of cream and some garlic-butter-soaked breadcrumbs on top of the pre-cooked mussels and put them into a hot oven until the topping is crisp and brown.

Other Shellfish

In the 1960s the cookery writer Monica Sheridan wrote, 'For years I
avoided scallops. I thought they were revolting. However, my natural
thrift got the better of me and one day I had a shot at them. I was an
immediate convert. They have a great deal to recommend them. They
are reasonably cheap . . .'

As any fishmonger will tell you (if you can find such a rare bird),
scallops are not a cheap option any more, and a glimpse at the right-
hand side of the menu in any seafood restaurant will confirm it. They
are, however, worth paying a good bit for.

Small scallops are sometimes known as 'queenies' or 'closheens' in
the west of Ireland and that same name 'queenies' is also found in the
Highlands and Islands of Scotland, and on the Isle of Man. These
small scallops need to be pan-fried for only a few seconds – it is a
question of keeping your nerve and not leaving them over the heat for
more than a couple of heartbeats.

In *An Account of the Customs, Manners and Dress of the Inhabitants
of the Rosses*, the Reverend A. B. gives the following account of
manners in the late eighteenth century: 'For scallops and oysters,
when the tide was out, the younger women waded into the sea where
they knew the beds of such fish lay; some of them naked, others
having stripped off their petticoats, went in their gowns tucked up
about their waist; and by armfuls brought to shore whatever number
of scallops they thought requisite; the scallops weighing from two to
four pounds each.'

A very old verse in Irish, a version of the triad, goes like this:

Trí chineál bia:
Bia rí ruacain
Bia tuata báirnigh
Bia caillí faochain
(Is í dá bpiocadh lena snáthaid)

Three types of food:
Cockles are a king's food
Limpets are a peasant's food
Periwinkles are an old woman's food
(And she picking them with her needle.)

This gives a fairly clear picture of the status of the various lesser shellfish. References crop up here and there in the early literature to hunting for *faechan* or periwinkles, and these small shellfish with a coiled, snail-like shell are usually called winkles, with 'willicks' their name in the north of Ireland and 'buckies' in Scotland. The work involved in extracting the small amount of meat on a periwinkle meant they were often reserved for old people who had the time and patience for them. Usually they were boiled in seawater for about 10 minutes and then 'winkled' out of their shells with a pin and eaten straight away or dipped in a little fine oatmeal.

Limpets – *báirnech*, a derivative of *báirenn*, 'rock' – were a real staple of people living by the sea, and as we have seen from Tomás O Crohan's account of his childhood, they were seen as treats. However, the old saying showed that they were not considered the most desirable of shellfish: *Seachain an teach tábhairne no báirnigh is beatha duit* (Beware of the public house or limpets will be your food).

To drive the message home, there was also the adage: *Bia í isea dúilicíní ach bia tuataigh isea báirnigh* (Mussels are the food of kings, limpets are the food of peasants).

Cockle Soup

Cockles, members of the *Cardium* family, are the first cousins of clams and are very numerous on Irish shores, particularly in the west. In Kerry they are known as 'carpetshell' and 'kirkeen'. This soup is very nourishing and has a real taste of the sea. Fried snippets of bread, croutons, are excellent with it.

2.25 litres cockles	550 ml milk
2 onions	40 g flour
2 sticks of celery	250 ml cream
40 g butter	2 tbs parsley, chopped
1.25 litres fish stock	Freshly ground black pepper

Wash the cockles and boil them in 1.25 litres of sea water or salted water. When the shells open, remove the cockles from the heat and put the meat into a bowl. Finely chop the onions and the celery and fry them in the butter. When soft, add the strained fish stock and most of the milk and bring up to simmering point. Simmer for 20 minutes, then thicken with the flour mixed into a smooth paste with the remaining milk. Return the cockles to the pan, season to taste and reheat for a couple of minutes. At the last moment stir in the cream and the chopped parsley.

Norway lobsters (*Nephrops norvegicus*) are often known as langoustines or Dublin Bay prawns, this latter name said to have arisen not because they were caught in the bay but because they came off fishing boats forced to take shelter in Dublin Bay during storms in the Irish Sea. Once the catch was landed, Molly Malone and her friends took these attractive shellfish (pink before and after boiling) out into the streets of Dublin and hoped to find takers.

The true lobster (*Homarus vulgaris*) is perhaps the most highly prized and priced shellfish found in Irish waters. Because the Irish coast is deeply indented, except on the east, it is well suited for the exploitation of lobsters and a great many farmers by the coast put a few lobster pots out in likely spots. The day you found a lobster in your trap was always a gala day, because you could be guaranteed to sell it to a restaurateur or fish merchant.

Since the middle of the last century, those old amateur ways have more or less died out; these days, an ever-increasing proportion of the catch goes to boats using gear especially adapted for lobster fishing. Small punts and the very odd curragh go out in the summertime but in winter larger boats are used as seiners or trawlers. Three standard versions of the lobster pot are in use: the French crawfish creel, many variations on the Scottish creel and the home-produced creel, the Kilmore Quay, an adaptation of the traditional inkwell-shaped lobster pot, once made of wicker but these days of metal, except for the neck, to give it a longer life.

The bait used to catch lobster is whole flat fish – gurnard, pollack, mackerel and herring. While they are fishing for lobster, many fishermen also go in for crawfish (*Palinuris vulgaris*) which can be found from Carlingford Lough to Carnsore Point on the east coast, but only rarely.

The following method of pickling is from Sara Power's manuscript book of 1746:

Pickled Lobster
Boyl your lobsters in Salt and Water till they slip out of their
Shelles, take the tails out whole, and make your pickle of half
white wine, and half water, put in whole cloves, whole pepper,
two bay leaves, Musharooms[sic], Capers and a branch of
Rosemary, and a little Cucumbers, put in your lobsters, let
them have a boyl or two in pickle, take them out, lay them to
be cold, let the pickle boyl longer. Put in the bodys, it will give

them a pretty Relish, when the Lobsters and pickles are cold put them in a long pot for use.

Crab

Finally, I write in sorrow of the fate of the crab in Ireland. Although in Kerry crab claws are sometimes charmingly called crab thumbs, the sad truth is that you hardly ever find any part of the crab other than its claws or the white meat from the body. Going for the first time to a seafood restaurant in Co Clare that had a great reputation locally, I looked forward to my crab salad, but was dismayed to find it consisted solely of the white meat, and even that had obviously once been frozen. My experience has been the same all over the country – time and again expectations are raised by the promise of a crab sandwich or a crab salad, but the crab is never properly dressed. I think if I had grown up in Ireland, I would be unaware that there was any brown meat on a crab.

I can't help but wonder where the brown meat is going. Opening up the shell of the crab and dressing it properly, with the dark meat alongside the white, is much more trouble, but the dark meat is of such intensity of flavour that it eclipses the white as far as I am concerned. Some fishermen have a cruel practice of twisting the claws off, and dropping the body of the crab back into the sea. I fully expect everyone to deny it, but I know it to be true. Let there be fewer crab claws served up with garlic butter. Crab that has had all its flavour leached out of it by freezing and indifferent handling needs a disguise; fresh crab needs none. Let us have crab as a rare treat, and let us have all of it!

Seaweed

Children today have probably never experienced the direct taste of seaweed, whereas their forebears would have taken, say, a piece of dulse, also called dillisk, and popped it into their mouths as a chewy titbit, not dissimilar to the chewing gum of today. They will, however, undoubtedly have eaten seaweed without knowing it, for carrageen is present in myriad commercially prepared foods, highly sought after for its terrific gelling properties, turning a thin sauce into one that is thick, and bulking out and stabilising all manner of liquids.

The coastline of Ireland stretches over some 3,000 kilometres and the deeply indented Atlantic seaboard, with its bays, inlets and coves, plus its cliffs and exposed rocky shores, offers ideal conditions for the natural growth of seaweeds of every description. Since the west coast is relatively unpolluted, marine biologists and botanists have a field day with its flora and fauna, and over 500 species of seaweed have been identified off the coast of Ireland. Recently, I heard that the Irish government is planning to sell the rights to harvest seaweed by mechanical means in Bantry Bay and other places along the Atlantic coast. My heart sinks, thinking of the ecological implications of this.

Over the centuries seaweed has proved an invaluable friend to the Irish peasant. In the west, particularly, it coaxed life from the sheer rock. Tiny fields, some scarcely bigger than the size of a handkerchief, were fertilised with loads of seaweed carried up from the shore either on the farmer's own back or that of his melancholy little ass, and pitchforked onto the stony soil. In time the seaweed broke down into a type of humus that plants were able to root in and it gave a little sparse grazing to animals.

Its secondary importance was as both a foodstuff and a basis of folk medicine, too. Carrageen, its name deriving from *carraigin*, the word for a little rock, has for generations been thought to be a cure for bronchitis and chesty colds. It was traditionally gathered from its habitat, stones on the lower shore, in April and May, and once the brown weed had been washed to rid it of excess salt, it was spread out on the grass near the seashore to dry and to bleach in the sun. (The farmers, knowing only too well the force of the winds off the Atlantic, took the precaution of covering it with a fishing net to prevent it from blowing away.) After several dousings with fresh water or rain, it gradually fades from brown to beetroot to pink and eventually to buttermilk. At that stage it was let dry in the sun, and then all that remained was to trim the stalks and store them in a dry place – if well dried it will keep indefinitely.

Carrageen (*Chondrus crispus*) was often referred to as a 'kitchen', a tasty morsel, a relish, something to liven up your potatoes. Small amounts of fish, bacon and even buttermilk also qualified for this title. In ancient times, this notion of a titbit was well established and the delicacies were salt and onions in small measure, honey if you could get hold of some, or more substantial foods, such as butter, curds, salted meat, suet, cabbage and other seaweeds. Providing a touch of piquancy to the blandness and monotony of one's main diet, be it oatmeal, potatoes, millet or rice, is as old as the hills and universal.

Carrageen should be treated in the same way as gelatine. After soaking it in tepid water a little first to soften it, you should then steep it in very hot milk with flavouring. A handful of carrageen to a litre is about the ratio, for it shouldn't be too stiff and although it has a very creamy taste, it cuts cleanly, as does an egg custard.

At one time in Ireland you would find it served in cafés, chiefly as a sweet, classed with the apple tarts and buns. Ginger, chocolate, coffee and raspberry were the more modern flavourings, although bay leaves, almonds and honey were traditional in the nineteenth century. Aside from its uses as a sweet, it is versatile and can be used to thicken jellied fish or eggs and to clarify soups and sauces.

This recipe is for a hot drink to be taken last thing at night as a digestive and to combat insomnia. These days carrageen may be bought in packets, ready to use, but you can still find it on the coast and pick enough for your own use, so long as you wash it thoroughly in cold water, and snip away the roots and dark stems.

Carrageen Milk

20 g carrageen moss   1 litre milk

Put the carrageen moss into a saucepan along with the milk, bring to the boil very slowly and then simply strain and serve. You may add a spoonful of honey if you wish.

Carrageen Moss Pudding

Vanilla pods would not have been readily available in most Irish homes, but it definitely adds to the attraction of this dish, which is mild and interesting, slightly reminiscent of panna cotta. In its short season you could infuse a large head of elderflower or lemon rind to add a note of muscat to the moulded pudding.

5 g dried carrageen moss   1 large egg
850 ml whole milk   1 tbsp caster sugar
A vanilla pod, split, with
   the seeds scraped out
   or ½ tsp vanilla essence

Soak the carrageen in lukewarm water for 10 minutes or so, then strain and put into a large saucepan with the milk, the vanilla pod and the vanilla seeds. (If you are using the essence, this goes in with the egg yolk, at a later stage.) Bring the milk to the boil, then reduce to a simmer and cook for 20 minutes.

Separate the egg, putting the yolk into a large bowl (to which you add the essence, if not using a vanilla pod), then add the sugar and whisk together. Remove the milk from the heat and pass it through a sieve or muslin into the egg yolk mixture. Make sure to press through all the jelly that the carrageen will have released. Beat the mixture together then set aside while you whisk the egg white until stiff – this works best in a small bowl. Gently fold the stiffened egg white into the mixture and then allow the pudding to set. Put it in the fridge once it has cooled a little. The final addition of the fluffy egg white gives a lovely frothy lightness to the whole pudding. It is ideally served with a fruit compote or else with good local honey and softly whipped cream. You can add a spoonful of sugar when whipping the cream, if you have a really sweet tooth!

In the summer its creamy taste is delicious with strawberries or raspberries or even stewed gooseberries. In spring, serve it with early forced rhubarb. And in the winter months it is soothing with baked apples or pears.

In the earliest years for which we have records, dulse was the most prized of the seaweeds and was hung up in a sheaf from the roof of the cabin, so that a handful could be plucked whenever it was wanted. Dulse, frequently referred to as dillisk (*duilesc* or *creathnach* in Irish), is a red weed and one that was eaten raw or boiled.

This well-liked seaweed was often hawked at fairs and other social gatherings. One verse of the song *The Ould Lammas Fair* goes:

Did you treat your Mary-Ann
To a dulse or yellow-man
At the Ould Lammas Fair
In Ballycastle-oh?

(Yellowman resembles the inside of a Crunchie bar, or the sweet called honeycomb or cinder toffee in parts of Britain.)

There was, in early Ireland, a general entitlement to the seaweed of every strand and the dulse of every rock, but sometimes whoever held the adjacent land laid claim to a 'productive rock'. Seaweeds supplied iodine, iron and trace elements, and burning them yielded a coarse salt, so they were valued. Several references are found to seaweed in the ancient texts of Ireland. In the *Táin Bó Cúailnge*, 'The Cattle Raid of Cooley', Cu Chullain offers Fergus a handful of watercress or seaweed. Dulse from the harbours of Cape Clear was, according to one story, one of the delicacies of the Fianna, led by Fionn MacCool. And a *Life of St Senan*, written not later than the tenth century, records a tale of two youths who went by boat to harvest dulse on the rocks, were marooned and drowned.

Saint Ciaran of Saiger is said to have not only abstained from all meat but also avoided all milk products. His meal every evening consisted of a piece of barley bread and a drink of spring water. As relish, he had two roots of what is called sea-fern, possibly the edible seaweed called dabberlocks (*Alaria esculenta*), which is fern-like in appearance and attached to the rocks by an anchor root.

The young stalks of *Laminaria digitata Saccharina* were eaten under the name of tangle, which reminds me of an old Scottish song whose refrain goes 'you've never smelt the tangle o' the isles'. In Ireland, babies born beside the sea were given a length of this cord-like seaweed to chew when they were teething – such a clever idea! – and in the old days people believed that if you ate a piece of tangle on Ash Wednesday you would never get a headache for the rest of the year.

The many Irish words for seaweeds, sloake and seakale (*femm, femmnach, femmar, murraith, medban* and others) indicate its widespread use and economic importance. The reddish-brown seaweed that is known as sloke in Ireland and laver in Wales (*Porphyra umbilicalis*) would have been a valuable supplement to a narrow diet, thanks to its high protein content and the fact that it is rich in vitamins B and C. Also called sea spinach, sloke was traditionally served as a vegetable with fish or bacon, and less often with lamb grazed on sea pastures, the type of lamb that the French call *pré salé*, and which they value highly for the special salty tang the grazing imparts to the meat. Because sloke requires very long cooking – as much as 4 hours – it was only worth cooking in large quantities, and some of it was often preserved in earthenware crocks. Despite the length of time needed to cook it, it was a popular dish and in the seventeenth century Dublin hostesses had special silver pots for serving it.

Sloke

Seaweed recipes varied from place to place, but none is too complicated. Here is a no-nonsense but tasty way of preparing it. If you are going to the bother of cooking it, make sure you get a good quantity. Remember that it will boil down.

Wash your sloke in several changes of water to remove grit and sand, then drain well in a colander or sieve. Into a saucepan put enough water to cover the bottom, bring to the boil, add the sloke and stir until it comes to the boil. Now put a sheet of greaseproof paper over the top of the pan and put on a tight-fitting lid to keep in the steam. Stir the sloke now and again and add a little more water if it looks in danger of boiling dry. It will take up to 4 hours before the sloke is tender. Once you are satisfied that it is cooked, season with salt and pepper and add butter, or soured cream or crème fraiche or even Greek yoghurt. It is delicious served with game or lamb.

Since you have cooked plenty of sloke, you should have some left over to make these delectable little patties. If you are feeling adventurous, you could add a sprinkle of ground cumin or maybe some caraway seeds.

Sloke Cakes

Take some boiled sloke, season it with salt and freshly ground black pepper and add a good knob of butter or sour cream, making sure not to leave the mix too sloppy. Add enough fine oatmeal to give a dough that you can pat into little cakes, about the size of meatballs. Roll each ball in oatmeal, then flatten it slightly and fry on both sides until crisp. If you have enough bacon fat, that is the ideal, otherwise you can use good lard or butter. Oil should be a last resort.

CHAPTER SEVEN

VEGETABLES, HERBS, FRUIT AND NUTS

Saunders has yet neither Colly-flowers nor Straw-berrys.
But He gave me on Sunday some fine young Turnips . . . I
hope you have asparagus now in plenty.
Bishop Synge in a letter to his daughter, 23 May 1750

Although you will find few in Ireland to praise the weather, when it comes to growing vegetables, fruit and herbs, Ireland has a great deal to offer. Admittedly, the soil is poor in places and the climate is hardly balmy, yet there are some very productive pockets of land. With no extremes of temperature, relatively few pests, not yet much pollution and the sky as nature's generous watering system, Ireland is well placed to grow vegetables, fruit and herbs, although they have never been tip top on Ireland's list of food production priorities.

I remember being shocked when I first went to live in Dublin at the end of the 1960s, to find onions and apples sold by the piece instead of by the pound. If you wanted to buy a bunch of parsley or mint, you might as well go and whistle for them. The only vegetables commonly available were carrots, cabbage, onions, swedes (known, as in Scotland, as turnips), turnips (called white turnips to differentiate them), perhaps a few parsnips, and that's about it. Tomatoes (strictly a fruit if you're a pedant) were sold, but most of them were imported. I am, of course, leaving potatoes out of the list, because they are dealt with in another chapter.

People in country areas usually had the odd apple or plum tree and a big clump of rhubarb, and you might find someone cultivating blackcurrants and gooseberries, but other fruits were seldom seen. Blackberries, of course, along with other berries, grew wild, but were often left to wither on the bush.

In my student days Moore Street market was full of life and the Moore Street women had a unique way of pronouncing the word 'mushrooms', giving it four syllables, as in 'mush-a-roo-ums'. But although those mighty women provided plenty of human colour, the stalls had yet to know the exciting range of fruit and vegetables that flood in nowadays, due in part to the demands of Ireland's immigrant population. A walk down the street today reveals Chinese emporia next to Nigerian food stores and the colour and variety of what they are selling seems to have encouraged the traditional Moore Street stallholders to widen their stock, too. These days, northside women are singing out the names of aubergines and melons, yams, limes and avocados, and piling them up beside the carrots and cabbages. The same story of widening horizons is happening all over Ireland.

Inevitably, there will be those who protest that I am exaggerating this poverty of choice – people who point to gardens full of leeks, spinach, chard and cauliflowers, and greenhouses with climbing vines, fragrant tomato plants and courgettes complete with their flowers. If such was their experience, I am glad for them. But I tell it as I find it.

As we shall see, many centuries ago, people in Ireland had to be more resourceful and they ate quite a wide variety of vegetables, but over the years that range narrowed significantly. Until of late, a distressingly narrow selection of fruit and vegetables has been on sale in Ireland and a more distressing lack of knowledge about unfamiliar varieties is the norm.

My father used to tell a story of two young men arriving in Manchester in the 1930s, straight off the boat from Dun Laoghaire. Passing a greengrocer's, they made a purchase and as they were walking along one of them took a bite out of his fruit and spat it out in disgust. He had inadvertently bought a tomato, thinking it was a plum, and the taste was a shock to him. He had never seen, let alone tasted, a tomato in his life.

As recently as ten years ago, in supermarkets, especially outside the cities, many of the people on the checkout counters had to ask the name of the vegetable if it was something as outlandish as asparagus or globe artichokes. Why, I wonder, do so few Irish retailers tell their workforce about the products on sale? And I wonder at an education system where knowledge of food and cooking has such a low priority.

Things are changing. My local supermarket in rural east Galway had lemongrass on sale at Christmas as well as pomegranates. Hooray. But they disappeared as soon as the festive season was over. It will take a long time to erase a deep-seated distrust of anything with a strange name – especially if it also looks strange – knobbly or floppy or curlicued in some alien way.

How did this lack of variety and – worse – lack of interest come about? Part of the reason is that in pre-famine days most farmers were tenants on land that was not their own. Any 'improvements' would be noted by the landlord and the ensuing hike in the rent would have deterred tenants from becoming interested in kitchen gardens and horticultural variety. Indeed, when a family could be evicted at the point of a gun, insecurity encouraged a hand-to-mouth mentality.

Another factor has been Ireland's isolation. While mainland Britain, England particularly, absorbed ideas and influences from outside, little from the wider world touched Ireland. Dominated by her far more populous and powerful neighbour to the east, Ireland was but a small island on the very edge of Europe. And although the early Celtic monks travelled far, there was virtually no immigration into Ireland, other than from Britain. Those who crossed the Irish Sea seldom did so without looking to line their pockets.

The British, before and after the Penal Laws, were at pains to keep the Irish subdued lest they rebelled (as they were wont to), and the authorities severely discouraged education. Manifestations of the Irish national spirit, in language, religion – even the manner of wearing one's hair – were crushed. With no outside stimuli and normal outlets closed, the Irish turned inwards. An intensity of feeling and thought was channelled into poetry and story-telling, music and dance. The Irish for centuries were the least materialistic of people, caring more for the magic of words, the high-minded pleasures of philosophy and the lilt of the fiddle and the flute than for interesting cuisine, fine clothing or comfortable housing.

After the Great Famine, farmers and gardeners realised the importance of diversity and there was an upwelling of interest in cultivation. The work of the Congested Districts Board helped and the Land League stimulated interest in all matters agricultural. While the larger estates employed gardeners who took a pride in fruit and vegetables as well the general landscaping of trees, shrubs and flowers, there was dedicated activity even in humble plots of land and small orchards. Fine old varieties of all kinds of fruit and vegetables were revived and developed and strains of these are still to be found all over the country.

To read Tomás O Crohan's *The Islandman* is to learn a great deal about the attitudes of the impoverished Irish at the end of the nineteenth century and the first quarter of the twentieth century. Here he explains how the assistance of the Congested Districts Board helped transform the farming lives of his community. 'Before the Board came we hadn't proper fencing for these little fields, and in the little bits of land we did sow – often enough with good potatoes – we used to have pigs and asses, and they'd often make an utter mess of them after all our labour . . . Now, when we had our gardens all ship-shape, so that neither deer nor eagle could go into them, nothing could tire us of sowing and reaping.'

Somewhere along the way, all that knowledge and enthusiasm seems to have ebbed away. Fruitful gardens are now gone to seed or have been concreted over. Where every small farming family used to be self-sufficient in potatoes, cabbages, turnips/swedes, onions, apples and rhubarb at the very minimum, most families now pile into the car and head off to the supermarket. A gradual haemorrhage of people from country areas, gravitating towards the towns and cities, has exacerbated this, although there are stirrings of interest again.

The late Jimmy Murray, shopkeeper, publican and one-time captain of a phenomenally successful Roscommon football team (Gaelic football, not soccer, of course), remembered Knockcroghery in the 1920s. 'The shop was completely different from what it is at the moment. I often said if my father came back here and looked at that shop he'd think we'd all gone crazy. There's a big stack of milk in the corner and a heap of potatoes and carrots and parsnips and cabbages. All of those were produced by the farmers themselves in his time. And the chickens there in the fridge – they were all produced locally. They were very self-sufficient, the old people were . . .'

Much has been lost, and lost recently.

The Irish Seed Savers Association is trying to reverse the losses. Anita Hayes, its founder, is interested in the whole range of possibilities for fruit and vegetable growing that Ireland is not yet exploiting to the full. Since Ireland is on the same latitude as Moscow, as she points out, she is working on the basis that plants respond not only to heat and sunshine but also to light. 'Plants produce quite lovely things,' she explains, 'even when they are really stretched. Once we find a crop that is good, we develop it.'

The organisation is active on all fronts, searching out indigenous or long-established varieties of a multitude of fruits and vegetables and appealing to anyone who knows of very old strains to get in touch with them. Their list of the top ten varieties of seed sold is instructive.

1. Beetroot – Bolthardy
2. Leek – Musselburgh – dates back to 1822
3. Salad Onion – White Lisbon – bred at the beginning of the 1800s and grown by gardeners ever since
4. Carrot – early Nantes, introduced in 1867
5. Carrot – Autumn King – popular old faithful for many years
6. Parsnip – Countess F1 – the only hybrid
7. Parsnip – Tender and True – bred 1890, only just leap-frogged by the new variety Countess
8. Lettuce – Little Gem
9. Pea – Hurst Greenshaft
10. Cress – this reflects that anyone, living anywhere, can grow food, even if only on a windowsill

The Class Divide

Nowhere is the divide between the food of the Big House and the food of the peasant in his cabin more sharply delineated than in this matter of vegetables and fruit. Actually, it would be more accurate to term it the food of the Protestant classes for, by and large, members of the Church of Ireland, the Quakers and the Anglo-Irish in general always had greater access to a variety of food than the mass of the people, and consequently developed more of a sense of adventure and ambition in their attitude to food and cooking. Most of the old Big Houses had walled gardens, many had extensive greenhouses. From quite early times there were systems for heating glasshouses and conservatories – the restored glasshouses at Strokestown House in Co Roscommon are a case in point.

The more well-to-do class were likely to have travelled abroad and to have had experience of how life was lived in the wider world. For many of the peasant class, travelling outside their own *county* was an adventure, although many ended up obliged to travel beyond the shores of Ireland on what was usually a one-way trip to find work in England, America or Australia.

Plenty of sowing and reaping took place in the fine walled gardens, complete with heated greenhouses, that commonly belonged to the Big Houses up and down the country and whose owners were able to employ head gardeners, under-gardeners and gardener's boys to keep the vases filled and the cook supplied with kitchen produce.

Someone else's work in the garden could put the hostess in a better position to impress her guests, as Mrs Delany discovered. In her diary, written at Delville on 22 June 1750, she notes, 'My garden is at present in the high glow of beauty, my cherries ripening, roses, jessamine and pinks in full bloom, and the hay partly spread and partly in cocks, complete the rural scene. We have discovered a new breakfasting place under the shade of nut-trees, impenetrable to the sun's rays in the midst of a grove of elms, where we shall breakfast this morning; I have ordered cherries, strawberries and nosegays to be laid on our breakfast table and have appointed a harper to be here to play to us during our repast, who is to be hid among the trees.'

In his autobiography, Peter Somerville-Large, from a well-off Irish family, recalls how his mother created a garden at their house in the country.

The orchard flourished: the Worcester pearmains and
Irish peach apples planted in 1933 were fruiting two years

later. She planted gooseberries, raspberries, a Victoria plum, a Mary Duke cherry and three pear trees. Some things were obtained locally: the fuchsia, bamboo and hydrangeas . . . Vegetables were laid out in black earth in a valley close to the house. No vegetables ever tasted better; the new potatoes wiped clean, were like truffles. In one year, 1934, carrots, onions, lettuce, cabbage, peas, French beans, curly kale, parsley, celery and sprouting broccoli were planted. Only the curly kale and the broccoli did not come to harvest. Unfamiliar with them, Jerry dug them up, thinking they had gone wrong.

The late Professor David Webb, head of Botany at Trinity College, Dublin, used to be eloquent on the subject of sea kale; this luscious vegetable grows well in Ireland, but knowledge of it is very confined. One of my personal favourites, ruby chard, with its astonishingly luminous green and fuchsia-coloured stalks, grows like a dream even in the heavy soils of the west of Ireland, but is hardly ever seen. Jerusalem artichokes are just creeping in. The globe artichoke, a member of the thistle family, has been grown in Ireland since the Norman conquest, but I have not seen it in any but specialist shops. Beetroot is grown but often fed to farm animals and I know an intelligent, educated woman not yet fifty years of age who has never tasted a leek, nor even seen one.

This is really the puzzle in Ireland. Faced with an unfamiliar item of food, the knee-jerk reaction seems to be 'Take it away'. At least some of this mistrust has to be ascribed to the Great Famine. When hunger drove people to dig up dandelion roots and to skim the ponds in the hopes that the green scum on the surface might give some nourishment, then those hateful memories lie deep, and an aversion to anything except the plainest and most familiar of foods has taken hold of people. Even textures of food can arouse disgust. I have lost count of the people I know who are suspicious of any lumps in their food and who require their soup to be strained or who buy jars of jelly rather than jam, because blackcurrant and gooseberry jams and the like have 'bits' in them. The most wholesome of food can be looked on with distaste. 'Country butter' (home-made), for instance, raises an eyebrow when I mention it to neighbours. I can only guess they have unhappy memories of badly made butter, too salty or half rancid.

Green Beginnings

In the early days of Celtic Christianity, plant cultivation was especially associated with the monasteries, the crops providing not only food but also the basis of medicine. The law texts of the time emphasise the medicinal properties of herbs, referring to 'the great service given by garden plants in nursing'. Significantly, contemporary texts make no mention of a gardener among the servants of a king or lord.

It was important for a client to have enough food not only to pay his food rent but also enough to put on a spread at the annual visit of his lord. The amount needed depended on the rank of the lord; the very least required would be four loaves of bread for each member of his visiting party of four men, and those loaves had to be accompanied by a relish (*annlann*) or condiment (*tarsunn*). These relishes and condiments were what added flavour and piquancy to the bland staples of bread and different types of porridge.

The types of relish and condiment included honey, fish, cheese or salted meat, and there was a requirement for 'true *cainnenn*' to be provided for each loaf. The identity of this is not certain, some scholars suggesting a shallot-type bunching onion; since a Middle English gloss states that *cainnenn* brings tears to the eyes, we can feel confident it was a member of the allium family, and it is the most commonly mentioned vegetable of that period. One specific use it had was to flavour the butter that had been buried in the bogs over the summer months, perhaps disguising a certain rancid taste.

If it was not an onion, onions certainly were known by the Middle Ages, because in Anglo-Norman documents we find onion and leek seed being brought into Clonmel, Co Tipperary.

Jonathan Swift wrote about onions.

Onyons
Come, follow me by the Smell,
Here's delicate Onyons to sell,
I promise to use you well.
They make the blood warmer,
You'll feed like a Farmer:
For this is every Cook's Opinion,
No sav'ry dish without an Onyon;
But lest your Kissing should be spoyl'd,
Your Onyons must be th'roughly boyl'd;
Or else you may spare
Your Mistress a Share,
The Secret will never be known;
She cannot discover
The Breath of her Lover,
But think it as sweet as her own.

Somewhat related is *foltchep*, thought to be chives. In an eighth-century saga there is a reference to the cutting of the foltchep down to the ground with a sharp knife, which would be the practice with chives, and the name *folt* , meaning 'hair' and *cep*, from the Latin 'cepa', meaning an onion, is further confirmation. Some scholars, however, differ and believe that the leek is intended.

In a *Life of St Patrick* dating from the ninth century, we learn that a pregnant woman suddenly developed a craving for a plant that she had seen in a vision and told Patrick that if she did not eat this plant, she or her unborn baby – or both of them – would die. When Saint Patrick asked her to describe the plant she said it was like rushes, so the saint blessed some rushes and they turned into chives. The woman ate some and was relieved of her craving and later gave birth to a son. From that day on, Patrick announced, any woman who ate of this plant would be cured.

Yet another member of this oniony family was *borrlus*, which we suspect to have been the leek. In an important law text, this vegetable is included in the annual food-rent due to a lord, and it specifies that a client must render two handfuls of *borrlus*, of which each plant must be four fists in length. The leek would answer that description. Another green plant that was native to Ireland was *imus*, possibly celery. We know that it was widely grown and was said to 'prevent sickness and does not stir it up, and prevents thirst and does not infect wounds'.

Of the rootcrops, we know that the carrot, the turnip and the parsnip were all cultivated in Roman Britain, but whether they were all found in early Ireland is problematical to resolve because the early texts are imprecise. As usual, *The Vision of Mac Con Glinne* gives some help. In it, what we take to be a carrot is associated with the diet of a queen, although the word meaning 'the bent, crooked one' may refer to skirret, a vegetable that was popular in Europe from the late Middle Ages until the nineteenth century. We can extrapolate from *The Vision* with its idyllic images that here and there were well-tended orchards and gardens producing reliably.

A row of flowering apple-trees,
An orchard in pink-topped bloom
Before the nearest hill:
A forest of lanky leeks,
Of scallions and carrot clumps
Under the back sill.

A great virtue of carrots is that in winter they bring a touch of sweetness. An old verse explains,

Is e mil fe'n talmh
A th'anns a'churran gheamhraidh,
E'adar Latha an Naoimh Aindreadh agus An Nollaig.

Honey underground
is the winter carrot
between St Andrew's Day and Christmas.

Carrot Pie or Pudding

From an old manuscript (1746) of Sara Power's comes this recipe. (Her instructions do not come in a completely logical order.)

Take half a pound of butter, the yolk of 10 eggs, half a pound of powder sugar, and one spoonful of orange flavour water, beat your eggs well and beat your butter either to cream or melt it in Oyle, then take well colour'd carrots, boyle and pare them well, so mix and beat all together, put it in a dish and do the brim with puff paste, bake it an hour, you must pound the carrots.

Beetroot is another root vegetable that has found widespread acceptance in Ireland. Peter Somerville-Large remembers from his childhood that 'beetroot in quantities made us pee puce'. On the other hand, beetroot nowadays is often found growing in kitchen gardens but is no longer picked or else it is used as animal feed. Sugar beet used to be a crop of real economic significance.

Parsnips (*meacan*) are moderately popular, and deserve to be hugely popular, for they are delectable when roasted in meat juices, next to a rib of beef, say. In the early post-Christian centuries, they were prized for their sweetness and during the Great Famine the Society of Friends tried to urge the sowing of parsnips as a substitute for the failing potato.

Norman Imports

When the Anglo-Normans arrived, they brought with them peas and broad beans, both of which were harvested when grown and then dried in a kiln and stored for use in the winter. In all likelihood, they were cultivated in monastic settlements, and it is just possible that peas existed in Ireland as early as the seventh and eighth centuries as there is a reference to them in the Brehon law tracts. By 1700 pease pottage was widespread, and from the twelfth century onwards in places settled by the Anglo-Normans (parts of the east and south), pea meal came to replace other types of meal for making bread in the homes of the poor. In the Charter granted in 1374 by Edward III to New Ross, peas and beans are included in the foods on which a toll might be levied.

Another manuscript written in 1746 by Sara Power gives this recipe. As with most early recipes, quantities and measurements are on the vague side!

Pease Soop

Boyl 2 quarts of pease, in six quarts of water till tender then take out some of the clear liquor and strain the pease clean from the hasks, then put in your pease, and liquor together and boyl them well, take what butter you think fit, and boyl it up in a pan, then put in some onions cut Small, some Sorrell, Sollory, and Spinage cut them pretty large and let them boyl for a quarter of an hour in the liquor, or in the butter. Take some flower and bland it and mix it with a little of the liquor or in the butter which you will then mix all with your soop, and put in salt, pepper, cloves and other spices as you please, with some sweet cream mix'd with all. Then take French rouls and crisp them, and lay them in the middle of the dish, and power in your soop and serve it hot, with a little lemon peel grated round the brim of the Dish.

The Adaptable Cabbage

Aside from the potato, cabbage (*braisech* or *praisech*) is the most important vegetable in Ireland, although neither is a native plant. The wild cabbage was probably introduced from Britain in the early Christian period (the word is a borrowing from the Latin *brassica*) and many monastic orders included it in their prescribed diets, although in one ninth-century monastic rule the clerics were forbidden to eat cabbage that had been cooked on a Sunday. In *The Vision of MacCon Glinne*, the word *braisech* is used of cabbage eaten as a soup, with a layer of animal fat on top.

White cabbage, savoy cabbage, floppy-leaved green cabbage, no one seems to have differentiated between them too much, although the cabbage and potato dish colcannon derives its name from the Irish *cal ceann fhionn* – white-headed cabbage. (Strictly speaking, you should make it with cooked, finely chopped kale, but it is also made with white cabbage.)

Cabbage seeds were often imported from Scotland. As early as 1777 Arthur Young in his *Tour of Ireland* writes: 'He has not for five or six years past been without a small field of Scotch cabbages. The seed he sows both in March and Autumn for use at different seasons . . . His people were all of the opinion that a good acre of cabbage will go as far as two acres of turnips . . .'

The cabbage is actually indigenous to Asia and it seems to have been late in arriving to the British Isles. In fourteenth- and fifteenth-century writings, we find 'caboches' and 'cabogis' and these must have been related to the more common term 'wort', 'wurtys' or 'woortes' or even 'coleworts'. All must have been some form of the Brassica family, both wild and cultivated. It is reputed that in the sixteenth century Sir Arthur Ashley of Wilburgh St Giles in Dorsetshire was the first to plant cabbages as we would recognise them today, from seed brought from Holland.

Once introduced to Ireland, the cabbage became a mainstay of the poor. Perhaps too much so. The cook and food writer Jane Grigson wrote tartly,

> To know that cabbages were once the only vegetable people had in some parts of Europe does not mean much. To experience it is another matter. We spent a fortnight in northern Donegal in the summer of 1950. We left with the impression that all the Irish

ever ate was cabbage, potatoes, poor quality lamb and Victoria sponges. No wonder they took to whiskey. The village street smelled intensely of cabbage every day at noon. This in a village of fishermen. Why did we not eat lobsters and crabs and other fish? Surely those fishermen must have caught a whiting or two?

A love of cabbage is not, of course, exclusive to Ireland. The Germans and the Austrians, the Poles and other people of Eastern Europe used their ingenuity and instead of forever boiling their cabbages, they turned them into sauerkraut. The principle behind making sauerkraut was known to the Romans, who took their leafy vegetables, layered them with salt and left them to ferment. This technique preserved the food to tide them over the winter. In the case of sauerkraut there is the added advantage of its keeping scurvy at bay – no mean consideration in the days when fresh greens and citrus fruits were unavailable.

We know that in the eighteenth century the Palatines were regular consumers. This group of Europeans had fled to Ireland to avoid religious persecution and Arthur Young reported on their successful forays into agriculture in their new country. 'Mr Oliver planted a colony of Palatines 15 year ago, from about Rathkeale (Tipperary) 66 families in one year. The benefit of them has been introducing much tillage . . . they drill their potatoes and on stubble land worn out. House their cattle, feeding them with hay and raising thereby dung . . . They live partly on sour crout [sic] . . .'

The same 'sour crout' never caught on in the rest of Ireland, though. Perhaps the Irish did not have the price of the salt, or perhaps the idea was not disseminated. To be fair, an Irish winter is seldom as harsh as can be found in parts of mainland Europe, where the warming influence of the sea is not felt.

A Gift from the Wild

In these days of plenty, it takes a huge effort of empathy to imagine how at one time every sinew was bent on getting enough to eat. Food was there if you were able to find it. While men in their prime would go hunting, fishing and trapping, it often fell to the women and the elderly to gather fruits, herbs and vegetables from the wild. A story from the eleventh century tells how Saint Columb Cille (Columba) met an old woman one day gathering nettles in a churchyard at Iona. Her only cow had not yet borne a calf, so she had no milk and had to survive on nettle broth (*praiseach neantóg*). The saint, in sympathy with the poor woman, could not bear to eat more luxuriously than she did, so ordered his cook to feed him thereafter solely on nettle broth without milk or butter. However, the rest of the brethren were concerned that the saint would damage his health, so his cook cunningly bored a hole down the inside of the stirring stick and, unknown to the saint, would pour milk down the tube every day. Because of this, the saint thrived and although he eventually learned the truth, he pardoned the cook for his disobedience in recognition of his good intentions.

Nettles and sorrel were significant foods for the poor in hard times, and in a Middle Irish *Life of Saint Coemgen*, it is claimed that he lived for seven years on nothing but nettles and sorrel.

An old song begins thus:

Twas down by the glenside I met an old woman,
She was gath'ring young nettles and ne'er saw me comin'.
I listened a while to the tune she was hummin',
Glory-oh, glory-oh, to the bould Fenian men.

Those old people had chosen wisely, for nettles have a high iron content. In the countryside, nettle tea was made by pouring boiling water over chopped nettles then simmering the leaves for 15 minutes, before straining off the liquid and adding milk and sugar. This tea was often given to children who had measles and is said to have been a favourite of St Colum Cille.

Nettles made an appearance almost six thousand years ago, when the first farmers cut down the forests to clear land for growing crops, and were once widely used in soups and pottages.

Nettle Soup

Gathering nettles can be a painful business, and in the old days people used to draw old woollen stockings over their hands to protect them. These days, gardening gloves or even rubber gloves will do the job. Gather young shoots, rinse in salted water and scissor them before putting them in the pot. This nutritious soup tastes even better for knowing that the main ingredient was gathered for free.

2 tsp melted lard
65 g oatflakes
1.25 litres good chicken stock
3 heaped cups nettle tops,
  chopped

3 chopped scallions
  (spring onions)
2 tbs fresh chopped parsley
Salt and pepper

In a saucepan, heat the fat and add the oatflakes, stirring them over a low heat until they turn pale brown and a toasty smell rises off the pan. At this point pour in the liquid and season. Add the nettle tops and scallions and simmer gently for 30 minutes or so. Remove from the heat and blend or sieve through one of the French mouli kitchen gadgets. Sprinkle with the chopped parsley just before serving. A swirl of single cream makes this soup look and taste delicious.

This old recipe from *The Lady's Assistant* by Charlotte Mason (Dublin, 1778) is very good for using up lettuce that is inclined to bolt and go to seed. Spinach could be used in its place. Again, do not be alarmed at the lack of precision.

Scald you Cabbage Lettuce, slice them and put them in a pan with a good piece of Butter and season'd with Nutmeg, Salt

and Pepper. Stew gently for half an hour and put all thru a
 sieve. Serve with Eggs fried in Butter on the Top. Garnish
 with Slices of Sevile orange.

The Elizabethan Edmund Campion, writing of the diet of 'the Mere Irish' explains 'Shamrotes, watercresses, rootes, and other hearbes they feed upon', and Fynes Moryson writes in his *Itinerary*, 'The Irish willingly eat the herb shamrock . . . which as they run and are chased to and fro they snatch out of the ditches.'
 The tale of the eighth-century king, Sweeney, known to generations of schoolchildren, was taken by Flann O'Brien (Brian O'Nolan) for his work of comic genius, *At Swim-Two-Birds*. In it, Sweeney is seen flitting around the treetops 'feasting on cresses and nettles', and this is the self-confessed diet of the mad King Sweeney.

Watercress
Apples, berries, beautiful hazelnuts,
Blackberries, acorns from the oak tree;
Haws of the pricking sharp hawthorn,
Wood sorrels, good wild garlic,
Clean-topped cress, mountain acorns,
Together they drive hunger from me.

Watercress (*biolar*) used to feature in ascetic diets of penitents and hermits. The twelfth-century poet Suibne Geilt addresses the plant thus:

O watercress, o green-topped one
from the edge of the blackbird's well

and in another poem:

 . . . a meal of green-topped longlasting watercress
a drink of cold water from a pure stream.

In 1726 Moffet in *Hudibras* numbers watercress among the 'curious salads' eaten by the Irish, and despite its penitential associations, it has remained a very popular food over the centuries. If you pick it from streams that you know are unpolluted, it is a gift from the wild.

Sorrel (*samhadh*) was mentioned in a *Life of Saint Kevin*, and it thrives on the acid soils that are commonly found in Ireland. Sorrel has a sharp, lemony tang and in France commonly appears in a sauce to accompany fish. It is also one of the most successful fillings for an omelette, and is altogether a plant that deserves to be cultivated much more than it is currently. The fact that it is one of the first green plants to poke its head up in the spring makes it doubly welcome. People out haymaking would often chew some sorrel to quench their thirst.

Seakale (*praiseach thra*), as mentioned above, is a marvellous vegetable. In Co Donegal the locals call it strand cabbage because it likes to grow on sandy or stony places. Those lucky enough to find a plant in the wild early in the spring would cover it with more sand and shingle in order to blanch it. After a couple of weeks you could dig out the stems and take them home. Like samphire, mentioned below, you need to wash and wash the seakale in several changes of cold water, but it is worth getting cold hands because once you have cooked it, simmering it in water until tender as you would with asparagus (20 minutes should do the trick), you have a most delicate flavour. As with asparagus, it is best to serve it with melted butter and a wedge of lemon to squeeze over it.

Samphire is a dark green seaweedy plant that grows wild on both marshes and on cliffs and rocks, as alluded to in *King Lear*.

> How fearful
> And dizzy 'tis to cast one's eyes so low!
> The crows and choughs that wing the midway air
> Show scarce so gross as beetles; halfway down
> Hangs one that gathers samphire, dreadful trade!
> Methinks he seems no bigger than his head.

Rock samphire (*Crithmum maritimum*) is frequently mentioned in old cookery books, sometimes chopped and put into a cream sauce but mainly pickled.

I have never gathered samphire from the cliffs, but I have often gathered marsh samphire and will continue to do so, despite the necessity of washing it in cold water until your hands are freezing. Wash it thoroughly in several buckets or basins of cold water and then boil until tender (not long – 2 or 3 minutes) before draining it really well and serving it with melted butter. You dip each piece of samphire into the butter and draw the flesh off the stems with your teeth and discard the string each time. Quite delicious and worth the trouble.

Other food from the wild included *curar*, the Old Irish term for what is probably the pignut, also bitter vetch or heath-pease, another root, and *briscen*, which is silverweed (*Potentilla anserina*) whose root was consumed widely in both Ireland and Scotland until the twentieth century.

Wild plants, such as goosefoot (*Chenopodium*) and orach (*Atriplex patula*), called *ceathram coatrach* in Ireland, both plants that bear a resemblance to spinach, were boiled, mashed and eaten with butter, but nowadays are quite forgotten.

Although rather despised these days, charlock (*Sinapsis arvensis*) kept many a community alive in hard times. Before the Great Famine, the third month of the summer used to be known as 'July *an chabaiste*' meaning 'July of the cabbage'. The cabbage as we would recognise it might not have been intended here, but some other form of greens. Wild cabbage, kale and mustard leaves were all used by the country people to supply the essential green vegetable that their health depended on, and charlock, commonly known as prashock, from its Irish name *praiseach bhui*, was often used in place of spinach, kale, cabbage or mustard greens and also added to stews or soups or stirred into porridge. In counties Armagh, Antrim and Monaghan, and also in Co Galway, charlock was called 'wild kale' and in England it was often called 'wild mustard' or even 'cornweed'.

From very early times the native wild garlic (*crim*) was eaten and prized for its medicinal properties. A client used to have to provide an annual *crimfeis* – a garlic feast – for his lord, and it seems to have consisted of garlic with cheeses and milk, usually taking place before Easter, although that might sometimes have fallen a little early. The season for wild garlic, sometimes called ramsons, is very short.

In the early part of the last century, garlic was grown in little garden plots and was in daily use in kitchens all over Ireland. As in the olden days, it was prized for its curative properties: toothache, swollen tonsils, stomach-ache, and all other digestive complaints were doctored with two or three cloves of garlic crushed and wet with a shot of whiskey. Sometimes wild garlic, which grows in profusion in many parts of the country, was used instead. An elderly lady of my acquaintance could see no good in garlic, cultivated or wild. 'The stink of it! There was always a lot of it growing at the turn, and you'd have to hold your nose. We had a man used to send up for it – I don't know what he did with it. He used to suffer with his chest and he took as much as you'd send him of it.'

Fungus Feasts

Considering how widespread they once were, there are few enough references to the field or horse mushroom (*beacan*) in Irish literature. Since they spring up in places grazed by sheep or horses, and possibly in sand dunes under the right weather conditions, the fields were often white with them. In the old manuscripts they were spelled 'musharooms' and this is what you will still hear the women call out from their stalls in Dublin's Moore Street.

The field mushrooms used to be so plentiful that a sort of ketchup was made from them and most homes would have a bottle of this in the press, to be brought out to serve with boiled potatoes or to add to stews.

The older generations in Ireland remember those early morning mushrooms. My father had such vivid memories of going out before

219

school, picking some mushrooms and bringing them back to toast over the fire, that for the rest of his life he never could bring himself to eat cultivated mushrooms. The newly picked field mushroom was put on a pan and as it heated, black juices began to well up inside the cup, so that all you had to do was sprinkle on a little salt and eat them as they were.

Nowadays, many of the fields are fertilised and the mushrooms no longer spring up in the profusion of yesteryear. The fact that the woods are full of wild mushrooms and no one is interested in picking them is something that leaves the Scandinavians, Germans, Poles, Italians and French flabbergasted. In their countries, the thrill of going out in search of ceps, the apricot-coloured chanterelles, girolles and other fungi is one of the joys of country living. In Ireland, if anyone is out hunting for wild mushrooms in the early autumn, you can be pretty sure he or she is a foreigner or collecting them to sell to one of the more upmarket restaurants.

Herbal Remedies

Herbs are used in traditional Irish cooking but are used even more in folk remedies and tonics. Parsley, rosemary and thyme were all considered essential, anyone who had a bay tree growing nearby knew the value of bay leaves, and mint was so easy to grow it was almost a weed. In addition, sage was used, especially for the stuffing for the goose or other bird, and borage, chamomile, tarragon, marjoram and sweet basil were known in some households, though much fewer than those that grew mint or parsley. (It was always the curly variety of parsley, too.)

A particular favourite was parsley jelly, for it was said to clear the blood, keep rheumatism at bay and be a great aid to digestion. It was made by washing a good few handfuls of parsley, then covering them with water in a saucepan and simmering the two together for half an hour or so. After that the juice was strained overnight through a jelly bag and when it was measured the following day it was boiled up again for a few minutes, then sugar was added – a pound to a pint was the old rule of thumb – then the two were boiled up again until the jelly started to set. A refinement was to add a few thin strips of lemon rind to the concoction towards the end of the proceedings. Finally, the jelly was poured out into bowls and there was usually no need to worry about sealing or sterilising it because it was used immediately.

Cultivated Fruits

Fruits grow well in Ireland and helped sustain life as far back as we can trace. Seeds of wild cherry from the Late Bronze Age have been found in a crannóg at Ballinderry. Blackberry and elderberry seeds, dated by radio-carbon to the eighth or ninth centuries, were found at Scotch Street, Armagh. In an eleventh-century pit in Winetavern Street, Dublin, the seeds of the following were found: rowanberries, blackberries, wild apples, sloes, hips and haws. The bilberry was important, its seeds being found in excavations of Viking and Anglo-Norman sites in Dublin. The cranberry, which grows on bogs, hence its Irish names *mónann* and *mónóg*, was also prized. A legal commentator in pre-Norman Ireland divides fruits into sour and sweet categories, with blackberries, bilberries, hazelnuts and strawberries all designated as sweet and acorns, haws and hips and rowanberries as sour.

The Irish term for an orchard is *aballgort* – literally, apple-field – and the wild apple (*Malus sylvestris*) is included among the 'seven nobles of the wood', the seven most valuable trees. It is a common native tree with heavy crops of small sour apples, although from very early times sweeter varieties were developed from seed or by grafting from native sources and probably from Britain and elsewhere in Europe. An eighth-century text refers to the wild apple (thereby implying the existence of the cultivated apple) and a text from the ninth century refers to an abundant crop of sweet apples in a churchyard.

Hermits and penitents relied greatly on apples to sustain them, as we see from the tenth-century anonymous poem 'The Hermit' (*Ata Uarboth Dam I Caill*). This extract is translated by Kuno Meyer.

Abull ubull (mar a ratha)
mbruidnech mbras.

Tree of apples huge and magic,
great its graces.

Apples were valued because they provided healthy food (vitamins, even if they didn't know it at the time) during the winter when other foods were scarce. A monastic rule of the ninth century states that a penitent could eat apples with his ration of bread, 'If they be large, five or six of them with bread are sufficient; but if they be small, twelve of them are sufficient.'

King Cathal MacFinguine, he whose prodigious appetite Mac Con Glinne set out to overcome, had to have a bushel of apples just to take the edge off his hunger, and the chieftain whom he was visiting was expected to provide these apples, not to mention the mountains of other food the king required.

In a charming legend, the Virgin Mary asked her husband, St Joseph, to pick an apple for her, and when he refused the tree immediately bent down so that she might pick one herself. Ever since then the apple tree in fruit bears its branches low.

Of all the trees in the Irish orchard, the apple tree is by far and away the most important, not only because it is so popular but also because there are so very many native varieties still extant – living links with our past. We value old ruins and preserve old artefacts in museums, but our living heritage is much neglected and kept alive largely by a few dedicated enthusiasts. Historically, apple trees were grown extensively in Limerick, south Tipperary and parts of Ulster. The Quakers (how often their name crops up when it comes to enlightened thinking!) were great orchard growers.

One of the oddest discoveries unearthed during my researches is the fact that in 1903 the British Empire wanted to impress itself on Ireland, so grants were given to establish English varieties in

Irish orchards. Today, in many of the big houses and castles you will find one-hundred-year-old trees dating from that time. However, some of the gardeners had enough pride and foresight to plant some native varieties alongside the invaders, so the traditional trees were not lost.

The Irish Seed Savers Association, whose members aim to locate and preserve traditional varieties of fruit and vegetables, is located in Co Clare, not far from Scariff. As you look around their few acres and see the cornucopia they have achieved on a hill site with initially poor soil, you realise the potential that is locked up and unexploited in Ireland. Let us take apples as an example. So many are imported that you might think it necessary to ship them halfway across the world. But a quick glance at the Seed Saver catalogue will make you boggle. Ireland is teeming with native varieties of apple tree. Here are listed apple trees that have been rescued from extinction, such as the Ard Cairn Russet. The note attached to this entry explains that this was originally 'from a seedling found growing in a garden in Cork in 1890. Once grown prolifically throughout the country.' The Farrell is listed as 'fine yellow eater, extinct except for one tree in Waterford'. How about the Ecklinville Seedling? 'Reputed to be raised in Ireland in 1820 by a gardener named Logan. Once grown commercially but dropped because it bruises. Beautiful blossom, the best baking apple in the collection.' And the Glenstal Cooker is saved from extinction thanks to an apple from the only old tree left in Glenstal Abbey, Co Limerick.

Anita Hayes of the Irish Seed Savers Association showed me some apple trees that are growing in very poor land and, against all the rules, new roots are growing out of the old wood. As she explained, 'the quality of the fruit from these old Irish trees is very, very variable, but they will produce anywhere, will root themselves and don't need grafting. Who knows how very important this vigorous ability to root will prove to be? Things not considered important at the time can become important in hindsight. Why do things root? Already, many of the monocrops are showing signs of not rooting so well. They are losing vigour.' The vigour of old and sometimes despised native species should not be underestimated.

Of all the native apples, perhaps the Irish peach apple is the most special. Only small, with no great beauty of appearance, this has a flavour that is said to evoke that of the white peach and its scent is superb. However, it fruits right at the end of the branch, so pruning is difficult and it is rarely found nowadays. While I was visiting the Seed Savers, one of the gardeners came in excitedly with an Irish peach apple that had just that moment fallen off the bough. I was lucky enough to be given a piece of this fragrant little apple and although I didn't detect the expected peach flavour, I was told that this little windfall had come off the tree too early and the full flavour had not yet developed.

The blackthorn (*Prunus spinosa*) is another tree native to Ireland and is placed in the third class of trees in the Irish tree-list. It bears small sloes that can only have been of use as a source of flavour or as an emergency food in times of famine, for they are mouth-puckeringly sour. (They come into their own if you make sloe gin.) The garden plum was cultivated, as there are early references to 'sweet sloes' – plums, in other words. An early eleventh-century pit at Fishamble Street in Dublin was found to contain stones of a plum not unlike a bullace, along with shell fragments of walnuts and stones from the cherry (*Prunus cerasus*), so some cultivation of the cherry seems to have taken place before the arrival of the Normans.

It was indeed the Normans who brought in many of the foods commonly eaten in Ireland today and who were responsible for introducing pears. (One of the oldest pears in cultivation today is the French *Cadillac*, dating back to 1665.) An attempt was made in the early Christian period to initiate some vine growing, despite the lack of a suitable climate, less because of a desire to drink the wine than to make wine for the celebration of mass. For a time the monks persisted, especially in the south of the country, but although the Venerable Bede claimed there was 'no lack of vines', Giraldus Cambrensis remarked on their absence.

When the Huguenots arrived in Ireland, mostly in the early eighteenth century, escaping from persecution at home, they set to work in their adopted country with great results. The Marquis de Ruvigny's Huguenot colony in Portarlington grew grapes and trained their apples and pears on espaliers. But such sophistication was not widespread and eventually the colony faltered. Some of the wealthier families integrated, but the rest, no matter how cultivated, were not welcomed by the local landed gentry and over a few generations ended up in small trades and education. The French language was used by them mainly for formal documents and dropped out of day-to-day usage.

Wild Fruit and Berries

A tree that is hugely familiar from the Irish landscape, for it grows at the drop of a hat on roadsides and in hedgerows, is the elder tree, a tree that has a lot of magic attached to it, as has the hazel. The elder (*Sambucus nigra*) gives two bounties: the elderberry, which makes jams and wines and syrups, and the elderflower, whose fragrance is unforgettably delicious.

Elderberry Syrup

In the old days, elderberry syrup was reputed to be helpful in relieving coughs and colds and sore throats. Try to pick the berries when they are absolutely ripe – they should be a glossy dark maroon-black and if the clusters droop downwards the fruit is probably ripe for picking. If you must pick fruit from the roadside, give it a good rinsing first. You may need to add more water – up to half as much again – if you don't feel the fruit is very juicy. It pays to use high-quality sugar – look for 'Product of Mauritius' on the bag.

3 kg elderberries   A jelly bag
150 g sugar per 500 ml juice

Put the elderberries into a large stainless-steel saucepan (avoid aluminium) together with water to cover, bring to the boil and reduce to a simmer for 45 minutes. Strain the mixture through a jelly bag, allowing it to drip away overnight into a deep bowl. The next day, measure the amount of juice and weigh out the right amount of sugar, which you should set in a warm place. Boil the juice gently for 10 minutes and then remove from the heat and stir in the warmed sugar until it dissolves completely. Put the saucepan back on the stove and boil gently for a further 20 minutes. Finally, skim the surface and pour into clean, sterile bottles. This should give around a litre of syrup.

The elderflower is one of nature's glories and elderflower fritters are marvellous, although I don't usually like deep-fried food. I have made elderflower fizz, but I got so nervous about slightly letting off the pressure in the bottles, lest they exploded, that I stopped altogether. If you make the cordial, you can always dilute it with sparkling water for much the same effect. The scent and the flavour of elderflower cordial are to me the essence of summer. Give the elderflowers a good shake to dislodge any lurking greenfly. (If you insist, you can rinse them and pat them dry.)

Elderflower Cordial

10 elderflower heads
1 kg sugar
1.5 litres water, boiled and cooled

A few leaves of lemon balm
20 g citric acid

Put everything bar the citric acid into a clean polythene bucket, stir and cover. Stir from time to time and after three days strain into a saucepan. Add 20 g citric acid (available in most food stores or pharmacies), bring to the boil and, using a funnel, bottle in sterilised bottles.

Wild strawberries and wild raspberries could be found on heathlands or in woods over the summer months and the wild cherry can be found in early July in hedgerows and old woodland. (If you use it in place of the cultivated cherry, you will need more sugar than usual, as it can taste pretty sour.) Mrs Delany, the wife of the Dean of Down, wrote from Clogher in a letter dated 2 August 1748, 'I gathered four sorts of fruit – raspberries, cranberries, strawberries and nuts, of which there are a great plenty, the raspberries were particularly high-flavoured.'

The crab apple is another autumn fruit, picked from August through to October; it is held to be necessary to pick it before Hallowe'en or else the *púca* (the malevolent Irish spirit) will spit on it and wither it. If you keep your eyes open at a Country Market sale or in farmers' markets, you might find a jar of crab-apple jelly, and this beautiful clear garnet jelly is well worth snapping up.

The rowan tree or the mountain ash is another source of berries that go on to make a superb jelly, one that is particularly good served with venison or other game.

There is one berry that has more names attached to it than any other: the fraughan, or bilberry. Its botanical name is *Vaccinium myrtillus*, and its Irish name is *fraochan*. From these, we move to bilberry, blueberry, whortleberry (and thence hurts and whorts), wimberry or whinberry, occasionally cowberry or crowberry. We know that the name 'blueberry' is used in America because of Fats Waller's song, *Blueberry Hill*, but the same berry is referred to as a huckleberry, the nickname that so appealed to Mark Twain.

Garland Sunday

Over the centuries and over the seasons, fruit gathering became woven into the fabric of Irish rural life and the fraughan, being the first of the wild berries to ripen, was the occasion for an outing. Because the wild ones grow in bogs, on moors or wherever heather grows, they could sometimes be hard to spot, but children with their keen eyes were famous for finding them.

The day chosen was the Sunday closest to the first day of August, a day that coincided with the ancient festival of Lughnasa, created for the pagan god Lugh. This day was generally called Garland Sunday in its Christianised form, but it went by other names, too: Whort, Bilberry, Fraughan, Harvest and Pattern Sunday, plus *Domhnach Deireanach an tSamraidh* (the last Sunday of summer) and, along the Irish-speaking western seaboard, *Domhnach Chrom Dubh* (Black Crom's Sunday), Crom being the name of an idol worshipped in Connacht. It was sometimes also called *Domhnach na bhFear*, meaning The Men's Sunday.

Lammas Day is celebrated on 1 August and the term Lammas came in with the Scots and English settlers, but never passed into the Gaelic speech and is associated with the northern parts of the country. The native Irish called it Lewy's Fair, a corruption of the Irish word Lugh. The scholar Kuno Meyer wrote:

> Lammas Day makes known its dues
> In each distant year,
> Testing every favourite fruit
> Food of herbs at Lughnasa.

In 1942 the Irish Folklore Commission issued a questionnaire about Garland Sunday, the last Sunday of July or the first Sunday of August. The response was overwhelming. People reported picking bilberries and other wild fruit, eating the first of the new potatoes and whatever else they had brought along for the picnic. Some of them drank home-made wine, others took a drop of poteen; musicians arrived with their fiddles, bodhrans and accordions and there were always a couple of lads with a mouth organ or a tin whistle in their pockets. Everyone, young and old, danced the night away.

These days, observance of Garland Sunday has disappeared and I never see any children picking bilberries or even blackberries, perhaps because mothers used to terrify children by warning them that blackberries were full of maggots.

Patrick Kavanagh, in his novel *The Green Fool*, writes,

> During the War money grew on the tops of the bushes. Blackberries were five shilling a stone. Rocksavage farm was the home of briars, rich, fruit-bearing briars ignored by all the money-grabbers. Very few people ate blackberries, the one man who did we thought a bit touched on that account. Myself and two sisters were sent out each morning with cans and porringers.

Traditionally blackberries and apples were combined to make jam. (The apples are needed because blackberries alone haven't enough pectin to set the jam properly.)

Blackberry and Apple Jam

This quantity should fill around ten 450 g jars.

1 kg cooking apples	Scant 2 kg cane sugar
2.5 kg blackberries	

First, prepare your jam jars. They must be completely clean and warm. If you can arrange for them to come out of the dishwasher just before you want to use them, that would be ideal, but most people warm them in the oven. Have ready their little wax discs and cellophane covers – most places sell these around jam-making time.

Now peel, core and slice the apples and stew them in 300 ml of water in a stainless-steel pan until they turn to mush.

Pick over the blackberries, ruthlessly discarding any dodgy berries, and cook them until soft in a maximum of 145 ml of water. If you wish, you may push the cooked fruit through a coarse sieve to remove the pips. Put the blackberries in a wide preserving pan (a stainless-steel pan will do), add the apple pulp and the warmed sugar and stir over a gentle heat until the sugar is dissolved. Let the mixture boil steadily for around 10–15 minutes. To test if it is ready, put a small amount on a cold saucer – if a skin forms that wrinkles as you push it, the jam will set. Ladle into your warm jars, seal and label and sit back satisfied. Using a jam funnel makes the ladling process much neater.

Plums and damsons were also great fruit for jam-making and most farms had a tree of one sort or the other. Bushes of soft fruits such as gooseberry, blackcurrant, redcurrant and whitecurrant were also widely cultivated, and in places raspberry canes were grown, too. All seemed to be hardy and thrive even in poor soils.

The other fruit that almost every single garden could boast was the rhubarb. It is not difficult to see why this was so popular – it is quite hardy and if it is forced under cover it provides a touch of colour and a portent of spring very early in the gardening year. I have a special memory of rhubarb because I was once offered some by an elderly bachelor, who thought to lure me behind his house, out of sight of the road. He seemed disappointed when I said that I had plenty of my own. 'Oh, so does that mean I won't get a feel of your chest, then?' I told some of my cousins that story and remarked that the price of rhubarb seemed a little high. 'It's as well,' they said, 'that he didn't offer you any of his potatoes!'

Nuts

From Neolithic times nuts were a godsend to help tide people over the lean winter months. A good crop of nuts was a sign of a good ruler and each crop was eagerly observed. The *Annals of Ulster* record that in AD 835 there was such a heavy crop of nuts (meaning hazelnuts) and acorns that the streams were dammed up and ceased to flow. The acorn crop was usually set aside for pigs, as was the beech mast, and because much of the land was covered in hazel there was a trade in hazelnuts. The year 1097 became known as the 'year of the white nuts' because they were so plentiful.

The bigger houses would have other nut trees growing, including walnuts. Mrs Delany, who moved in the upper set, wrote in her eighteenth-century diary, 'I have just been gleaning my autumn fruits – melon, figs, Beury pears, grapes, filberts and walnuts. Walnuts are indeed but just come in with us. I loaded my basket and filled my hands with honeysuckles, jessamine, July flowers and pippins.'

These filberts were among the few foods known to the ascetic hermits of the early Celtic church. They were often crushed down to form a nut flour and then mixed with water or milk to sustain the monk on fast days. Paradoxically, the nut was also one of the chosen foods of the well-off and the courts of the medieval kings used vast quantities of nuts, particularly almonds.

Hazelnuts, though, remained a constant source of food for all strata of society and never lost their popularity. My father remembers his childhood years in Co Galway in the 1920s. 'There was a big copse, or wood, belonging to Connells down near the Shannon. There was land extending from the house to the Shannon and at the far end there were all hazel trees. They never objected, the Connells, at all. They came from far and near at every season and it would be an army there collecting hazel nuts. Climbing trees, shaking trees. It wasn't our property at all, but Connells never bothered about it anyway. (People would now, of course. It would never be allowed now, climbing fences and breaking trees.) We could save the nuts up for Christmas . . .'

CHAPTER EIGHT

THE POTATO AND THE FAMINE

Potatoes are good when the white flower is on them,
They are better when the white foam is on them,
They are still better when the stomach is full of them.

An old Irish saying

Is maith an t-anlann an t-ocras.
Good it is for a sauce, the hunger.

An old Irish saying

Until 1770 three plants shared the name of potato: the yam, the sweet
potato and the white potato, this last known in America as the 'Irish

potato' as early as 1635. Nowadays the world associates the potato with Ireland – Murphy, its nickname, tells us that.

Vocabulary reveals what people find important. The Inuit, we are told, can precisely describe varying conditions of snow. Similarly, in the Irish language many words evolved to pin down conditions of potatoes: among them *gruán*, lumpy potato; *ceaist phrátaí*, batch of potatoes roasted in ashes; *caochán*, eyeless potato; *muireog*, potato head; *brúitín*, mashed potatoes; *gátaire*, often a small griddle cake, but also potatoes roasted in embers as a treat; and *steodaire*, small, worthless potatoes. Reckoning small potatoes as worthless relates to a time when the smaller tubers were set aside for feeding the pigs, hens and other livestock; even today Irish country people prize a good big spud rather than the 'rubbish'. An old triad tells us that the three worst things of all are small soft potatoes, from that to an uncomfortable bed and then to sleep with a bad woman.

The potato was celebrated in song over and again, for folk song often deals with what folk are most familiar with.

The Potato

I'm a careless potato and care not a pin
How into existence I came;
If they planted me drillwise or dibbled me in,
To me 'tis exactly the same.
The bean and the pea may more loftily tower,
But I care not a button for them;
Defiance I nod with my beautiful flower
When the earth is hoed up to my stem.

The potato originated in the High Andes and the story is that Walter Raleigh brought the potato to Youghal in Co Cork in 1585. That may be so, but all we know for sure is that Francis Drake, another Elizabethan adventurer, left three sacks of potatoes with the English settlers in Virginia (named for the Virgin Queen Elizabeth) on the way home. It was 1615 before the colonists harvested the first white potato and, having eaten the leaves and failed to be impressed, they returned to maize and corn.

Fortunately for the potato it had some influential friends. Thanks to Thomas Jefferson's experiments with potato cookery after his visit to Paris, the potato eventually caught on. Jonathan Swift, ever independent-minded, rejected the views of other preachers who condemned them as aphrodisiacs, and was said to be fond of potatoes cooked in a Dublin coddle. Most important of all was the great French chef and army pharmacist, Antoine-Auguste Parmentier. Having survived on potatoes and a little milk when he was imprisoned during the Seven Years War, he came away determined to popularise them. 'I know many people in Paris who live on potatoes and milk alone,' he wrote, 'and whose stomachs have never tolerated any other foods.'

When he presented the tuber to Louis XVI, Marie Antoinette was charmed and tucked the spray of purple potato blossom behind her ears. But Parmentier was more concerned about the value of potatoes to the peasant and wrote a thesis to prove that the potato was the answer to famine. (In his native village of Montdidier, outside Paris, they erected a statue of the great chef handing a potato to a group of peasants.) Cleverly playing on the allure of the forbidden, he surrounded his potato patch in Sablon with an armed guard by day, thus arousing the curiosity of the Parisians, who stole the potatoes at night and took to them greedily. In 1773, Parmentier pointed out in his *Examen Chimique des Pommes de Terre*, 'Years ago, only the very destitute ate potatoes in France; however . . . the present consumption of these roots proves that they are currently less disdained.'

As we shall see in the section on the Great Famine, from the late seventeenth century the potato was adopted widely, so much so that foods which had been used for centuries were forgotten and ways of cooking them also. Nevertheless, the potato-rich diet was not unhealthy. Over three-quarters of the potato is water, but it also contains vitamins, fibre and protein in a naturally packaged starch that does not raise cholesterol levels and is easily digested. One potato averages 90 calories and there is almost no fat in a potato, so enough potatoes, plus a little milk and occasional fish or meat, gives a balanced diet. Moreover, you don't need teeth to eat a potato (in the days when there was no dental care, such a consideration was useful) and eating potatoes might well have eradicated scurvy from the broader European population after the seventeenth century.

The traditional way of growing vegetable crops was in raised beds or ridges known as lazy beds. Something along these lines was practised 4,500 years ago, but the system became fully developed in the 1660s. The English, who did not understand it, despised it, but there was nothing lazy about the scheme – it was clever and well adapted to the thin wet soils of Ireland, particularly in the west.

The technique was to spread manure on a strip of grass, then, using only a spade known as a 'loy', turn a scraw (a grass sod) roughly the size of an old-fashioned family Bible, onto the sward. The first cut would be flicked to the left, the next cut flicked right and so on down the strip before moving back along a second strip. This time the scraws flicked to the right would meet the scraw turned onto that side in the first strip, the two joining together, forming a thicker, drier ridge, with drainage trenches running either side, where the cut was made. Planting in April and May was usually the women's job, and when the shoots were well grown, the potatoes were earthed up with a further spadeful of soil from the furrows. You could improve the ridge by adding manure and seaweed. After a bed had been cropped regularly for a period, it was divided down the central ridge and the soils thrown outwards over a layer of manure and seaweed to form two new beds drained by a central channel. Ingenious!

The potato, once planted, needed very little attention and paid back handsomely the work that went into planting and harvesting. One hectare of potatoes could produce as much food as two hectares of barley or three hectares of oats or wheat. Digging the lazy beds was heavy work, and often the beds were located some distance from the cabin, but thereafter the cottier or labourer was free to engage in other work, with sowing and harvesting being fitted in outside the hours given to the landlord or 'strong' farmer. The potato would grow on very poor-quality land and the family would eat what would seem to us unbelievable amounts of potatoes, as much as 5 kg per person per day. Arthur Young, the English traveller, said that the poor 'have an absolute bellyful of potatoes and the children eat them as plentifully as they like'. Any surplus was fed to pigs and poultry, and these had to be fattened, because the money from the sale of the meat or eggs was essential to the survival of the poor.

By the nineteenth century potatoes had eclipsed white meats and bread in the diet of the common people and this switch to the potato had been going on for some time. As early as 1672, an English observer, Sir William Petty, was writing, 'Their food is bread in cakes, whereof a penny serves a week for each; potatoes from August till May, mussels, cockles and oysters near the sea, eggs and butter made very rancid by keeping it in bogs.' Similarly, in 1690, John Stevens, in his *Journal of my Travels in Ireland since the Revolution*, recorded, 'The meaner people content themselves with little bread, but instead thereof eat potatoes, which with sour milk is the chief part of their diet . . .'

The potato in Ireland was not simply adopted as a cheap food by the poor. The better off also took to it hugely. Richard Twiss in his *A Tour in Ireland*, 1775, reported that,

> The outskirts of Dublin consist chiefly of huts . . . made
> of dried mud, and mostly without either chimney or

window; and in these miserable dwellings far the greater part of the inhabitants of Ireland linger out a wretched existence. There is generally a small piece of ground annexed to each cabin, which produces a few potatoes; and on these potatoes, and milk, the common Irish subsist all the year round, without tasting bread or meat, except perhaps at Christmas once or twice . . . As to the customs peculiar to the Irish gentry . . . [one] is the universal use of potatoes, which form a standing dish at every meal. These are eaten by way of bread, even the ladies indelicately placing them on the tablecloth, on the side of their plate, after peeling them.

More peculiar is the story of the hostess who, having found Lady Mount Cashell eating plain boiled potatoes for her luncheon in the middle of the day, 'heard for the first time that that was the principal food of the Irish, and immediately resolv'd on giving Lady Mount Cashell a breakfast in compliment to her country. We went there and literally found nothing but Potatoes dress'd in Fifty different fashions.'

Plentiful Potatoes

Prata na hEireann (The Irish Potato)
I'll give you a song, 'tis a true Irish strain.
Our cruiscins and glasses, my boy, let us drain.
Our voices in chorus now manfully lend
And sing the potato's the Irishman's friend.
With my Ballinamona oro, it's a laughing potato for me!

'Tis the root of all roots and that everyone knows,
And best of all places in Ireland it grows,
So grateful of care it repays well our toil

And like a true Paddy is fond of the soil
With my Ballinamona oro, it's a mealy potato for me!

Prata na hEireann, the Irish potato,
Its progeny various would puzzle a saint – oh
Pink, purple and white, red, russet and black,
But all the same hue with no coat on their back.
With my Ballinamona oro, it's the land of potatoes for me!
From a nineteenth-century ballad

There are hundreds of varieties of potato. Anita Hayes of the Irish Seed Savers Association finds Champions very productive, getting a bucketful to feed people just from one plant. At the Association site in Co Clare they grow many historic indigenous varieties, including the Land Leaguer, named from the Land League Festivals at which competition raged as to who could grow the best and the earliest. The now rare Lumper, the potato almost exclusively grown around the time of the Great Famine, was said to have tears in his eyes for the Irish who died in the Potato Famine. Actually, by the early nineteenth century the red varieties of potato were known to be more resistant to blight, but the huge crops that the white Lumper (also called the 'horse' potato) gave caused people to choose it above all others. It is not a particularly good potato to eat, but a delicious taste was not a priority. I grew some potatoes from some Lumper chits they gave me at the Seed Savers, and they were essentially fine, if rather soapy of texture.

Before the Great Famine, varieties other than the Lumper prevailed. Up to 1730 the Black was popular, a white-fleshed variety with a black skin. It gave a good yield for the time and stored well for the following year. Until 1768, a round, red potato, the Apple, was popular, noted for its mealy texture and excellent keeping quality. The Cup was a favourite until 1808, a variety described as 'more difficult to digest' than the Apple. However, it yielded 10–15 per cent more than the Apple and also grew in upland areas. As big yields had priority above taste, after 1808 the Lumper dominated. This white-skinned, white-fleshed variety produced high yields of knobbly potatoes, giving 10–15 per cent higher yields again than the Cup. First introduced as animal feed, it soon became the most widely grown variety and accounted for almost 90 per cent of potatoes grown in Ireland in the 1840s.

A strange thing in a nation of potato lovers is that Irish people truly value only one style of potato. No other nation takes such an interest in the variety of potato they buy, but ask any Irish person to describe his or her ideal potato and the answer will come back, 'a ball of flour'. A dry, mealy potato is the choice every time. Few appreciate the waxy potato at all, even though Ratte or Pink Fir Apple is a fine potato for certain dishes, potato salad being one of them. And no one in Ireland really seems to be switched on to the virtues of the early new potatoes. Instead of seeing them as special treats to mark the beginning of summer, boiled whole with mint, many people are impatient of the small new potatoes and can't wait for later in the summer when the praties start to get big again and have their familiar taste and texture. This failure to appreciate new potatoes may be due to a folk memory of the days when hunger would drive the poor to dig up some of their crop of potatoes in July, even though they might be only the size of a pullet's egg.

Those caveats aside, people do care passionately about their potatoes. Local greengrocers (and in Ireland they have not yet all been ousted by the supermarket) will advise which variety is best at the time of buying – one week it will be Records, another it might be Roosters or again it could be British Queens or Kerr's Pinks. And everyone has an opinion on the potato and finds it an absorbing topic of conversation. An excellent book on the subject is *The Potato Year* by Lucy Madden, containing much history as well as a good number of recipes.

Cooking Methods

The main peasant way of cooking the potato is hard to beat – it is boiled or steamed in its jacket, thus preserving the vitamins lying under the skin. A potato is judged to be cooked when its skin has just split, when it is said to be smiling or laughing. In the past the potatoes were tipped out into a large wicker basket or *sciathog* which allowed the steam to escape and this was set in the middle of the table or on a stool and the family sat around. Since few families could extend as far as having a knife per person, many people grew the thumbnail long on one hand, especially to be able to peel potatoes with it, and the advice to young people was to be 'eating one potato, peeling another, have a third in your fist and your eye on the fourth'.

The etiquette these days is to spear a potato with your fork, and transfer it to your main plate once you have peeled it on your side plate. (I believe some modern types use knives rather than thumbnails.) The *sciathog* or skeb is sadly a museum piece these days, undeservedly so, for it was practical as well as a craft piece of beauty and appropriateness.

In grand houses the skeb was replaced by a potato ring, a deep band of silver, often elaborately chased, with a white linen napkin tucked inside it to absorb the steam. The thumbnail was not employed.

As the potato became a staple of the kitchen, more interesting ways of cooking than mere boiling were devised.

Champ

Made essentially of potatoes and scallions (spring onions), its name varied from place to place, but call this dish what you will, champ, poundies, stampy, cally or thump, it has universal appeal. When men came to a farm to do a day's labour – cutting turf, saving the hay or sowing potatoes – the woman of the house would provide a hot dinner and champ was often the centrepiece.

In the old days huge quantities were prepared and it took the man of the house to pound the potatoes, using a beetle or pounder, made from a heavy block of wood on a long handle. Often, in the beaten dirt floor of the cabin, a hollow was made into which the big iron potato pot could be set to hold it steady while the vigorous pounding was administered.

In 1938 Patrick Kavanagh wrote in *The Green Fool*: 'George told me, "Me grand-uncle was in Monaghan gaol for a debt of eleven shillings. Me granny brought him his dinner of champ every day. Twenty one and a half Irish miles to Monaghan, she'd have the champ warm enough to melt the butter."'

A children's rhyme goes:

> There was an old woman
> Who lived in a lamp.
> She had no room
> For to beetle her champ.
> So she's up with her beetle
> And broken the lamp
> And then she had room
> For to beetle her champ.

Champ

You might need to add a little more milk for a creamier mash, but it ought not to be too sloppy because the butter is an essential part of the dish and more can be added to each helping. If you wish, you may substitute chopped chives or young nettles or even fresh parsley for the scallions (spring onions).

1 kg floury potatoes
1 heaped cup chopped
    scallions (green
    stems included)

220 ml milk
Salt and freshly ground pepper
A gigantic knob of butter

Ideally, steam the potatoes until the skins are just about to split. Remove them from the heat and let them dry before you peel them. Meanwhile, simmer the chopped scallions in the milk, then mash, pound or stamp the spuds. For a small amount such as this you won't need a beetle – use a mouli, a potato ricer or else a hand masher – and never try to mash potatoes in a food processor or you will end up with glue. When the potatoes have been thoroughly mashed, pour in the hot milk and scallions, season with salt and pepper (white pepper was once the norm) and stir in the butter. Some like to sit a lump of butter in a little well hollowed into each serving.

Colcannon

Considering how close this dish is to that preceding it, it is remarkable that the two have remained so distinctly identified. The 'col' of the name refers to the kale that was traditionally used, although cabbage often replaced the kale and in past centuries charlock could have provided the necessary green element. (You can make it with white cabbage, too, but then you will miss the flecks of green that are traditional.) At Hallowe'en a ring and a coin were slipped into the mixture. If you drew out the coin it foretold riches; the ring a forthcoming marriage.

A sentimental old song goes thus:

Did ye ever eat Colcannon
When 'twas made with yellow cream
And the kale and praties blended
Like the picture in a dream?
Did ye ever take a forkful
And dip it in the lake
Of the heather-flavoured butter
That your mother used to make?
Oh, ye did, yes, ye did,
So did he and so did I

And the more I think about it
Sure, the more I want to cry.
God be with the happy times
When trouble we had not,
And our mothers made colcannon
In the ould three-legged pot.

Colcannon

As with all simple recipes, the better your ingredients, the happier the
result. Serves four to six people.

450 g kale or green leaf cabbage (Savoy is good)	6 scallions (spring onions), chopped
450 g floury potatoes	Salt and pepper
150 ml creamy milk	100 g butter

Remove the tough ribs from the kale or cabbage and shred finely. Cook
until tender in salted water then drain very well. Boil or steam the
potatoes in their skins and towards the end of their cooking simmer
the scallions in the milk for 5 minutes. Drain and peel the potatoes
and put back into the pot to dry before mashing them until they are
smooth. A potato ricer will do the job well, as will a mouli. Now add
the scallions and milk, beating well so that the potatoes are creamy,
and finally beat in the kale and season to taste. Heat the whole again
gently and serve in a warm dish, with the butter in a well scooped into
the centre so that it can melt lusciously over the colcannon.

Boxty

This is made of an unusual mixture of cooked and raw potatoes. The
idea might have originated in the west of Ireland and the tradition
is also strong in the more northerly counties of Cavan, Leitrim and

Monaghan. It is only speculation on my part, but I think that grating soft potatoes, perhaps on the verge of rotting, would have been an expedient turned to during the Famine times, as an alternative to throwing the still-precious potato away.

I have seen home-made graters fashioned from thin pieces of tin through which several holes were punched to form a smooth side and a rough side. Eric Cross, who in 1942 wrote a delightful account of his friends, the eponymous *The Tailor and Ansty*, told how, 'They used to make a kind of bread with potatoes called Stampy. They would grate the potatoes on a tin grater and then squeeze them into a tub of water. The stampy was made on a breadtree, a kind of sloping board put before the fire to hold bread, and was only usually made for Christmas or November night, unless you had a good supply of potatoes, when you might make it once a week.' That sounds mightily like a variation on boxty, don't you think?

Boxty on the Griddle
Serves four to six people

225 g raw potatoes, peeled	1 tsp salt
225 g cooked, mashed potatoes, cooled	50 g plain flour

Line a bowl with a clean cloth, letting the ends hang over the edge and grate the raw potatoes into it. Gather the ends of the cloth and twist them, as if you were holding a balloon by the neck end, then lift the cloth over the bowl, squeezing out as much of the liquid starch as possible into the vessel below. Take another bowl and put your grated potatoes into it, followed by the cold mashed potatoes. Meanwhile, the starchy liquid from the grated potatoes will be separating out, the heavier starch sinking to the bottom. It will take a couple of hours for this to complete.

Thereafter, carefully drain off the clear liquid and scrape the starch onto the top of the potatoes. Next, sprinkle on the salt and mix in well before adding the flour to form a dough. Set your griddle to heat. (A heavy frying pan will do, at a pinch.)

Turn the dough out onto a floured surface and roll into a fairly thin circle. Cut eight farls or triangles out of it. Sprinkle a little flour on the hot griddle to stop the boxty from sticking and proceed to cook until both sides are nice and brown – about 30 minutes.

If you like, you can serve the boxty straight away, with lovely yellow butter, or you can let it cool and slice it in two for frying alongside rashers the following day.

Boxty in the Pan

Boxty pancakes are crisp little cakes that are eaten hot, either with rashers from the pan or else with butter and sugar as a sweet dish. In some families a handful of charms were scattered into the batter – a ring for courtship, a coin for future wealth, a button for an old bachelor, a thimble for an old maid and a cross for a religious vocation. Serves four to six people.

450 g potatoes, peeled and grated   Scant 1 tsp salt
2 tbs plain flour   150 ml whole milk
1 tsp baking powder

Peel and grate the raw potatoes into one bowl and in another sieve the flour, baking powder and salt together. Combine the contents of the two bowls and add the milk gradually, making a soft batter of dropping consistency. Set your griddle or heavy-based frying pan to heat and grease it lightly with a small knob of butter. From here on you simply drop the mixture onto the pan one tablespoonful at a time. You should get a bare dozen pancakes from this recipe, and if they won't all fit in the pan together, cook them in two batches. The boxty pancakes need to be cooked for about 5 minutes on each side, until they are golden and crisp.

Some people eat them with butter and sugar or jam, but I prefer them with rashers and a fried egg, its yolk still runny. I also find that adding some grated onion to the mixture or even chopped scallions gives a pleasing savoury twist.

Potato-apple Cakes

These were cooked as a treat in the autumn when cooking apples were plentiful and comfort food was desired. Basically, a few apples were peeled, cored and sliced and some mashed potatoes were mixed with salt, melted butter and a good scatter of flour to make a stiff dough. This was then halved and both halves rolled out to give two circles of dough. Each was cut so that eight triangles were formed from each circle, and on half of those triangles you would pile some sliced raw apple, before using the other triangles as lids, pinching the edges to seal them.

In the old days they would rake some glowing red embers under the pot oven and pop in the cakes, with a few embers on the lid. When the potato-apple cakes were browned and risen, their sides were slit and the tops turned back to allow slices of cold butter and plenty of brown sugar to be added. The tops were then replaced and the cakes returned to the bastable just long enough for the sugar and butter to melt into a fragrant, syrupy sauce that oozed from the sides.

FAMINE

Ni thuigeann an sách an seang
(The well fed does not understand the lean).

Old Irish saying

In a desperate attempt to pretend that everything was all right, an Irish broadsheet of 1847 gave this cheering proposal:

So now my good people, you need never fear,
Old Ireland will prosper on this present year,
But instead of potatoes, believe what I say
We'll have a cheap loaf with a good cup of tea.

As was tragically apparent, Old Ireland did not prosper and no cheap loaves or cups of tea were to be had. By the mid-nineteenth century, one foodstuff had replaced nearly every other in the diet of the very poor in Ireland. In 1845, out of a population of eight million, more than five million depended entirely on the potato. How had this come about?

The People's Salvation

In seventeenth-century Ireland the potato had proved the salvation of the people when crops failed or were burned during Cromwell's occupation, and when in the late 1770s Arthur Young described Irish labourers as the most impoverished class he had yet seen in Europe, he added the rider, 'the Irish have a bellyful . . . I will not assert that potatoes are a better food than bread and cheese, but I have no doubt of a bellyful of one being much better than half a bellyful of the other.'

Around the same time another commentator, David Henry, in *The Practical Farmer or The Complete English Traveller*, remarked, 'It [the potato] is favourable to population; for it has been observed that in the western part of Ireland where it is almost the only diet of the labouring poor, it is no unusual thing to see six, seven, eight, ten and sometimes more children, the issue of one couple, starting almost naked out of a miserable cabin, upon the approach of an accidental traveller.'

Favourable to population it certainly was. Between 1700 and 1845 the population of Ireland rose from a little below three million to over eight million, that is, to a density of population far greater than it is today. This phenomenal increase is one that historians have yet to explain fully.

In part it was due to the period of stability and peace that followed the wars and plantations of the sixteenth and seventeenth centuries. People had switched from a dairy-based diet to one centred on cereals and the potato, confident of getting their daily rations from the existing land area. This newfound reliability of food supplies and the fact that young men were no longer being dragooned into wars meant that people were marrying younger in a country where the marriage rate was already very high. Some 90 per cent of the population married and the average age of couples dropped to about twenty-two years of age for women, twenty-three years for men.

Unsurprisingly, the birth rate jumped up. Reliable contraception was unknown and the accepted wisdom of the time was that since your children would look after you in your old age, you should have plenty. It is also possible that better health care led to a drop in infant mortality and a generally increased longevity, although for the tenant farmers and casual labourers in the most impoverished parts of the country, health care was mostly self-administered.

Whatever other elements brought about this increase, the figures are startling. In 1600 the population was under one and a half million; by 1718 it was almost 3 million. In 1781 it had reached well over four million and the census in 1841 published the figures as 8,175,124. Large areas of land were put to potato growing, the area sown increasing from about 180,000 hectares in 1725 to 860,000 hectares in 1845. As demand for land grew, the more people had to move into poor land and in remote parts of Mayo and Sligo lazy beds were established in the most unpromising places, on rocky slopes, very exposed to the weather.

Nowadays, if you look in some of the lonelier parts of the landscape, you can still see traces under the surface of the ground, stretching right up the mountains. The Great Famine wiped out whole families, their homes never reclaimed, so that the lazy beds lie there, silent but eloquent of a lost culture and generations blighted.

Although people were desperate for land, Ireland has, in fact, quite enough to house eight million people in a fair degree of comfort, but only if you assume the land was divided equally, which it emphatically was not.

Back in 1727, when he set off to see for himself the state of Irish peasantry, Jonathan Swift found, 'The families and the farmers . . . pay great rents, living in filth and nastiness upon buttermilk and potatoes and not a shoe or stocking to their feet.' Forty years later the Englishman John Bush in his *Hibernia Curiosa* reported that 'The province of Connaught is the thinnest of inhabitants of any part of Ireland. The landlords, first and subordinate, get all that is made of the land, and the tenants, for their labour, get poverty and potatoes.'

The economic status quo was as follows. 'Strong' farmers rented ten hectares or more from the landlords, but, once they started to subdivide it to set up their sons and their families, the amount of land per family dwindled. By 1841 there were 310,000 farms of less than six hectares in the country.

The landless labourer did not rent land, but instead got tangled up in a system known as conacre, which saw him paying for the right to grow potatoes on a specified piece of land. It was only let for a single season, and because the landowner undertook to manure the ground, he charged very high rents for it – as much as £8 per acre (0.4 hectares) was recorded. Money did not always change hands – the labourer could have the option of working for the farmer, paying off the rent from his wages, reckoned at 8d to 10d per day. This arrangement might take up two-thirds of the year, leaving very little time for the labourer to earn any money for his family.

It is estimated that about 140,000 hectares (350,000 acres) of land were let on the conacre system in 1845. However, this land would only provide potatoes from September to April or May for the 650,000 landless labourers and their families. The summer months could be lean enough.

At the bottom of the ladder was the landless labourer, known as a *spailpín*, who had no regular employment and no security of any nature. While he was fit enough and strong enough, he walked to the hiring fairs and hoped to be taken on during the busiest seasons of the year, sowing and harvesting. If he was lucky, the work lasted for a third of the year. The rest of the time he spent in his mud cabin by the roadside and trusted to chance and the odd spot of poaching. When he was no longer able-bodied, he was on the scrap heap. It is small wonder that many worn-out spailpins spent what time they could in the shebeens, drinking to forget their misery. These men accounted for 41 per cent of the population in 1845, in a country where four-fifths of the population were rural-based.

Given this dependence on what you could grow on a small plot of land, the potato was a godsend. It would grow anywhere, even on poor, thin soil, even on wet, boggy land. On decent land it raised the heart. Humphrey O'Sullivan, the son of a hedge schoolmaster and a schoolmaster himself, wrote this entry in his diary:

Friday 30 July 1830

A cloudy fine mild morning . . . The diet of my family and
myself is as follows: a hot breakfast, consisting of oat-meal
stirabout made on milk; wheaten bread and milk at one
o'clock, this is a cool midday meal; and potatoes and meat,
or butter towards late evening, as a meal in the cool of the
evening . . . My potatoes are growing wonderfully.

The potato allowed a family of five or six to live for a year on an acre
and a half. If the potato had not existed and the head of the family
were required to grow an equivalent amount of grain to feed everyone,
he would have needed an acreage anywhere from four to six times
larger and some knowledge of tillage as well. The equipment needed
for tillage could not be compared with the simple requirement of a loy
for digging the lazy beds.

In total, approximately fifteen million tonnes of potatoes were
consumed annually in Ireland in the early 1840s, just under half used
for human food, around five million tonnes for animal feed and a
further two million tonnes for seed, while a small quantity was exported.
(Wastage would be included in that calculation, as some potatoes would
have rotted in the potato clamps, as the storage pits were known.)

Pigs, cattle and fowl could be reared on the potato, using tubers
too small for everyday use. And for the human consumers, the potato
was bland enough to ensure that as a diet, it did not pall. Yet relying
on it was dangerous because it could not be stored from one season to
the next.

Figures vary, but it would be no exaggeration to say that the adult
working male ate over 6 kg a day, if available, the potatoes being eaten
in three equal meals, morning, noon and night. Some claim the figure
was higher still. The reason for this was not greed; the body was calling
out for the necessary quantity of vitamins and other nutrients that it
needed to function properly. The human stomach, being a very elastic
organ, stretched to accommodate the bulk.

John Carr in his 1805 work *The Stranger in Ireland* wrote: 'Upon an average, a man, his wife, and four children, will eat thirty-seven pounds of potatoes a day. A whimsical anecdote is related of an Irish potato. An Englishman, seeing a number of fine florid children in a cabin, said to the father: "How do your countrymen contrive to have so many fine children?" "By Jasus, it is the potato, Sir," said he. Three pounds of good mealy potatoes are more than equivalent to one pound of bread.'

Golden Land

Land was seen as the source of all wealth for there was virtually no industrial activity in Ireland with the exception of parts of Ulster. The country had no natural resources of coal or iron, the linen and cloth weaving trades were in decline and the fisheries tragically underdeveloped. In Galway and Mayo in the early nineteenth century, it was recorded that the fishermen were too poor to buy salt with which to preserve their catches.

Even on the land, regular employment, as it was understood in England, did not exist. While there were farms in England large enough to justify hiring agricultural labourers full time, Irish farms were too small to require anything except occasional hired labour. (Over 93 per cent of farms consisted of fewer than twelve hectares.)

In the absence of any regular work, an Irish labourer had to get hold of a patch of land on which to grow potatoes for himself and his wife and children or watch them starve. Accordingly, as Cecil Woodham Smith put it in her masterly *The Great Hunger*, 'Land became like gold in Ireland.' Owning a piece of land was all that stood between life and death. As a result of the desperate competition for land, rents in Ireland could be hiked up to enormous heights. They were, by and large, from 80 per cent to 100 per cent higher than in England.

In the forefront of the Irish labourer's mind was the overwhelming importance of paying the rent, for if he fell into arrears there was no doubt at all that he would be evicted. The majority of occupants were cottiers or tenants 'at will' and they could be evicted readily if their rents were over six months in arrears.

In 1846, when the famine had begun to really bite, the House of Commons in London was told, 'Ejectment is tantamount to a sentence of death by slow torture.' But ejectment happened, as we shall see, and many landlords rejoiced at the excuse to get rid of troublesome tenants and put the land to more profitable use.

Such is the background against which the tragic drama of the Great Famine was played out. Famines great and small had been known in Ireland across the centuries and Europe had known famine of epic proportions on many occasions. The difference between the Great Famine and all those that had preceded it was that it took place in the middle of the nineteenth century. That people were allowed to die in their hundreds of thousands in what was then the richest and most powerful empire on earth cannot be excused. Nothing compelled the government in London to interfere, and hearts were hardened against the troublesome Irish.

God's Will

In 1842 the grain crops in the USA and in Canada began to falter and then the failure spread to Ireland. This was no immediate cause for alarm because there was still an abundance of cheap food, easily obtained in the shape of the potato. By the standards of the day, a very restricted diet was not a particular hardship.

An outstanding witness of the period just prior to the famine years, Asenath Nicholson was a remarkable American woman who travelled around Ireland in 1840, spreading the good word and distributing Bibles. In her book *The Bible in Ireland*, she records this conversation between herself and a peasant: 'And all you have for your labour is the potato?' 'That's all, ma'am, that's all; and it's many of us that can't get a sup of milk with 'em, no, nor the salt; but we can't help it, we must be content with what the good God sends us.'

A natural fatalism, combined with a repressive establishment made up of politicians, the law and the Church, made the Irish very accepting of their situation. This inclination to bow to God's will and put their faith in the potato applied equally in the countryside and in the cities. Henry D. Inglis in his *A Journey Through Ireland During the Spring Summer and Autumn of 1834* wrote, 'The appearance of even Dublin prosperity is somewhat deceptive. I believe . . . that there is less profitable trade in Dublin now than was found some years ago. I was . . . struck with the small number of provisions-shops. In London every fifth or sixth shop is a bacon and cheese-shop. In Dublin, luxuries of a different kind offer their temptations. What would be the use of opening a bacon shop, where the lower orders, who are elsewhere the chief purchasers of bacon, cannot afford to eat bacon, and live only upon potatoes?'

The potato was marvellous in many ways but, as we have seen, June and July were hungry months or, as Humphrey O'Sullivan wrote in his diary on Monday 26 July 1830, 'July of the famine this month is called now. Yellowmonth is its name in Irish and it is an apt name, for if the cornfields are yellow, the faces of the poor are greenish yellow, because of the livid famine. For they are subsisting on green cabbage and other inferior odds and ends of a similar character.'

When the potatoes ran out, the family was thrown into a vacuum. Sometimes meal had to be eaten instead, meal bought on credit from the petty dealer and usurer who was the scourge of the Irish village, the 'gombeen man'. He bought up stocks of grain, then released them little by little at the most exorbitant prices he could get away with. As a result, he was cordially hated.

A Blighted Crop

For so many people to be so completely reliant on a single foodstuff was a highly dangerous situation, and it took only a single change of circumstance to tip this precarious balance and cause a landslide of cataclysmic significance. At the beginning of August in 1845, news arrived in the British Prime Minister's office from the Isle of Wight. A blight had appeared in the potato crop there and Sir Robert Peel's first thoughts were for the English working class.

At the same time as Parmentier had popularised the potato among the French, the English working classes had also begun to appreciate its advantages. Increasingly, potatoes were being put on the table in place of bread. On the last day of September 1845, *The Times* in London reported that in England the two main meals of the working man's day now consisted of potatoes.

The blight quickly spread through England, Scotland, Belgium and Holland and, inevitably, it reached Ireland. Once blight had been seen, beyond any shadow of a doubt, to have invaded the Irish potato crop there followed a sequence of delays and prevarications on the part of the British authorities. The Assistant Secretary to the Treasury, Trevelyan, was someone who felt an antipathy towards the Irish and under his aegis earnest warnings, heartfelt pleas and sensible suggestions as to how to ameliorate the situation were given the cold shoulder. Among the ruling classes was a deep-seated belief that the Irish exaggerated, and so, against all the evidence, the men in power continued to feel that the picture could not be as black as it was painted. Trevelyan saw the famine as 'a mechanism for reducing surplus population'. Very conveniently, it did just that.

Some steps were taken, it is true. Men of science were called in to sort out the problem, but their advice was worse than useless – it exacerbated an already serious situation. Where the Irish kept potatoes in potato clamps that might have protected some of them from the fungus that was causing the plants to putrefy, the scientific delegation recommended a different type of storage and one unsuited to the wet Irish conditions.

These wise men devised a method of dealing with diseased

potatoes. The Irish peasant was to provide himself with a grater or rasp, a linen cloth, a hair sieve or a cloth strainer, a tub or two for water, and a griddle. He was then required to take the slimy, stinking potatoes and rasp them very finely into one of the tubs, wash the pulp, strain, repeat the process, then dry the pulp on the griddle over a low heat. In the water used for washing the pulp a milky substance would be found, which would sink to the bottom of the tub. This white substance was starch, and good, wholesome bread could be made by mixing this starch with dried potato pulp, peameal, beanmeal, oatmeal or flour. It was the nineteenth-century equivalent of the alchemist's insistence that gold could be made out of base metal.

'There will be of course,' wrote the Commissioners, 'a good deal of trouble in doing all we have recommended, but we are confident all true Irishmen will exert themselves and never let it be said that in Ireland the inhabitants wanted courage to meet difficulties against which other nations are successfully struggling.'

Even if this transmutation of rotten food could have been achieved, starch alone would not supply the necessities for human life, but the desire to create starch at least had some relation to sanity. In her book *The Great Hunger*, Cecil Woodham Smith reproduces a communiqué that would have been funny if it had not been so tragic: 'the Duke of Norfolk suggested the Irish learn to eat curry powder, on which, mixed with water, he appeared to believe the population of India was nourished'.

In a series of letters in *The Nation*, Sir John Murray printed a recipe he claimed to have tested: 'cut off the diseased parts and steam or boil into a mash with bran and salt. When warm [it] is nourishing for pigs and cattle but tainted potatoes cold are apt to disagree.' Another suggestion called for the baking of diseased potatoes, for 18 to 22 minutes at a temperature of 180 degrees Fahrenheit. When 'blackish matter' with a foul smell oozed out, the potatoes would, it was claimed, then turn white and could be peeled.

Market Forces

Throughout Europe in 1846 there was a widespread failure of the harvest in general – wheat, oats, barley, rye and potatoes were all a total loss. Where Britain had been dragging its feet and unwilling to pay the asking price, these European countries responded quickly to the impending calamity and gave orders for grain to be bought abroad, easily outbidding Britain. One person willing to buy at the prices asked was the Irish meal dealer and petty money lender – the gombeen man. By 15 September 1846, the price of meal had soared to levels that relief committees and private philanthropists simply could not reach. 'The Dealers, hungry for money, buy up whatever comes to market and offer it again in small quantities at a great price which a poor man cannot pay and live.' So wrote Captain Pole, Commissariat officer at Banagher, Co Offaly.

A principal reason why the British authorities did not send grain as an emergency foodstuff lay in a fanatical belief in private enterprise. Corn could not be sent from Britain as relief to the starving, as that would interfere with the market. The government of the day cast around for a foodstuff that would not enrage the British farmer and found it in the shape of Indian corn, or maize, which was not grown in Britain. However, the government had procrastinated for so long that when they eventually acted it was a case of too little, too late. Other European countries affected by blight had already started looking for alternative food sources, in competition with the British authorities, and had got to America first.

An insufficient cargo of maize was finally secured, but it was not going to be easy to use. The US chargé d'affaires in Brussels wrote to say that it could not be treated as ordinary grain. Because it was flint corn, it was too hard to be ground in the normal way and at home in the USA similar grain was chopped with steel blades.

Since no mechanism existed for chopping the grain, ordinary millstones would have to be used, but to produce a reasonably digestible meal it was necessary to grind the corn twice. If this did not happen, the corn could scarcely be eaten no matter how willing the starving might be to give it a try; it was so sharp and irritating it could even pierce intestines. Trevelyan, who was in practice the head of Treasury, felt that this was a great deal of fuss about nothing. He was a hawk, disdainful of the bleeding-heart sentiments of the doves around him. 'We must not aim at giving more than wholesome food. I cannot believe it will be necessary to grind the Indian corn twice . . . dependence on charity is not to be made an agreeable mode of life.'

Indian corn was the only recourse the people had, but even a single milling of the stony grain posed a problem. Administrators who had never been to Ireland could see in their minds' eyes a network of mills around the country that could be used to process the grain, but these mills existed only in the imaginations of the British. The few mills that did exist were too busy milling grain for export or for speculative sale at home. Eventually, the Indian corn was sent to British Admiralty mills at Deptford, Portsmouth and Plymouth, and to hired mills in Rotherhithe and Maldon, Essex, before being taken by Admiralty steamer to Ireland. Even more bizarrely, Indian corn imported from North America was shipped out to naval mills in Malta and then shipped back to England before being sent on to Ireland.

Trevelyan decided, at length, that this was all too much trouble and he came up with the notion that boiling without crushing was the way to go. 'Ten pounds of corn so prepared is ample food for a labouring man for seven days . . . Corn so used', states the memo, 'will be considerably cheaper to the committee and the people than meal and will be well adapted to meet the deficiency of mill power . . .' What the memo fails to tackle is the uncomfortable fact that unground Indian corn was found by the Irish people all but impossible to digest. Even after they had boiled it for nearly two hours, the grain remained gritty and inedible.

While Trevelyan could not bring himself to believe that matters were as bad as they were cracked up to be, William Smith O'Brien, MP, reported that he saw in Limerick people eating potatoes which no Englishman would give his hogs. In Clare, people were eating food 'from which so putrid and offensive an effluvia issued', said Lord Monteagle, 'that in consuming it they were obliged to leave the doors and windows of their cabins open.'

If you underboil a large potato and split it in half, a 'bone' or a 'moon' around the core is visible, and that parcooked core remains in the stomach when the softer potato has been digested. This waxy centre fools the stomach into thinking it is full for longer and its slow digestion releases a little more energy, hours after the meal.

Thomas Reid reported that on a visit to Co Tyrone he found: 'The father was sitting on a stool and the mother on a creel of turf . . . the children were standing around the potato basket. The potatoes were half-boiled. "We always have our praties hard, they stick to our ribs and we can fast longer that way."'

Such heartbreakingly heroic cheerfulness in the face of slow starvation!

The Evictions Begin . . .

As the blight took hold, the evictions began. Records only started in 1848, but we know that in Ballinglass, Co Galway, a Mrs Gerrard evicted 300 tenants on 13 March 1846. She brought in police and they had the back-up of the army in order to evict the tenants and use the holdings as a grazing farm. A village of sixty-one houses was emptied and the land left free for Mrs Gerrard to stock with cattle. In April 1848, a Captain Kennedy in Co Clare calculated that 1,000 homes had been levelled since the previous November.

It is hard to escape the conclusion that highly placed figures among the British authorities could see the benefits of the potato blight and the excuse it gave landlords to put their land to more profitable use. The example of the Highland Clearances is always there if we doubt that man's inhumanity to man could reach such proportions.

For those tenants who were still on the land, the prospects of eviction were terrifying. For the small-time Irish farmer, wheat, oats, barley, eggs, butter and pigs were not food – they were the means by which the rent was paid; failure to do that meant eviction, which was nothing but a death sentence. The potato, not money, was the unit of value. Unfamiliarity with money was so great that coins and notes of value went unrecognised.

The year 1845 saw widespread blight, so when 1846 arrived, the people clung to the belief that a good crop always followed a bad. However, there were not many seed potatoes around, and even a bumper harvest would not have provided enough food. As it was, the potato blight recurred. By August of that year, you could smell the stench from the rotting potatoes even as you passed along the road beside the fields. The people had already pawned or sold anything they had set aside for a rainy day. From now on every day was rainy. In the case of part-time fishermen, they had been obliged to sell their boats and nets the previous year.

Meanwhile, the scientists were persisting in their attempts to understand what was going on. It was generally believed that fungi were the result of decay – not the cause.

Some people wonder how the Irish people remained so passive in the face of impending catastrophe. Why did they not rise up? The answer in part must be that many of the Irish, especially in the west, could not even speak English and could not understand what the authorities were doing or saying. Their priests urged prayer and obedience to the ruling class. Weakened, demoralised and despairing, hunger debilitated them still further. When you are fit and confident, you may be full of fight and take the initiative, but the peasant of Ireland was mostly downtrodden and fatalistic. Once he was physically drained of energy by encroaching hunger, and morally drained by the prospect of himself and his family dying the slow, drawn-out death of starvation, he lapsed into apathy.

Moreover, early attempts to seek assistance had met with a stone wall. Having survived the first winter following the 1845 famine, desperate citizens at their wits' end in Craughwell, Co Galway, banded together to appeal to the highest authority in the land.

CRAUGHWELL APRIL 13 1846 TO HIS EXCELLENCY, LORD HAIGHTESBURY, LORD LIEUTENANT AND GOVERNOR GENERAL OF IRELAND

The humble petition of the farm labourers resident in the parish of Killeeneen, Barony of Dunkellon and County of Galway

Sheweth

That the price of potatoes in the districts is over 5d per stone. That a day's wages without food, and now in the busiest season, is 8d

That many of us have wives and families . . . that a stone of potatoes is the allowance to daily support one man, that some of us having families require 2 stones, others require 3 stones daily . . . That we have heard that Indian corn meal, from foreign parts, has been brought over to this country by the Government and to be sold at such prices as would enable poor men to feed themselves and their families . . . Petitioners humbly pray that Your Excellency may order that an immediate supply of Indian Corn Meal be sent to this district and sold to us at prices our wages can reach.

The response to this petition is not known.

What is known is the attitude of *The Times* in London. A leader writer thought that too much was being made of the whole affair. On 8 September he declared that if 'the Irishman is destitute, so is the Scotchman and so is the Englishman . . . It appears to us to be of the very first importance to all classes of Irish society to impress on them that there is nothing so peculiar, so exceptional, in the condition which they look on as the pit of utter despair . . . Why is that so terrible in Ireland which in England does not create perplexity and hardly moves compassion?'

While the leader-writer could not imagine that things were all that exceptional, Ireland was being stripped of anything remotely edible. Dogs, horses and donkeys were all slaughtered and eaten. Smaller creatures from the wild, such as hedgehogs, foxes and frogs provided some sustenance. Nettles, berries and mushrooms were devoured. In parts of the west of Ireland, the hardest hit of all, curlew soup was eaten. Blood was siphoned from the necks of cattle and horses. Those who lived near the sea ate as many fish and shellfish as could be got. However, the people had earlier sold their boats, fishing tackle and nets in order to have any kind of food, so shoals of fish not very far out to sea remained tantalisingly out of reach. Poaching was contemplated but anyone caught was severely punished.

The song 'The Fields of Athenry', much beloved in Ireland and adopted as the Irish rugby followers' anthem, tells how a man was sentenced to be transported to Australia for the crime of stealing.

> For I stole Trevelyan's corn
> So the young could see the morn
> Now the prison ship lies waiting in the bay.

Starvation and Soup Kitchens

We do not know the identity of the first person who died of starvation, but it is recorded that on 24 October 1846 a man named Denis McKennedy died while working on road No 1 in the western division of West Carberry, Co Cork. Cecil Woodham Smith quotes the post-mortem as showing that 'death resulted from starvation. There was no food in the stomach or in the small intestine, but in the large intestine was a portion of undigested raw cabbage, mixed with excrement.' At the coroner's inquest, a verdict was returned that the deceased 'died of starvation caused by the gross neglect of the Board of Works'.

Children were among the first victims of the famine. Of those admitted to Skibbereen workhouse after October 1846, half of them went on to die. And a couple of months later the situation deteriorated yet further. The winter in Ireland between 1846 and 1847 was the worst in living memory. The same applied to London where, by the middle of December, the Thames was so thickly frozen that you could skate on it.

Because of the doctrinaire belief that relief must be earned, not handed out, the Irish peasant was required to labour on public works during this winter of Black '47. Half-starved and dressed only in rags, with no shoes on his feet, he was required to brave icy gales blowing in from Russia. The number of deaths rose hugely.

While certain 'improving' landlords and other decent private individuals supplied soup to alleviate the hunger of the local people, much of the soup was 'not so much soup for the poor as poor soup'.

Alexis Soyer, the celebrated chef of London's Reform Club on Pall Mall, had created a sensation at home by coming up with a formula for soup costing three farthings a quart and distributing it daily to several hundred of the London poor. One recipe that, it was claimed, had been 'tasted by numerous noblemen, members of Parliament and several ladies . . . who have considered it very good and nourishing' used an entire quarter-pound of leg of beef, costing 1d. 'Medico', writing to the press from the Athenaeum, a club two doors away from the Reform, described Soyer's recipes as 'preposterous'. It was clear that the soup would not keep a cat alive.

Nevertheless, the great man had fame and gravitas and in Victorian England that carried you a long way. He landed in Dublin to a great fanfare and had a model soup kitchen constructed in front of the Royal Barracks. This long wooden building, with a door at either end of it, housed a giant soup boiler and several long tables on which were laid a hundred bowls to which spoons were attached by chains. The hungry crowds outside were funnelled, a hundred at a time, into a narrow passage, and as soon as the bell was rung they were admitted, given a ladleful of soup and a portion of bread and left to eat up. It did not take long for them to empty their bowls, but, unlike Oliver, there was no chance of asking for more, because the next hundred were waiting outside. In the interests of hygiene, the bowls were rinsed before they were let in.

In my nearest town, a massive set of buildings comprises Portumna Workhouse. It is now open for fascinating tours, and as Steven Dolan, the director, will explain, men were separated from women the moment they entered the gates. Women were allowed to keep young children until the age of two, at which point they were taken from their mothers. No contact could ever be made between any family members as long as they remained in the workhouse.

The point was reached when the British authorities began to fantasise. Routh suggested importing the yam, a staple in the Caribbean and some of the southern states of America. Hardnosed Trevelyan doubted whether yams would be a 'practical import in quantity' and he suspected that tropical yams would prove a difficult crop to grow in the west of Ireland, but he did not dismiss the idea entirely and the surreal notion of yams as a possible food for Ireland continued to be entertained.

The government gave a trial to the scheme by instructing a barrel of seed from the West Indies to be given to a Dr Lindley, who was expected to supply 'cultural directions'. Enclosing them, he confessed that he had misgivings about the prospects of the yam succeeding in Ireland, since it was a native of the tropics and could be induced to grow neither in France nor in Spain, where the climate was considerably warmer. Nevertheless, packets of seed were distributed all over Ireland.

By 1849 Trevelyan was thoroughly fed up with the whole business. Ireland had always caused trouble and he had decided that the only thing to do about the situation was to 'leave things to the operation of natural causes' and do nothing. His failure to intervene effectively and on time led to incalculable misery and the lingering deaths of untold men, women and children.

Thousands of poor people, in an attempt to flee death in Ireland, met death on the Atlantic, as they set out in the so-called 'coffin' ships. For those who did land in a new country, it was a death of another kind, for few if any ever returned to their native land. Up until the end of 1845, annual emigration was roughly 60,000 persons. Emigration reached its highest point in 1851, when the numbers amounted to 249,721.

Those on board those overcrowded ships, in no way equipped for such numbers of passengers, were destined for a months-long journey, one which many did not survive. Those who did make it did so with memories that they carried to the grave.

The famine changed the lives of everyone in Ireland. The British troops and civil servants stationed there were indelibly marked by what they had witnessed. A very few people grew rich from exploiting the desperate times – the gombeen men among them. For those in the Big Houses, the period after the famine was marked by a gradual decline of wealth and influence. Many of their inhabitants had sat out the famine by holing up on their estates and existing on game, chiefly rabbits.

As *The Great Hunger* concludes, the famine was never 'over' in the sense that an epidemic occurs and is over. The poverty of the Irish people continued, dependence on the potato continued and failures of the potato, to a greater or lesser extent, continued.

CHAPTER NINE

STRONG DRINK
AND POTS OF TEA

I once heard it said that an Irishman would crawl over the naked bodies of ten beautiful women in order to get to a bottle of whiskey. There might just be a grain of truth there. Although the stereotype of the brawling, drunken Irish is a grotesque distortion, the Irish love of drink is undeniable. Irish songs are full of its praises: '*Preab San Ól*' – 'Drink with Joy'! – is a toast to drinking and conviviality. So, too, are 'The Jug of Punch', 'Whiskey in the Jar', 'Bottles of Black Porter' and 'The Parting Glass'. I particularly like '*An Bunnan Buí*' – 'The Yellow Bittern' – so called because its writer went out one winter's day and found a bittern, dead because it was unable to drink from a frozen lake. These lines are translated from the Irish by Thomas MacDonagh:

The yellow bittern that never broke out
In a drinking bout might as well have drunk.
His bones are thrown on a naked stone
Where he lived alone like a hermit monk.

O yellow bittern, I pity your lot
Though they say that a sot like myself is curs't
I was sober a while, but I'll drink and be wise
For fear I should die in the end of thirst.

Surreptitious Pleasures

Although kings and lords enjoyed feasting, the majority of the Irish remained outside the doors of the banqueting hall. Humble people might also hope for some intoxicating liquor to take the edge off life, but powerful forces were lined up to discourage them, notably the religious authorities, and for much of the twentieth century there was a vigorous campaign in Ireland to get young people to become Pioneers – avowed teetotallers – which is still pursued today. The Church in Ireland has always had an ambivalent attitude to drink. While they generally frown on it, alcohol, in the form of wine, is present on the altar whenever mass is celebrated, and many an altar boy has taken a surreptitious swig of it. Moreover, in times gone by the knowledge of fermentation and distillation was most highly developed among the clergy. (It was a monk, Dom Perignon, who first created champagne.)

A good many priests had no objection to a drop or two themselves and even for pioneers and other teetotallers, whiskey was somehow regarded as a highly respectable drink, as was port. In every humble house in Ireland, city and country alike, a bottle was kept, usually in a sideboard or chiffonier in 'the room' or parlour, a room that was glacial, damp and unused other than on special occasions. This bottle was purchased to offer to visiting clergy and was known as the 'priest's bottle' or the 'priest's drop'. There was little fear of thirst with the priests, by and large, for dinners given by the parish priest usually ended with port and hot punch.

From the earliest days, church tradition required Lent to be a time for abstinence from meat and general mortification of the flesh, so much so that in 1563 the Council of Trent decreed that no marriage should be solemnised during that period. In one respect, however, the cardinals and bishops veered towards leniency, causing the grateful populace to cry,

> Good luck and long life to the Council of Trent
> For it took away meat, but it left us the drink.

The diarist Amhlaoibh Ó Súilleabháin (Humphrey O'Sullivan) describes a meatless St Patrick's Day feast he shared with the local parish priest and some friends in 1829 in which they dined on fresh cod's head, salted marinated ling, smoked salmon, fresh trout with green cabbage and fragrant cheese, served with white wine, port, whiskey and punch in plenty. If they were deprived of meat, they did not stint on the drink, for St Patrick's Day provides a glorious oasis in the middle of a long period of abstinence. No matter what you have decided to give up for Lent, by long tradition you can give yourself a dispensation on the national saint's day. Even those who have taken the pledge for Lent may drink the *pota Phadraig*, or Patrick's pot.

Yet the early Celtic Christians disapproved of too much drink. It seems that while Saint Patrick was on his travels through Connacht a king came to visit, obviously with drink taken. Displeased at the discourtesy and immodest behaviour, the saint foretold that the vice would pass to the king's descendants, who would all become drunkards and come to a bad end. Sad to relate, the prediction came true. On the other hand, Saint Patrick was not himself averse to beer and had his own favourite brewer, a priest called Mescan, who accompanied him on his missionary travels around Ireland.

In the ninth century, an Irish poet, Sedulius Scottus, wrote these wistful lyrics.

Nunc Viridant Segetes

The standing corn is green, the wild in flower,
  The vines are swelling, 'tis the sweet o' the year,
Bright-winged the birds, and heavens shrill with song,
  And laughing sea and earth and every star.

But with it all, there's never a drink for me,
  No wine, nor mead, nor even a drop of beer,
Ah, how hath failed that substance manifold,
  Born of the kind earth and dewy air!
    (Translated by Helen Waddell from the medieval Latin)

Mead and Wine

Although trading brought both wine and brandy into Ireland from early days, the earliest indigenous strong drink was mead (*mid*), possibly one of the first intoxicants known to man. Made by fermenting honey and water and herbs, it took a very large number of beehives to make even a small amount so it conferred more prestige on those who served it than just beer. In *The Vision of Mac Con Glinne*, mead is described as 'the relish of noble stock' and the banqueting hall at Tara, seat of the High Kings, was known as the 'house of the mead-circuit'.

Also mentioned in the early literature is *brocóit*, anglicised to bragget, made from malt and honey and seemingly halfway in strength between mead and ordinary beer.

If the kings drank mead, they also drank wine. The Vikings paid tribute to Brian Boru with vats of wine, and old records in Bordeaux show wine being sent to Ireland 2,000 years ago for 'feasts in the courts of the kings'. One such took place at Tara on Easter Sunday AD 433, when Saint Patrick arrived to find King Laoghaire presiding over a banquet with lesser kings, princes and druids quaffing wine. It is told that in AD 535 the High King Muircheartach Mac Earca was in the middle of entertaining his chieftains and warriors when his palace was set alight by a beautiful woman whom he had scorned. The king, trying to escape the flames, jumped into a huge barrel of wine and was drowned.

A thirteenth-century poem tells of the bard travelling from 'one feast of purple wine to another' and Giraldus Cambrensis in the late twelfth century comments on the abundance of wine brought into Ireland from Poitou in France. Wine was imported not just for the delight of kings but also because it was needed for the proper daily celebration of Mass. Some efforts had been made by the monks (always great horticulturists) to grow vines for the making of altar wine, but the climate was against them and they abandoned the attempt.

Ironically, there *have* been successful Irish wine makers, but not in Ireland. When many of the great Irish families were stripped of their land around the time of Cromwell, some, the so-called Wild Geese, fled to France and established vineyards there. Names such as Hennessy, Palmer, Barton, Lynch, Sullivan and McCarthy are familiar to the wine trade and many went on to found top châteaux. (The rumour – no more than that – is that Haut-Brion is a French corruption of O'Brien.)

Regulations and Excess

When the Normans held sway within the Pale of Dublin, they introduced a number of regulations regarding food and drink. Although men only were allowed to sell wine and meat, women brewers were given the right to sell oysters and salmon along with their ale. (Many also sold sexual favours.) Winetavern Street, now adjacent to Guinness's brewery, was once full of drinking houses. 'The whole profit of the town', complained one English commentator, 'stands upon ale-houses, taverns are open day and night and every minute of the hour. Every filthy ale-house is thronged full of company.'

The ancient Brehon laws and those that succeeded them put no restrictions on the amount of ale you could brew for yourself, but there were tight regulations on ale for sale and also on the proper way to run alehouses. Moreover, there were fines for drunkenness. The Normans in particular were concerned with order and cleanliness in all public transactions and laid down strict regulations for the proper conduct of markets. They were, in effect, public health officers and weights and measures inspectors. (Here is a little etymological nugget I found during my research. In an effort to be the first to meet the country people coming into the towns for market day, some merchants set up their stalls outside the town boundaries. These crafty salesmen were not playing fair, and came to the attention of the Normans, who banned this practice of 'forestalling'.)

These efforts had to be constantly renewed, because abuses were rife. By 1600, Dublin brewers were reported to be selling beer at twice the price charged in London, although they bought the malt at half the price the London brewers paid for it.

It was all very well to criticise the Irish for drinking, but the boot was on the other foot when it suited. Drink has always been a classic tool of the abductor, the spy catcher and the blackmailer. In the sixteenth century, English merchant ships would sometimes arrive along the Irish coast, invite the unsuspecting local chieftains on board, and keep them plied with drink while the soldiers of the Crown were wiping out their followers. In a similar vein, during Elizabeth's reign, the captain of a decoy ship at Lough Swilly invited the young Aodh Ruadh O Donaill aboard at Christmas 1587, got him drunk and defenceless on wine, then delivered him in chains to Dublin Castle.

A traveller in 1579 commented on the scarcity of inns in Ireland, but admits, 'Outside the port town there are no lodging houses to be found, but any traveller is welcome to put up in any house he meets, where he is warmly received and entertained without payment. The table is not usually laid until evenings, when the meal is served but in the meantime drink is not denied the traveller. There are eight sorts of draught on offer: beer made of barley and water, milk, whey, wines, broth, mead, usquebaugh and spring water.'

The not necessarily trustworthy Fynes Moryson complained in his *The Commonwealth of Ireland*, published in 1617, that the Irish squander their money on drink. 'Whenever they come to a market town to sell a cow or a horse they never return home until they have drunk the price in Spanish wine, which they call the "King of Spain's daughter".'

In 1656 Sir William Petty, one of the most successful of the Cromwellian adventurers, gave some startling figures in his *Survey of the Political and Economic State of the Country*. He reckoned that in Dublin there were 1,180 alehouses and 91 public houses – nearly one-third the total number of houses, catering for a population of around 4,000 families. He also found about 1,800 women and servants to be engaged in the drinks trade.

While kings and monks drank wine, the mass of the people, when they got a chance, drank cider and home-brewed beer. Few early records exist relating to cider, but apple trees grew in abundance, and by the seventeenth century farmhouse cider-making was well established, with the Quakers, ever forward-looking, establishing large orchards in Limerick and south Tipperary.

Beer Brings Fame

Beer was a drink of great social importance. A wisdom-text declares 'beer brings fame', meaning that you can hold your head high if you are able to offer beer to your guests. A law-text dealing with status expected a king to drink beer on Sundays (along with his household, presumably) and made it plain that if he could not ensure beer every Sunday of the year he was not fit to rule. A triad specifies that one of the three shouts of the house of a wealthy landowner was 'the shout of the strainers straining the beer'.

In *The Vision of Mac Con Glinne*, the poet slavers over drink:

Spurting behind, a spring of wine
Beer and ale flowing in streams
And tasty pools;
From a well-head of nectar
A crest of creamy malt ran
Over the floor.

Beer was actually a good choice of beverage, since drinking water was often unsafe. During the winter, milk and vegetables were scarce, so beer provided some essential vitamins. In fact, it was regarded as a substitute for vegetables and fruit and even given out in the refectory of some monasteries – especially at Easter – although it was laid down that, while the laity and the clerics got the same amount of food, the tonsured monks got only half the measure of ale.

The local lord was in a position to make beer because his clients provided malt in their annual food-rent, although some lords wanted beer rather than malt. The return on a rented knife, for example, consisted in part of four mugs of beer, with the rider that there must be no dregs or froth.

Brewing Secrets

The Irish probably learned the secret of beer and ale-making from the Scandinavians. Even today, they have a great reputation as brewers and the old Irish word *beoir* comes from the Old Norse *biorr*. A heroic story, possibly even true, is told that the Vikings had a recipe for heather ale that was a closely guarded secret, handed down from father to son. After the battle of Clontarf in 1014, when the occupying Danes were defeated and pushed into the Irish Sea, only one family escaped, but shortly afterwards were captured by an Irish chieftain who took them to the top of the towering Cliffs of Moher in Co Clare. Their captor promised to spare their lives in return for the secret recipe. 'I would be ashamed to tell you before my son,' said the father proudly, whereupon his son was put to the sword before his eyes. At this, the old Dane consented to whisper the secret, and the two moved apart from the others and stood on the cliff edge. The chieftain listened, then told the Viking, 'You have bought your life and are free to go.' But the old man tightened his grip and hissed, 'Had my son lived, he might have bartered the secret for his life, but now only you and I know how the heather ale is made and we shall take that knowledge with us to our graves.' With that, he hurled himself off the cliff top with his son's murderer clasped to him.

Actually, the Irish managed perfectly well without the recipe, for they went on to make beers that were quite different from those being made elsewhere in Europe. Early references indicate that beer had a reddish colour and red beer is mentioned in an Old Irish hymn to St Brigid. (In France they sell a beer called St Killian, advertised as a russet Irish ale.) *Gruit* ale, as it was once called, was made with herbs, usually bog myrtle, rosemary or yarrow, and it precedes the discovery of hops. Red Biddy Ale was made according to the old recipe and was the only herb beer made in Ireland. The Biddy Early Brewery in Inagh, Co Clare, which set up as Ireland's first microbrewery in 1995 and sadly closed in 2010, made an ale which harked back to the original beer of Ireland.

While brewers in continental Europe were turning to hops, the Irish continued with their gruit ale, but eventually saw the value of hops, not only for their flavour, but because they prolong the life of beer.

A weak beer known as small beer was made throughout the medieval period, but it eventually faded away. Over the centuries, three great beers of Ireland emerged: ale, porter and stout, all of them top fermented, meaning they are brewed at a high temperature, using yeasts that respond best to heat. Generally, lagers are bottom fermented, at lower temperatures, with different yeasts. Ale is characterised by a light colour and a pronounced taste of hops. Porter, no longer brewed, used to be dark brown in colour with a slightly sweet, malty flavour. Stout at its best is dark and rich with a bitter taste of hops and a creamy head – you should nearly be able to chew a good pint of stout.

Thanks to the efforts of Arthur Guinness, who started selling the dark beer porter in 1778, the name of St James's Gate, Dublin, has spread across the world, and his own name along with it, as the dark brown liquid with the creamy head became an ambassador for Ireland.

Nowadays there is a fast-growing market for stout in Africa, but if I restrict the parameters to the island of Ireland, the burning question is to decide where the best pint is to be had. Some used to swear you must drink it right by the gates of the St James's brewery in Dublin, but there isn't a county in the land where some pub hasn't laid claim to the title of Best Pint in Ireland. Moreover, Guinness is by no means the only stout in Ireland – Beamish and Murphy's both have a loyal following and microbreweries are springing up that make both ale and stout. The story of Arthur Guinness and where the 'Best Pint' is to be had are themes that you can study very pleasurably, with field research recommended. Your mission, should you choose to accept it, is to find a pint that is neither cold nor too hurried in its pouring, and to drink it in the most congenial of company.

Ale was sometimes drunk hot and spiced, too. While a bowl of punch was a great favourite over the centuries, hot drinks were all the rage in the 1700s. Mulled ale and porter, punch, hot spiced wine, possets, buttered whiskey and rum – drinks with names as fanciful as Lamb's Tail and Bishop – were found in inns and private homes alike and an Irish speciality was *scailtín*, a blend of hot milk, butter, sugar and Irish whiskey, flavoured with cinnamon or cloves. The brandies found in profusion came from both France and Spain.

Whiskey with an 'e'

Brandy has never lost favour in Ireland, but whiskey, the native product, has gone on to far outstrip it in popularity. Aqua Vitae, *uisce beatha*, usquebaugh, the juice of the barley, a drop of the crathur, the hard stuff, balls of malt. Call it what you will, Irish whiskey is what we are talking about, and note, by the way, that letter 'e' that distinguishes even its name from Scotch whisky.

Queen Elizabeth I declared that whiskey was her only true Irish friend, and even Fynes Moryson, who had little good to report of Ireland, wrote, 'The Irish aqua vitae, commonly called usquebaugh, is also made in England, but nothing so good as that which is brought out of Ireland. And the usquebaugh (or Irish whiskey) is preferred before our aqua vitae because of the mingling of saffron, raisins, fennel seed and other things, mitigating the heat and making the taste pleasant and refreshing to the weak stomach.'

Another Englishman tells us: 'It is sweetened with liquorice, made potable, and is of the colour of Muscadine. It is a very wholesome drink and natural to digest the crudities of Irish feeding. You may drink a naggin [a 200 ml bottle] without offence.'

Barley, known in Ireland since 3000 BC, is at the heart of Irish whiskey. (Actually it is distilled from a base of barley and malted barley.) Early whiskey, as suggested above, was more like a liqueur whiskey, sweetened and flavoured with raisins, dates, liquorice, aniseed and herbs. This recipe comes from *Delights for Ladies*, 1602.

> To every gallon of good *aqua composita*, add two ounces of liquorice, bruised and cut into small pieces; add two ounces of aniseed, cleaned and bruised. Let them macerate for five or six days in a wooden vessel, stopping the same close, and then draw off as much as will run clear, dissolving in that clear aqua vitae, five or six spoonfuls of the best molasses you can get; then put this in another vessel, and after three or four days, when the liquor hath fined itself, you may use same. Add dates and raisins to this recipe. The grounds which remain you may redistill and make more *aqua composita* of them and out of that you may make more usquebaugh.

Although legend gives Saint Patrick the credit for the introduction of distilled liquor back in the sixth century, there is no evidence for it earlier than the thirteenth century. Possibly Irish monks brought the knowledge of distillation back from abroad, with a view to its uses in medicine, as various orders of monks ran hospices for the needy and sick. The modern-day liqueurs of Chartreuse and Benedictine have their roots in that early recognition of the tonic effects of distilling with health-giving botanicals.

The first reliable mention of whiskey in Ireland is to be found in the *Annals of the Four Masters*, 1405, in which it was recorded that a certain Risdeard Mag Raghnaill, heir to a property in Co Leitrim, had died on Christmas Day of a surfeit of aqua vitae. The scribe appends a wry footnote: 'Mine author says it was not to him aqua vitae, but aqua mortis.'

The Elizabethan scholar Edmund Campion, whose Catholic sympathies put him in danger, wrote an influential *History of Ireland*.[3] In it he describes the habits of the 'mere Irish'. 'They drink whey, milk, and beef broth, flesh they devour without bread, corn such as they have they keep for their horses. In haste and hunger they squeeze blood of raw flesh and ask no more dressing thereto, the rest boileth in their stomachs with aquavitae, which they swill in after such a surfet by quarts and pottles [half-gallons].'

For something like 300 years, whiskey in Ireland was made privately. Large farms would have a steady supply, and even poor people would be no stranger to whiskey. Butler writes in his *Journey Through Fermanagh*, published in 1760, 'At Callyhill . . . there are neither inns

---

[3] His work was first published in Holinshed's *Chronicles* in 1577, and as any Shakespearean scholar will know, Holinshed was the source of much of the Bard's knowledge of history.

nor alehouses on the road, yet almost every house has for public sale aqua vitae or whiskey, which is greatly esteemed by the inhabitants as a wholesome diuretic. They take it before meals, and what is surprising is that they will drink it to intoxication and are never sick after it.'

However, governments have a way of sniffing out new avenues of taxation, and around 1680, excise duty began to be imposed on the distillation of spirits. Certain householders were allowed to distil spirits for their own use; tavern owners or innkeepers could make whiskey for their customers; and specialist distillers were there to serve the public at large. There was an initial resistance to having an ancient freedom curtailed, but by the second half of the eighteenth century the illicit distiller was being driven into the more remote parts of the land.

Poteen and Shebeens

The necessities for spirit making were fairly easily come by: access to clean water, plenty of turf to keep a fire going, and the still itself, which was not heavy and could be transported without difficulty. The ingredients – malt, grain, potatoes, sugar, treacle, molasses, yeast – were readily found. The only thing the maker of illegal spirits – poteen – had to be concerned with was to make sure the smoke from the fire didn't give the game away to curious excise men.

A hillbilly song from the Appalachian Mountains in the United States explains how to avoid detection when making moonshine.

Build your fire with hickory,
Hickory and ash and oak,
Don't use no green or rotten wood
Or they'll get you by the smoke.

Naturally, poteen made by a skilled hand is marvellous stuff (so I've been told) while poteen made carelessly can be rotgut or even do you serious harm. The vital thing is to follow tradition and spill the first run of poteen on the ground, to placate the Little People. Whether you believe in fairies or not, this practice of discarding the first run chimes with that in any modern distillery, for the heads, as they are sometimes called, contain impurities and are not fit for human consumption.

A certain amount of sly poteen is still being made in Ireland. (I am discounting the 'poteen' that is licensed for sale for export.) These days a gas cylinder can handily provide the fuel to heat the still and it makes not a puff of smoke. Rural gardai (police) keep their ears open and generally get to know if someone is overstepping the mark and selling what he makes. One policeman I met confiscated a still from a poteen maker and kept it locked at the station, pending it being produced as evidence in a future court case. A few days after the raid, the poteen maker came tapping on the door to ask if he could have his still back, because it was a new one. They wouldn't mind, he hoped, if he gave them an old one to take its place, as that would do just as well as a piece of evidence.

Back in the eighteenth and nineteenth centuries, shebeens (unlicensed drinking houses) sprang up around the country, and some persisted into the twentieth century. They were usually smoke-filled cabins, found up lonely boreens or beside bogs, and they often advertised their wares by a sod of turf hanging over the door. (Pegeen Mike in Synge's *Playboy of the Western World* lived in a shebeen.) When life was hard, many sought solace in the glass, but those who did so were mostly fathers and husbands, drinking away what little the family had.

Punch Drunk

While illicitly made whiskey was the province of the poorer classes, commercial whiskey began to emerge in the middle of the eighteenth century, and punch soon became a favourite drink of the landlord classes. Made with whiskey and hot water, flavoured with slices of lemon and spices such as cloves, cinnamon and nutmeg, and sweetened with honey or sugar, it was comforting and could be offered as a reviver as much as an indulgence. The nation's 'strong' farmers, shopkeepers and the clergy were not far behind the landlords in taking up the cause of punch, so classy and so far removed from the raw spirit the peasantry drank.

O'Toumy was the landlord of an inn in Mungret Street, Limerick, which was a meeting place for poets during the 1700s. His drinking song went:

Here's brandy! Come, fill up your tumbler,
Or ale, if your liking be humbler.
And while you've a shilling,
Keep filling and swilling,
A fig for the growls of the grumbler!

A reply by his friend Andrew McGrath went thus:

O'Toumy! You boast yourself handy
At selling good ale and bright brandy,
But the fact is, your liquor
Makes everyone sicker.
I tell you that, I, your friend Andy!

Whiskey was affordable by the end of the nineteenth century, if we go by what Tomás O Crohan tells us. Sailing back to the Great Blasket island with provisions from the mainland, he had five bottles of whiskey with him, half a crown a bottle being the price.

But he had this to say: 'Drink was cheap, too. It wasn't thirst for the drink that made us want to go where it was, but only the need to have a merry night instead of the misery that we knew only too well. What the drop of drink did to us was to lift up the hearts in us . . .'

Dr Oliver St John Gogarty, who flourished in the first half of the twentieth century, had his rooms next door to Dublin's Shelbourne Hotel for a couple of years, and although the hotel bar was not then in existence, it was some bar he had in mind when he wrote 'The One Before Breakfast'.

> The one before breakfast
> Alone in the Bar,
> Will slide down your neck fast
> And ease the catarrh.
> Your glass with its end up
> Will scarce leave your jaws
> When your body will send up
> A round of applause.

In time, the less affluent classes, too, indulged in punch, for all the dilutions and additions made the whiskey stretch further. A nineteenth-century ballad extols the virtues of punch.

> Let the doctor come with all his art
> He'll make no impression upon my heart.
> Even the cripple forgets his hunch
> When he's snug outside of a jug of punch.

> Aye, and when I'm dead and in my grave
> No costly tombstone will I have,
> Just lay me down in my native peat
> With a jug of punch at my head and feet.

Many, many more ballads and songs revolve around the pleasures of drinking and forgetting one's troubles in jocund company. The very greatest of these is the nineteenth-century 'Finnegan's Wake', which was the inspiration for James Joyce's stupendously erudite, rambling, bewildering, vexing and inexhaustibly pleasurable novel *Finnegans Wake*. Note that it's not Finnegan's Wake with an apostrophe – it's James Joyce calling on all Finnegans – all mankind – to wake.

Tim Finnegan lived in Watling Street
A gentle Irishman, mighty odd,
He'd a beautiful brogue both rich and sweet
And to rise in the world he carried a hod.
But Tim had a sort of a tippling way,
With the love of the liquor he was born,
And to help him on with his work each day
He'd a drop of the crathur every morn.
> *Whack fol the da, will you dance to your partner*
> *Welt the floor, your trotters shake,*
> *Isn't it the truth I told you*
> *Lots of fun at Finnegan's wake!*

One morning Tim was rather full
His head felt heavy, which made him shake,
He fell from the ladder and he broke his skull
So they carried him home his corpse to wake.

Sadly, a row breaks out:

Then Mickey Moloney raised his head
And a gallon of whiskey flew at him,
It missed – and falling on the bed
The liquor scattered over Tim!
Begod, he revives! See how he rises!
Timothy rising from the bed!
Crying, while he lathered round like blazes,
'Name of the devil, do you think I'm dead?'
> *Whack fol the da, will you dance to your partner*
> *Welt the floor, your trotters shake,*
> *Isn't it the truth I told you*
> *Lots of fun at Finnegan's wake!*

Whiskey, Wakes and Song

As we can see from the above ballad, whiskey was considered essential at a wake. Indeed, it was required to mark many important occasions – a wedding, a wake, a christening, the annual letting of land, the sale of property, or a matchmaking. And it was usually found at a 'station' – an occasion when neighbours, often in a rural parish, take turns to have mass said at their house, followed by a party. (The practice just about survives.)

At the country dances that flourished in rural Ireland in the middle of the twentieth century the local parish priest made sure the premises were dry, but the lads usually arrived well tanked up and several made trips out to the cloakroom, where a brown paper bag in a coat pocket provided a bit of Dutch courage for a shy Romeo.

In addition, whiskey was always drunk at the traditional 'coming out Sunday' or 'show-off Sunday'. On the second Sunday following their marriage, newly-weds would make their public appearance at last mass, the bride dressed up to greet the world in her new role as married woman. The couple would then go off with family, friends and well-wishers for 'the bride's drink', consisting of ham sandwiches, cakes and biscuits, teas, whiskey, porter and wine.

Another occasion on which the bottle was produced was the farewell to the emigrant, the 'American wake', so called because when someone was leaving home the chances of their returning were remote. For the mother, to see her son head off for that emigrant ship was to see him for the last time. For most mothers it was a heartbreak as keen as if for a death.

Tea Time

In comparatively recent times another, non-alcoholic, drink came into the homes of Ireland – tea. The Irish are the world's number one nation for per capita consumption of tea, although historically it was not always the first choice of hot drink. At one time coffee was cheaper by far, but the British had interests in India, Ceylon (now

Sri Lanka) and China, so they promoted the use of tea to boost the market. Initially, the uses of tea were imperfectly understood, and it is told that hostesses in the early days would serve dainty dishes of the leaves to their guests, leaving the brown-coloured liquid behind for the kitchen maids to drink.

Tomás O Crohan, born in 1856, recalls that he 'was a grown man before tea was known, and, when a pound of tea came our way for Christmas, it was sparingly used and the remnant saved up till the next Christmas'. An old man in the west of Ireland remembered, 'The old women would buy an ounce of tea for Christmas. It cost two and a half pence the ounce. Whatever they had left over, they kept it in their pockets for the Easter. Yes, they'd keep the bit of tea from Christmas to Easter. We loved to get the sup of tea at Christmas.'

It did not take long, though, for the proper use of tea to dawn on the general population and then a twist of tea was on every shopping list. While tea bags are the norm in Ireland today, it is still easy enough to buy leaf tea. My uncle Jack used to like his tea 'strong enough for a mouse to trot over' and swore by Barry's of Cork, as do I.

A dedicated tea drinker was George Bernard Shaw, whose memories of a neglected childhood included eating in the kitchen with the servants, dining on 'stewed beef, which I loathed, badly cooked potatoes, sound or diseased as the case may be and much too much tea out of a brown delft teapot left to "draw" on the hob until it was pure tannin.'

In his play *Heartbreak House*, Ellie Dunn is about to have a cup of tea when Captain Shotover grabs it, tips it away and insists on serving something better. 'Now, before high heaven they have given this innocent child India tea – the stuff they tan their own leather insides with . . . You shall have some of my tea.'

One of the reasons Ireland has such a giant per capita consumption of tea is that the moment you walk into anyone's house, the offer is made, 'Will you have a cup of tea?' or 'Wait while I wet the tea.' Few are the ills that a cup of tea cannot remedy, or so you would imagine.

The best joke about tea comes from James Joyce, in the scene at the beginning of *Ulysses*, when Buck Mulligan is entertaining two friends, Haines and Stephen Dedalus, in his Martello tower in Sandycove.

Haines sat down to pour the tea. 'I'm giving you two lumps each,' he said. 'But, I say, Mulligan, you do make strong tea, don't you?'

Buck Mulligan, hewing thick slices from the loaf, said in an old woman's wheedling voice, '*When I makes tea I makes tea*,' as old mother Grogan said. '*And when I makes water I makes water.*'

'By Jove, it is tea,' Haines said.

Buck Mulligan went on hewing and wheedling. '*So I do, Mrs Cahill*,' says she. '*Begob, ma'am*', says Mrs Cahill, '*God send you don't make them in the one pot.*'

Home-brewed

Tea was one of the few items that did not fit into the ethic of self-sufficiency (tobacco was another) unless you count dandelion or mint 'tea'. Wine, however, did not need to be imported. At one time many a housewife made her own cider and wine. Sloes, blackberries, blackcurrants, elderberries and elderflowers, rhubarb, apple, beetroot, bilberries and more were all the basis of home-brewed wine. Carrots, celery, dandelions and nettles were all gathered for making into wine or tea, and many a child grew up in a house where a ginger beer 'plant' was kept on the go for years.

Many of these home-made teas and wines were ascribed health-giving properties. Dandelion tea, made from either the roots or the leaves, was said to be a cure for bed-wetting, although the French name for the dandelion, *pissenlit*, suggests it is a diuretic and is the *cause* of bedwetting. Cowslip wine was said to be good for the complexion and both ginger wine and ginger tea aid digestion.

Ale, too, was made in many households in the early twentieth century. Tepid water, to which treacle and brown sugar had been added, was poured into a bottle containing the 'seed' of the ale plant and then left for ten days to ferment away, after which it was ready to bottle or (more likely) drink.

Open House

Inextricably linked with drink in Ireland is the notion of hospitality. The obligations of hospitality were laid down in the Brehon laws, sometimes called the Laws of the Fianna, formulated about AD 438 in the tenth year of the reign of King Laoghaire. It was strictly required that people in higher stations of life entertain guests 'without asking any questions'. For the high-ranking, hospitality operated on the basis of *noblesse oblige*; for those in the religious life the laws of charity obliged them to take in the stranger, feed him and give him shelter.

In 1554 Patrick Sarsfield, the Mayor of Dublin, kept open house from five in the morning until ten at night and no one came to the house without being given food and drink. As he explained, when he took up his office, he had three barns of corn but these were being fast depleted. 'God and good company be thanked,' he said towards the end of his term, 'I stand in doubt whether I shall rub out my Mayoralty with my third barn which is well nigh with my year ended.'

The wisdom poetry of the ninth century tells us that three things are always ready in a decent man's house: beer, a bath, a good fire. While drink was a consolation, it was also an expression of Irish expansiveness.

De Latocnaye in *A Frenchman's Walk Through Ireland*, written at the end of the eighteenth century, perceived 'in the corner of a ditch, a miserable cabin, the horrible shelter of the abjectest poverty . . . I knocked and an old woman . . . clothed in rags, opened the door. I told her I was a poor traveller who had lost his way, and was tired. She immediately asked me to come in and offered me all that her house afforded – a few potatoes, part of the alms she had received during the day . . . The poor woman told me that her husband was a sailor, that he had gone to sea three years ago, and that she had not heard a word from him since.

'She spread a mat on a box, the only piece of furniture in the house, and invited me to rest on it . . . ' The following morning, her guest made haste to decamp, but was obliged to add 'I had a great deal of trouble to get my poor hostess to accept a miserable shilling.'

Another Frenchman, Charles Etienne Coquebert de Montbret, wrote, 'I have noticed here, as I have often noticed before, with what vigour the Irish express their gratitude. A gift of two shillings has earned me an infinite number of blessings.'

The Irish are justly famous for their generosity, but sometimes this can get out of hand.

A certain Mr Cuffe, MP for Mayo, related how in 1753 he and some other gentlemen went for a day's fishing on Lake Corrib and in the evening landed in a bay in order to cook the fish they had caught. Presently a messenger arrived, sent by the head of the Sept [clan] in that district to know why they had landed in his territories without his leave. Once they had explained, the messenger departed and not long after, the great man himself came down to bid them welcome and invited them to his house. By the standards of that country, it was, writes Cuffe, a magnificent palace, with an entertaining room, neatly strewed with rushes and provided with blankets to serve as lodging for visitors.

A Bottle of Brandy was the wet before dinner, and the Entertainment was Half a Sheep Boiled at top, Half a Sheep roasted at Bottom, broiled Fish on one side, a great wooden bowl of potatoes on the other, and a heaped plate of salt in the middle. After dinner some pretty good Claret and an enormous Bowl of Brandy Punch which according to the old as well as the modern Irish Hospitality, the guests were pressed to take their full share of, nor did his hospitality allow him to forget their Servants and Boatmen, but gave a Bottle of Brandy between every two of them.

All was going well, and the chief began to grow mellow, and

call'd his Favourite Girl to sing which she did very well and was a neat handsome jolly girl. Before he called her in, he stipulated that they were welcome to any liberty with her from the Girdle upwards, but he would not permit any underhand doings.

There followed more entertainment from a bagpiper and then an 'old Irish Bard' and the chief was reluctant to let them lie down for a nap, but eventually relented.

When they got up the next morning their host saluted them with another bowl of punch, so they waited until he was dead drunk, then stole away. However, he happened to wake and find them gone and immediately mounted a horse bare-backed and pursued them. They had just reached the boat and pulled off from the shore as he came up. 'He pour'd upon them vollies of Excretions for being uncivil Scoundrels and Milk Sops.'

Cuffe has given the account, he explains, 'to give you a specimen of ancient Irish hospitality and their manner of Living.'

Dr Massari, Secretary to the Papal Nuncio, who had come to Ireland in 1645, was impressed by boundless hospitality and wrote home about it. 'The kindness of these poor people among whom the noble lord had come by chance, was without compare. At once they slaughtered a large ox, two sheep and a pig and brought a plenitude of beer, butter and milk. And those of us who remained in the ship experienced the generosity of these poor fisher people, by getting the finest fish and oysters of huge size in such abundance that no more could be desired.'

Over the centuries the same perception of open-handedness recurs. Sir John Carr, a Devonshire gentleman and member of the English Bar, arrived in Ireland in 1805, and remarked at once on the extreme poverty of the Irish peasant. He found this story worth recording in *The Stranger in Ireland Or, A Tour in the Southern and Western Parts of that Country In the Year 1805.*

> Poor as the cabin is, do not, reader! think that hospitality and politeness are not to be found in it. The power of shewing these qualities, to be sure, is very slender; but if a stranger enters at dinner-time, the master of the family selects the finest potato from his bowl and presents it, as flattering proof of welcome courtesy . . . The . . . stranger finds every man's door open, and to walk in without ceremony at mealtime and to partake of his bowl of potatoes, is always sure to give pleasure to every one of the house, and the pig is turned out to make room for the gentleman.

Sir Walter Scott, visiting Ireland in 1825, found 'perpetual kindness in the Irish cabin; buttermilk, potatoes, a stool is offered, or a stone is rolled so that your honour may sit down . . . and those that beg everywhere else seem desirous to exercise hospitality in their own houses.'

The remarkable Mrs Asenath Nicholson, who travelled to Ireland from New York to 'personally investigate the condition of the poor', toured the country, mostly on foot, carrying her possessions on her person, notable among which were the contents of two bags slung from a cord around her waist – copies of the New Testament in English and Irish. She had chosen to arrive in the very worst years of the Great Famine, and remained for eight years, doing her utmost to draw attention to the plight of the people she found little more than 'walking rags', and spending any money she made from her writings on food and clothing for the poor. She relied on the hospitality of those poor who still had a roof over their heads, sleeping in the same room and, indeed, sometimes the same bed, as her hosts, and the animals that also lived under the thatch.

At one house, she was fed. 'I applied my nails to divesting the potato of its coat, and my hostess urged the frequent use of the milk, saying "It was provided on purpose for you and you must take it." It must be remembered that a sup of sweet milk among the poor in Ireland is as much a rarity as a slice of plum pudding in a farmhouse in America.'

In another house, she is treated with extreme civility. 'My feet needed bathing, the pot which had been used for the boiling of the potatoes was presented, and in presence of ten male eye-witnesses gathered about, the girl washed my feet in spite of all remonstrance.'

None was more noted for her humility or generosity than St Brigid. This daughter of a slave girl and a wealthy chieftain was fostered by a druid, and became the most important female saint in Ireland. We are told in the fifteenth-century *Book of Leinster*, that on one occasion she received some unexpected visitors: seven bishops with their retinue. Since she had no food to offer, she sent her servant out fishing and he returned with a seal. This was a precious catch, and Brigid, an excellent cook, dairywoman and brewer, put such a fine dinner in front of the bishops that they departed happy and full of her praises.

On another occasion she was cooking a side of bacon for yet more visitors, when her heart was touched by the howls and yelps of a starving dog, and she fed most of it to the poor creature. By a miracle, the little that remained of the bacon was enough to feed the company.

This religious impulse to hospitality was found also in the laity. The duties of the husbandman are expressed in some early Irish lines translated by Kuno Meyer:

Bid thy guests welcome, though they should come at
    every hour
Since every guest is Christ – no trifling saying this;
Better is humility, better gentleness, better liberality
    towards him.

Hospitable Ways

The old Irish custom of hospitality was accepted and adopted by
the Normans, who were soon welcoming bards and poets into their
strongholds. In medieval times any traveller could claim food and
lodgings, a king or overlord could claim the right (known as coshering)
of putting his servants into billets and there was also the well-exercised
right of a lord to be entertained by his vassals.

Three classes of men were expected to keep open house. First were
the holders of Church land. In the early medieval period, there had
been falling away from the highest standards of the early Church,
especially with regard to celibacy; clergy kept concubines or even
married outright. As history demonstrates, the pendulum swings only
so far before it swings back again, and this period of excess began to
meet with opposition. By the twelfth century we find more austere
clerics of the new order, but because these did not keep open house the
bards, out of self-interest, tended to back up the more luxury-loving
clergy and mock the puritan new wave.

The second group with an obligation of hospitality was the
professional class – doctors, poets, craftsmen and the like.

The traditional hosteller or hostel-keeper, the *brughaidh*, was the
third. He was nearly always a man of means who sought to buy his
way into aristocratic society – a social climber. In a bid to impress,
he kept a very lavish table, hoping to attract men of power and rank.
Nevertheless, he had also to take in itinerant students, bards and
musicians and these were very demanding. If they felt that anything
had been held back from them, they could write a mordant satire and
shame the *brughaidh*, so they were handled with kid gloves

There was much high living in the Big Houses during the glory years before the Great Famine. Mrs Delany, who had been married off to her first husband when he was sixty years old and she a mere seventeen-year-old, became a widow when she was twenty-four and came to Ireland when she married again, this time to Dr Delany, a clergyman and friend of Dean Swift's. She kept a lively chronicle of life in Ireland in the mid-eighteenth century, telling how old Mrs Connolly, widow of the Speaker of the Irish House of Commons, used to be 'at home' all year round to visitors to her splendid residence, Castletown House in Co Kildare. Her habit was to receive callers in her drawing room every morning for four hours, then those who were still present at 3 p.m. sat down to dinner with her other guests, who might number anything up to twenty. Two substantial dishes were placed on the sideboard and no fewer than seven courses were carried to a table set with magnificent Irish silver. Liveried servants waited upon the guests and musicians playing French horns entertained the diners. Wines were of the best and dispensed with lavishness.

Mrs Delany herself was no mean hostess. Her dinner parties at her residence in Glasnevin became much talked about and her invitations met with no refusals. The menu for a dinner of hers is reproduced in Chapter One and would typically consist of a first course of fish, meat, fowl, soup, blancmange, cherries and cheese, followed by a second course of turkey, salmon and quail with accompanying salads and vegetables, followed by fruit in season with cream and sweetmeats. As many as twenty might sit down to dine, with an entertainment of a dance or an evening of cards to follow.

The hospitality of the rich, of course, must lose some of its lustre when we remember that little of the work devolved upon the host or hostess and the expense involved was trifling. Food was cheap and Irish taxation low. Servants did the manual work and were kept on for little more than their bed and board. There was no difficulty in acquiring servants, either, as being taken on at the Big House was seen as a boon, offering security for young country lads and lasses, who would then stay there for life.

The Act of Union, passed in 1800, had a catastrophic effect on Dublin high society, however, for no sooner was the Irish Parliament dissolved than many of the noble families packed up and sailed to England or else retired from the city to their country estates. While high living was taking the pantechnicon back to mainland Britain, the native Irish continued in their ancient habit of being open-handed.

The generosity endures. Robert Lynd, in his *Home Life in Ireland*, published at the very beginning of the twentieth century, recounts his experience: 'On a lonely road in the West one parching day, we called in at a public house which looked something like an ordinary farmhouse and tried to get some lemonade. The house was out of temperance liquors, however, and as we refused to take claret, the girl in charge of it offered us some milk. We took good drinks of this, and then asked how much we had to pay for it. But the girl said, "There's no charge" and would take nothing although the house was a licensed public-house and the sales of drink must have been small.'

Perhaps, with all this plethora of evidence of lavish hospitality, we should remember that not all guests were welcome. The host and hostess would be too polite to show their impatience, but a visitor given a hearty breakfast or an early tea might take the hint if he knew that the old Limerick phrase for speeding an unwanted guest was 'Give him two eggs for the road!'

The Final Round

In the pub an etiquette attaches to the buying of rounds and accepting a drink. There is no such thing in Ireland as going to the pub with a friend for 'just the one'. Once inside, a social gavotte of *politesse* is conducted. 'You'll have another one, now.' 'No, I must be going. Really, now, thank you but I won't.' A discreet nod to the barman brings him to the tap, and then the pint is being poured and it would be an insult to walk away.

Some visitors from abroad fail to understand the reciprocal nature of round-buying. One told me, in all innocence, that he had not been allowed to buy a round all evening. His single offer to buy a round had, as form demanded, been refused, and he had failed to insist. Haste was made to cover his gaffe and never by the slightest flicker did his drinking companions betray any displeasure. The true generosity on occasions such as these is not reckoned in terms of money but in a generosity of spirit.

The last word goes to Tomás O Crohan, whose perception was that the old heartfelt love of company had vanished. He wrote in *The Islandman*, 'We would spend a day and a night ever and again in company together when we got the chance. That's all gone by now, and the high heart and the fun are passing from the world.'

CHAPTER TEN

FOOD AND THE SPIRIT

There are more things in heaven and earth, Horatio,
Than are dreamt of in your philosophy.
Hamlet, Act I Scene V, William Shakespeare

These days, people in the developed world are increasingly cocooned from nature, and Ireland, so long a rural society, is going that way, too. Before mechanisation, a watchful intimacy with the natural world went deep and affected the daily lives of country people. In this the Irish were no different from country people all over the world. And, as with rural societies on every continent, many people held beliefs (often unspoken) about spirits inhabiting this world and interfering in human affairs for good or ill.

Less than a hundred years ago (less than fifty in many cases) folk, in rural areas especially, believed in a supernatural world running parallel to this one. While they believed in the Christian teaching of heaven and hell, an older set of beliefs persisted. Country people went to great pains to avoid offending the fairies, the little people, the good people, the Sidhe – call them what you will – and would propitiate them if ever it was thought they had been wronged.

Many food customs and taboos derive from a profound belief in the little people. Lady Gregory, in her preface to *Visions and Beliefs*, records, 'As to their food, they [the Sidhe] will use common things left for them on the hearth or outside the threshold, cold potatoes it may be, or a cup of water or of milk. But for their feasts, they choose the best of all sorts, taking it from the solid world, leaving some worthless likeness in its place; when they rob potatoes from the ridges the diggers find but rottenness and decay; they take strength from the meat in the pot, so that when put on the plates it does not nourish. They will not touch salt; there is danger to them in it. They will go to good cellars to bring away the wine.'

In Ireland, despite virulent attacks by the Church over the centuries, these beliefs were never eradicated. Trees are still hung with rags and other favours in a tradition predating the coming of Christianity. These votive offerings are put there either to appeal for something desired, frequently related to health, or else in thanksgiving for a wish granted. Often the old ideas and rites were subsumed under a cloak of Catholic piety; many wells had long been sites of pilgrimage and supplication before they were dedicated to a saint. The old Celtic festivals, dressed in new robes, were incorporated into the Christian calendar, and it was around those especially significant times of the year that the veil between the material world and the world of the spirit was at its most filmy.

These high points of the year were avidly awaited by those whose lives were marked chiefly by toil and frugality. Joy greeted any departure from dull routine, and while weddings and wakes provided occasions for people to gather together, the most reliable sources of relief were bound up with the feasts of the religious calendar. Or calendars, it might be more accurate to say, since the old pagan rites were observed alongside the Christian celebrations. Early Celtic Christianity took a pragmatic approach to the rituals and beliefs of the old dispensation, seeking to incorporate and emasculate them, rather than ban them outright.

Easter

The greatest feast in the entire Christian year is that of Easter, and its principal symbol, the egg, is the symbol of new life. At this time of year spring is visibly producing signs of revival and rebirth – birds are building their nests, animals resuming their breeding and the plant world sending out new shoots and buds.

Easter's significance was clear to a Mrs Crotty, of Rathluire, Co Cork, who was recorded in 1928 as explaining, 'On Easter Sunday, before the family went out, they used to take a piece of this meat called "bit of breedeen" and it is said that whatever family had the "bit of breedeen" on Easter Sunday, hunger would not trouble them for the year.'

The weeks of preparation for Easter were also significant. On Ash Wednesday, all Irish Catholics (the overwhelming majority of the population) resigned themselves to mortifying the flesh by going on lean rations. But it made sense to use up any rich food in the house, so on Shrove Tuesday people ate their fill. 'Carne vale' – farewell to flesh – is the origin of the word 'carnival', and it is also known as Mardi Gras, translated as Fat Tuesday. Eggs, flour and milk were the ingredients for pancakes and tradition required the eldest unmarried daughter to be first to toss the pancake; if it fell to the floor, she would remain unwed for the coming year.

Mayday and Bealtaine

Easter is a movable feast, but the first day of May is fixed, and this date was chosen for one of the most important annual festivals in old Celtic

Ireland, for it marked the beginning of the summer, when prosperity for the year ahead would be determined by healthy livestock and flourishing crops. May Eve and the first day of May were dedicated by the Celts to Bel, the god of life and death in the Celtic world, and the feast was known as Bealtaine, meaning 'the fires of Bel'. (This same god gave his name to London's Billingsgate and may be related to the eastern god Baal.) At Bealtaine, special cakes were baked and offered to the dead or given to beggars in the name of the dead.

Around this date the people of the Sidhe were said to move residence, and times of change are times of danger. The first three days of the month of May in particular were considered to be highly dangerous to cattle, for it was believed that the fairies' power was strong at that time, so everything was done to avert this threat, to the point of the people staying up all night on May Eve to protect their cows.

In the old days the priests or druids would make fire from the rays of the sun on the last day of April, and all domestic fires were extinguished, then relit from the druids' fires. Under the guidance of the druids, it was customary to drive the beasts between two fires on high ground as a precaution against their being 'overlooked' and water or ash blessed by the druids was sprinkled both on the cattle and on the land boundaries as a safeguard against ill intentions.

Many of these old pagan rites were Christianised, and Saint Patrick, recognising the power of these fire rituals, adopted them, bringing them forward to Easter and making them 'Paschal fires'.

On Mayday in Christian times, the custom was to hang rowan boughs in the cow byres and sprinkle holy water (blessed by the Christian priests) on the stalls and in the mangers. Women milking the cows would make the sign of the cross into the frothy milk at the top of the bucket and also made a sign of the cross in the air towards the cows. Some would tie a piece of red cloth or thread around the cows' tails or else a twist of rowan. At Inishmaan on the Aran Islands, those milking the cows would say the rosary to avert any mischief.

It was considered unlucky to give away milk on Mayday, for it was believed that whoever got the milk of a cow on that day would take the good from her for the rest of the year. If you needed to hand over milk, a pinch of salt or a drop of holy water was added to prevent ill luck. Additionally, no fire was taken out of the house on this day and no beggar was welcome at the door, for fear it might be a person from the Otherworld.

In some parts of the country particular attention was paid to making the May Eve churn and the butter of that churn was salted and put away for the coming year. Every night and morning before the milk was put in the pans, the woman of the house got a small piece of butter from the May Eve churn and put it in the pan, followed by the new milk. The 'power' of this butter prevented the milk and cream from being taken by any supernatural power.

Butter and milk were always felt to be targets of fairy desire and many pishogues (spells or rituals) were directed towards keeping them safe at this dangerous time. Butter could not be stolen if a lump was placed on the flat top of the gate pier or thrown over the roof of the house or dairy. Another defence against fairies was to scatter primroses on the threshold of any door leading directly into the dwelling. (I remember arriving at the front door of Strokestown House on May morning and finding primroses on the top step. No one claimed responsibility.)

Witches were said to be active around the beginning of May and some people swore they had seen them out before dawn on May morning, gathering up the dew with a cloth or a rope, repeating the charm:

The tops of the grass and the roots of the corn,
Give me the neighbours' milk, night, noon and morn.

Others were convinced that witches could assume the shape of hares at will. According to Giraldus Cambrensis, 'It has been a frequent complaint from old times, as well as in the present, that certain hags in Wales, as well as in Ireland and Scotland, changed themselves into the shape of hares, that, sucking teats under this counterfeit form, they might stealthily rob other persons' milk.' Stories are told all over Ireland of a hare milking the cows on May morning. The archetypal conclusion is that when pursued by a hound or brought down by a gun, the hare turns into an old woman with blood flowing from the wound.

An old man from Tanderagee, Co Armagh, told this tale: 'A man in Granemore could get no good from his cows. Somebody was takin' the best of the milk. He put a charge in his gun one night an' he watched an' he saw a hare slip in till the byre. As it came out, he blazed at it. He hit it about the hip an' it got away. But the country said it was Jane Hanlon. She was lame after, anyhow.'

This suspicion of hares meant they were more or less a taboo food and even in the late nineteenth century it was pointed out that 'country people in Kerry do not eat hares; the souls of their grandmothers are supposed to have entered into them'.

Not all the fortunes of May were ill. The first water taken from the well on May morning was known as the 'luck of the well', and maidens believed that washing their faces in the dew at dawn on May morning would render them beautiful in the coming year.

Summer

The next major feast was held around midsummer's day, 21 June, or a couple of days later, on Saint John's Eve. As happened at Bealtaine, bonfires were lit on the hills and cattle driven through the ashes to prevent their being 'overlooked'. In the west of Ireland, white bread soaked in hot milk or hot milky tea and flavoured with sugar (a concoction known as 'goody') was heated in a large pot and given out to young people. Herbs gathered at this time of year were judged especially powerful. St John's wort (*Hypericum*) was known as the fairy herb, for when it was crushed it gave off an odour like incense and was said to protect against witchcraft. Its yellow petals turn red when crushed, and because the plant flowers around the feast of St John the Baptist, it was said to be a reminder of the saint's blood when he was beheaded. Made up into an ointment, it had the reputation of relieving bruises and rheumatism and was even said to provide a remedy for 'the airy fit', which we today would call depression. St John's wort remains popular among herbalists and, according to a modern handbook, is still valued as an aid in dealing with depression.

To mark the end of the summer, the feast of the god Lugh was both a harvest festival and an occasion of merriment and courtship. Originally held at the beginning of August, it gradually became Christianised and the last Sunday in July was celebrated under a variety of names, Garland Sunday or Fraughan Sunday among them. This whole feast, centring on *fraughans*, is discussed more fully in Chapter Seven. The annual pilgrimage to Croagh Patrick, St Patrick's sacred mountain, also takes place on that last Sunday in July when the name most often used is Reek Sunday.

Hallowe'en

The division between the world of mortals and the Otherworld was at its most tenuous around the last day of October and the first day of November, the time known to the ancient Celts as Samhain and to the Christians as Hallowe'en, for it was the eve of All Saints or All Hallows. Mothers were always nervous at this time of the year lest the fairies took it upon themselves to steal away a child, and one old charm to protect against this was to rub salt and oatmeal onto the crown of a child's head. New mothers and their babies were also at risk of being stolen away, and among the talismans that could be called upon were the spoonful of oatmeal given to the mother as soon as the baby was born and the small lump of unsalted butter slipped into the new baby's mouth.

According to some people it was champ and to others it was colcannon that was eaten especially at Hallowe'en. In either case it was the custom to set the first two portions on the flat pier at the gate for the good people to take or else at the foot of the nearest fairy thorn (hawthorn or whitethorn) on both Hallowe'en (31 October) and All Souls' Night (2 November). A variation on this was the custom of leaving bread and water on the kitchen table at midnight for the return of the dead.

The fruit loaf known as the barm brack was also prepared at this time. It was customary to hide small tokens in the food – a ring to signal marriage and a button or thimble to indicate the young person would become, respectively, an old bachelor or an old maid.

All over the country it was believed that if you slept on a sprig of yarrow you would dream of a lover. Likewise, if you named two nuts, one for someone you had an eye on and the other for yourself, and put them on the hob it was thought to be a good sign if they hopped off the fire together. Another charm consisted of peeling an apple in a strip without breaking the skin, then throwing the peel over your shoulder and seeing which letter of the alphabet it formed, for such would be the initial of your future partner. To discover his potential riches, a girl would go out blindfolded to pull a head of cabbage. The size and shape of the root would indicate if her future husband would be strong and straight or wizened and crooked. He would be rich if a good lump of clay came up with the root but a poor man if it came out of the ground bare.

Yet another custom, more elaborate this time, was for a girl to cut nine stalks of yarrow with a black-handled knife and maintain her silence from the moment she began to eat her colcannon until all the family had gone to bed. Once alone, she must peel the yarrow and recite:

Good night, good yarrow, thrice good night to thee!
Pray tell me who my true love will be.
If his clothes I'm to wear, if his children I'm to rear,
Blithe and merry may he be with his face turned to me.

If his clothes I'm not to wear, if his children not to rear,
Sour and gruama may he be with his back turned to me.

The first suitable man she met after this would be carefully scrutinised for the telltale signs.

A further charm was for a girl to eat an apple before a mirror at midnight while combing her hair. As the clock struck twelve she would see the face of her future husband looking over her right shoulder. In many parts of the country, the first and last spoonfuls of the Hallowe'en colcannon were put in a marriageable girl's stocking, then hung from a nail in the door in the belief that her future husband would be the first man to enter the house.

From Hallowe'en onwards, mothers warned their children not to pick blackberries nor take apples from the tree because the *Puca* (a malevolent fairy) had spat on them.

Martinmas

Not long after, on 11 November, came the feast of Martinmas. This was one of the few days of the Christian calendar on which meat should be eaten. In a ritual reminiscent of the sprinkling of blood on the lintels of houses for the Passover, the *bean an tí* would spill some blood at nightfall on St Martin's Eve. Traditionally, it was the blood of a newly slaughtered sheep or a lamb, but more often it was that of a fowl – goose, duck or chicken – and the best of the flock. Those who did not keep birds bought one at the market or received one as a gift from a better-off neighbour. The full rite was to sprinkle blood on the door, the doorpost, above the lintel or on the threshold, on the bedpost, over the fireplace and on the doors of the outhouse and cattle byres. In some families, they spilled a little blood on a cloth and put it aside for later use, for it was thought to have curative powers. During the killing of the bird, the following prayer was recited: 'I shed this blood in honour of God and St Martin to bring us safe from all illness and disease during the coming year.'

After it was killed, the bird was plucked, drawn, roasted and eaten by the family on the day of the feast. If they were strict in their observance of the customs, a bone was kept to one side to be cast into the midsummer bonfire on the following St John's feast.

A story is told of a poor family who were unable to afford a bird and therefore killed a cat as their sacrifice and used its blood for the ritual. St Martin accepted their humble offering and they prospered all year long, but the following year greed took hold of them and they decided once more to kill a cat, even though they could have afforded a bird. Needless to say, their miserliness was rewarded with a year's bad luck.

Christmas and New Year

Surprisingly, I have come across no special food rites or pishogues associated with Christmas itself, although it was said that between Christmas Eve and 6 January, the feast of the Epiphany or the Magi, commonly known as the Women's Christmas, the prevailing weather was an omen for the coming year. It was also understood that anyone who died at this time would find the gates of Heaven open for them to go straight in.

The last night of the old year was known as *Oíche na Coda Móire* – the Night of the Big Portion – because the old people believed that a generous supper on this night ensured abundance for the year to come. No food was to be taken out of the house on New Year's Eve, and on this night, as at the May festival, food and drink were given grudgingly to any traveller or beggar for he or she might be from the Otherworld and wanting to take the food for the year.

In some parts of Ireland, the woman of the house would bake a large barm brack on New Year's Eve and as night was drawing in, her husband would take three bites out of the cake, then dash it against the front door in the name of the Holy Trinity, wishing that starvation might be banished from Ireland. After this, the family gathered up the fragments of the cake and ate them. On the following day, *Lá na gCeapairí* – the Day of the Buttered Bread – slices of bread and butter were placed outside the door at daybreak to propitiate the 'good people' or the 'gentlemen of the hills'.

All Year Round

Quite aside from these significant times of year, a constant vigil had to be kept against the fairies and also against human enemies. Foodstuffs were one of the main tools in charms and pishogues. Other propitiatory offerings made at all times of the year were a spill of milk on the ground, a morsel of food thrown down when someone sneezed, a little liquid from the first run of poteen out of the still, and unsalted food left out at night. The Sidhe feared salt, and so it was thought to be a great protector.

A common fear was that an ill-wisher would bury bread, meat or eggshells in one's field. If those foods had been stolen from the victim's house, the power of the ill-wisher was doubly strong, and generally the crops would be taken or would fail. The best way to counter this was to burn the buried food and in its place bury a blessed candle, a string of rosary beads or some other religious object.

Other foods were also found at the centre of superstitions and pishogues. In Galway it was considered unlucky to plant potatoes on a 'Cross day'. The year was marked by two solstices and two equinoxes, and the midway points between those four quarters were cross days, so, specifically, Candlemas on 2 February, 1 May, 1 August, the feast of Lughnasa and 31 October, Samhain. In Kerry a piece of cypress wood was stuck into the potato ridge on planting day and was burned after harvesting. J. M. Synge spent time on the Aran Islands and reported that when a child had been taken by the fairies (that is, when it had died), the flesh of a seed potato was seen to turn red.

In counties Mayo and Galway they believed that a pig killing should take place under a full moon. If the animal was killed when the moon was waning, the meat would reduce in size, although if the moon was waxing or full, the meat would increase.

Brian Merriman, the eighteenth-century schoolmaster and author of the great satirical poem '*Cúirt an Mheán-Oíche*', 'The Midnight Court', wrote:

> Under my pillow, I've kept all night
> A stocking stuffed with apples tight
> For hours a pious fast kept up
> Without a thought of bite or sup
> My shift I've drawn against the stream
> In the hopes of my future love to dream.

Not only apples were said to be potent in dreams but also cabbages, for dreaming of cabbage was said to be a portent of death.

Bread, too, was significant. It was considered unlucky to mistreat the loaf or to waste bread, and in parts of the country where the scrap of dough was kept from one baking to leaven the next (the sourdough method) it was called 'the blessed bread'.

When a gipsy or traveller died, instead of coins, two crusts of bread were placed on their eyes. Anyone off on a journey should always carry a crust in his pocket lest he stumble on the 'hungry grass' and die of starvation. At one time the 'hungry grass' was said to grow on the spot where a dead body had touched the ground, or where a meal had been eaten and no crumbs left behind for the people of the Otherworld. After the Great Famine, the people believed that 'hungry grass' grew over the unmarked grave of a famine victim.

Another old ritual concerned the bride cake or wedding cake. Unlike the rich fruit cakes of today, it was often a simple wheaten cake with honey and fruit in it, and when the bride returned to her home after the marriage ceremony, her mother would symbolically break the cake over her head for luck, then distribute the pieces among the guests.

Milk and Butter

Many of the anxieties and superstitions concerned the theft of milk and butter. A malevolent person, so the story goes, could steal milk by walking backwards, always looking at the smoke from the chimney of a farm, and chanting 'The butter of that smoke upon my milk.'

In former times their owners would make the sign of the cross on the cow's udder and, to prevent the beestings from being stolen when a cow had calved, they used to put a piece of cow dung in the newborn calf's mouth.

To spill milk was always significant – whether it was by accident or design. If a cow kicked over the pail, it was thought that the little people were responsible, and the saying was 'there's a dry hearth waiting for that'. A tale is told of a woman who could hear an infant crying. An old travelling woman came to her door and advised her, 'When you fill your first pail at milking time this evening, take it out to the bawn [the wall around the cow enclosure] and upset it with your foot.' The woman did as she was told and the child ceased its crying, for it was a fairy child and now it had some milk. In the same vein, if a cow kicked over the pail of milk, the old saying was 'It was needed where it went': *Theastaigh sé san áit a ndeachaigh sé.*

It was believed that if you spilled milk on a neighbour on purpose, it would bring them bad luck, but this act of ill will could also backfire. A story from Ardee, Co Louth, collected by the Department of Irish Folklore goes thus. 'My father spilled the milk to try and stop a certain person from using the pass in case it would become legal and they could claim a right of way. The curse follows us and our name, and we will be gone out of the townland in a few years. Seven sons and not one with a male heir.'

Butter-making was one of the most vitally important parts of a woman's work around the farm, for butter was like gold – it was a form of currency just as much as it was a foodstuff. The greatest care had to be taken not to break your luck in any way when churning and to protect butter from harm, physical or supernatural. The crossbeams of a churn were often made from two different woods and if the butter refused to 'break', the twig of a rowan tree or quicken tree, known as the fairy tree, was tied to the churn dash. Butter refusing to 'break' was the result of a witch or envious neighbour having put the 'evil eye' on the dairy or 'overlooked' the cow and stolen the butter.

This did not mean that the butter was taken physically, but rather that the power of the milk and cream to turn into butter was spirited away by some malign act, and the ill-wisher would be able to produce butter marvellously well because they were able to profit from the butter-making powers of their victim.

Other ways of counteracting such evils were dropping a piece of salt into the milk, or tying a red ribbon or rag onto the cow's tail after calving. Hags, witches and the fairy people feared both salt and iron and in Co Tyrone they would loop a hair rope around the iron coulter of a plough, put one end in the fire and tie the other end to the churn to prevent ill luck. In other places it was accepted that placing the iron coulter of the plough under the churn would help bring the butter, even if the churning had failed thus far.

Wednesday was believed to be the most fortunate day of the week for churning (*Lá na Cáuiginne*) and even in very recent times it was accepted that visitors to the house must make a few turns of the churn to ensure good luck.

Some rather gruesome stories concern devices for stealing butter. One was to put the hand of a dead infant under the churn; alternatively, the thief would stir the milk in the churn with the hand of a dead man, preferably one who had died on the gallows, meanwhile naming the person from whom the milk was to be taken. If your churn was too successful, they'd say, *T-anam don diabhal, tá lámh a'duine mhairbh agat!* Devil take it, you have the dead hand!

A friend of mine, Michael-Joe Tarpey, remembered Bridgie Goonan, a local woman. 'She lived to be a hundred and four, she did. And any time she was ever churning – she had a little dairy, you know – and she'd get the tongs and she'd have them ready to go start, and she'd bring a little coal out of the fire and she'd put it under the churn, d'ye see, for fear anyone would bring the butter. A small little bit – just put it one side of the churn there. To protect it.'

A Mrs Brady of Inchaboy, Co Galway, had heard of people churning all day with nothing to show but a churn of froth. 'Well, they told the priest. And the priest said to go making the butter on a Sunday while the Mass was on, and whoever has it gone will walk in while you're at it and then the butter will come right.'

The Sanctity of Sunday

In the very early days of Celtic Christianity the sanctity of Sunday was jealously guarded, for it was understood that if anyone violated it God would send a failure of every produce of sea and earth and there would be raids by foreigners with avenging swords, come looking to capture slaves. In view of those dire consequences, the people accepted that baking on a Sunday was banned, as was boiling food.

The rule of the monastery of Culdee at Tallaght was similarly strict, the monks being allowed to eat neither cabbage that had been boiled on a Sunday, nor a vegetable cut on a Sunday, nor bread baked on a Sunday nor nuts or blackberries picked on a Sunday. The ban on Sunday cooking was relaxed at Easter and Christmas, those being times of festivity.

However, the rules of hospitality took priority and it was permitted to get food for guests on a Sunday and to minister to them for the sake of Christ. In the late eleventh century, Bishop Patrick of Dublin records among the 'wonders of Ireland' the tradition of the miraculous mill that would grind on a Sunday if a guest had arrived, but would otherwise refuse to budge on that day.

We have seen above how fire was regarded as sacred. I find unforgettable the story of an old woman in Co Limerick who grieved at leaving her cabin to move into a fine new house, for at that point the fire that had burned continuously on the old hearth for 330 years was now gone out for ever.

Earth, wind, water and fire – these primeval elements run through the history of Ireland. The earth is there in the fields, the hills, the mountains and the raths. The waters define Ireland, from her seas, rivers and loughs to the drinking troughs for the cattle and the buckets for drawing water from the well. The wind is never absent from an Irish day, billowing the fields of barley, turning the mill wheel and, in today's landscape, the great monolithic wind turbines, ranged on hillsides, like giant art installations. Perhaps pre-eminent is the element of fire, from the *fulachta fiadh* to the turf fire in the cities as well as in the Big Houses and most particularly in the cottages of the poor throughout Ireland. Food was cooked over these turf fires, while invalids and old folk were settled in the inglenooks to keep warm. Seated in a semicircle before the hearth, people exchanged news, span tales of romance, soldiery and superstition. It was where songs were sung, where fiddles, flutes, concertinas and bodhráns were played. As the spirit moved them, dancers tapped and whirled in an expression of joy and pride, there on the beaten earth floor. And, of course, meals, full or scant, were eaten beside the fire, as the *bean an tí* looked on. The story of Ireland is ever a story of what grows on her soil, the creatures that live on her hills and in her waters and the work of human hands, passing life on to the next generation. This is Ireland's larder, green and life-giving.

BIBLIOGRAPHY

Allen, Darina, *Irish Traditional Cooking*; Kyle Cathie

Burnett, John, *Plenty and Want*; Scolar Press, London

Danaher, Kevin, *The Year in Ireland*; Mercier

Drummond, J. G. & Anne Wilbraham, *The Englishman's Food*; Pimlico

Fernandez-Arnesto, Felipe, *Food: A History*; Pan

Harrington, John P., *The English Traveller in Ireland*; Wolfhound

Heaney, Seamus, *Opened Ground*; Faber & Faber

Kavanagh, Patrick, *Tarry Flynn*; Penguin

Kavanagh, Patrick, *The Green Fool*; Penguin

Keane, Molly, *Good Behaviour*; Abacus

Kelly, Fergus, *Early Irish Farming*; Dublin Institute for
   Advanced Studies

Laverty, Maura, *Full and Plenty*; The Irish Flour Millers' Association

Madden, Lucy, *The Potato Year*; Mercier

Mahon, Brid, *Land of Milk and Honey*; Poolbeg

Ní Chuilleanáin, Eiléan, *Selected Poems*; Gallery Press

O Crohán, Tomás, *The Islandman*; Oxford University Press

Paston-Williams, Sara, *A Book of Historical Recipes*; National Trust

Sexton, Regina, *A Little History of Irish Food*; Gill & Macmillan

Sharkey, Olive, *Ways of Old*; O'Brien Press

Sheridan, Monica, *Monica's Kitchen*; Castle Publications, Dublin

Tannahill, Reay, *Food in History*; Paladin

Yeatman, Marwood, *The Last Food of England*; Ebury Press

ACKNOWLEDGEMENTS

I want to begin by recognising my brilliant supporters, who pledged to buy a book sight unseen, hoping that the pig in the poke would not be a disappointment. You've had to wait, but I trust that you will reckon yourselves rewarded for your patience! It's a fine pig, in my judgment!

If there is anything in these pages that is incorrect, I apologise. I have tried to be honest and accurate, without denying myself the pleasure of sharing my opinions!

In the course of my research, the following were generous in sharing their knowledge and their time: Gene McEntee, Mary Burns, Sally Barnes, Silke Croppe, Patrick Perceval, who introduced me to Jane and Louis Grubb, Roman Düll, Anita Hayes of Seed Savers, the late Veronica Steele plus the late Barbara Harding. Likewise, the staff of the Ulster Folk Park and the National Library, Dublin. Jane Hansell joined me in my food experiments and Tommy Cunningham brought me beestings. Veronica Halloran passed on stories, as did my cousin Bernie Hogan and the late Mrs Margaret Connell.

Once I had made the link with Unbound, Margaret O'Farrell was of enormous help and support. My friend Clarissa Webb was deeply supportive, as were Noelle Lynskey, Dolores O'Shea, Robin Hansell, and Brian Nolan. Ken Crampton gathered lots of pledges on my behalf and has always been an extraordinary friend. Sue Lawrence, cook, broadcaster and novelist, offered enthusiastic advice, as did Maureen Cahalan and Bernie Starr. Anne Finneran Treacy introduced me to Vanishing Ireland. Jennifer Sharp was an enthusiastic supporter, too.

Ruth Smith and Fergal Cahill are responsible for the brief video that kickstarted the crowd funding process, and they were and are a delight.

Vincent Woods and Martin Doyle both showed an interest early on, when it matters most. My thanks to Georgina Campbell, always supportive and helpful. Nuala Ni Chonchuir, sometimes writing as Nuala O'Connor, offered great encouragement, as did other members of The Peers group.

The great poet Paddy Bushe gave generously of his time to check the Irish language words and phrases in the book and my pal Denis Cahalane stepped in there, too. Steve Dolan, of the Irish Workhouse Centre in Portumna, a passionate lover of history, made helpful suggestions. Vinny Browne was a warm and generous supporter from the off, as was Judy Murphy – two stars in Galway city.

Special thanks to Darina Allen for lending her generous support to the book and, of course, to Richard Corrigan. Both of them fight the good fight to raise standards in today's complex food world.

Julian Roberts has done a first-class job of illustrating the book, as I knew he would.

It is due to Paul Kingsnorth, writer and countryman, that I heard of Unbound and he suggested that I contact John Mitchinson. A great day when I did. And the people I have dealt with at Unbound, notably Phil Connor, Georgia Odd, Imogen Denny and Charlotte Hutchinson, have been enthusiastic, efficient and friendly.

Last, I want to thank my mother, who gave me my love of good food, and my father who gave me my love of Ireland.

INDEX

SUPPORTERS

Unbound is a new kind of publishing house. Our books are funded directly by readers. This was a very popular idea during the late eighteenth and early nineteenth centuries. Now we have revived it for the internet age. It allows authors to write the books they really want to write and readers to support the writing they would most like to see published.

The names listed below are of readers who have pledged their support and made this book happen. If you'd like to join them, visit: www.unbound.com.

Niels Aagaard Nielsen
Elizabeth Adam
Keith and Elizabeth Adam
Louisa Adam
Irina Aleyeva
Giampi Alhadeff
Darina Allen
Gaby Allen
Gail Armstrong
Pete & Mandy Ashford
Brian Ashmore
Mary Ashmore
Maxine Backus
Marian Baldwin
Preeti Bansil
Marie Barrett
Alan Beck

Fiona Beckett
Angela Blakemore
Margaret Bluman
Anne and Graeme Booth
Michael Booth
John Brennan
Clive Bright
Ger Burke
Margaret Burke
Joseph Burne
Paddy Bushe
Majella Byrne
Maureen Cahalan
Denis Cahalane
Anna Callanan
Keggie Carew
Michael Carson

Patrick Chapman
Susan Clark
Lucy Coles
Madeleine Collett
Pat Compton
Robin Connolly
Andy Cook
John Coulter
Robert Cox
Anna Cronin
Ken Crampton
Sally Anne Cullum,
    beloved chum
Christy Cunniffe
Ann Cunningham
Patricia and
    Tommy Cunningham
Brian Curran
Catherine Darigan
Elizabeth Darracott
Anne Davis
Katherine Dennis
Anne Deroe
Abigail Dillon
Sheila Dillon
Steve Dolan
Patricia Donnellan
Maura Dooley
Joe Doyle
Shane Duffy
Wiltrud Dull
James Dunlinson
Mona Eames
Peggy Fallon

Gayle Farrell
Jack Feehan
Enda Felle
Erin Foley
Caroline Fox
Hugh Frazer
Antonia Galloway
Mark Gamble
Karen Gannon
Marian and Johnny Geary
Vanessa Gebbie
Marie Gibbs
Mary Gillespie
Shauna Gilligan
John Gleeson
Thomas and Meta Glendon
Susan Godfrey
Jose Gonzalez Zubiaurre
Peter Gordon
Peter Goulding
Betty and Patrick Grace
Iris Greene
Vincent Guiry
Peter Hagerty
Clara Hainey
Jane Hansell
Ginger Harpur
James Harpur
MJC Harpur
Patrick Harpur
Catherine Hayes
Grainne Hayes
Orla Hayes
Tim Hely Hutchinson

Rose Henderson
Margaret Hickey
Teresa Hickey
Andrew Hillier
Jackie Hogan
Robert Holmes
Anne Marie Hough
Jim Hynes
Miranda Innes
Iris Jackson
Phil Jakeman
Signe Johansen
Sonja Johnston
Karin Joyce
Kathy Kate
Aine Kelly
Leonie Kelly
Sarah Kelly
Valerie Kelly
Lucia Kempe
Anne Marie Kennedy
Caroline Kennedy
Eleanor Kennedy
Joanna Kennedy
Dan Kieran
Bill King
Michael Kinghan
Paul Kingsnorth
Korhomme
Pierre L'Allier
Matthew Lambert
Nick LaPointe
Barbara Lappin
Paul Lappin

Tom Lappin
Millie Larke
Patrick Lawless
Francine Lawrence
Sue Lawrence
Josephine Lynch
Noelle Lynskey
Noreen Lyons
Patsy MacCarthy-Morrogh
Nuala MacKenzie
Darran MacMaghnusa
Claire Madden
Ribbet Malone
John Mannion
Richard Marriott
Alfie McCaffrey
Sally McCaffrey
Meghan McCusker
Siun Mcdonald
Neil McGinty
Carmel McGlackan
Iggy McGovern
Claire McKay
Pamela McNeill
Paula McWaters
Monique Mielke
Yvette Mills
Caroline Miskin
John Mitchinson
Aideen Monaghan
Breda Mounsey
Sara Mullen
Judy Murphy
Muireann Murphy

Orlando Murrin
Ted Naughton
Carlo Navato
Melissa Newman
Eileen Nolan
Margot Norris
Breeda O Connor
Shelly O'Connell
Nuala O'Connor
Anne O'Doherty
Margaret O'Farrell
Robert O'Farrell
Veronica O'Halloran
Michele O'Leary
Mark O'Neill
Mary O'Reilly
Dolores O'Shea
Aine O'Toole
Anthony O'Toole
Gary Owens
Dan Pearce
Blake Perkins
Karen Plewman
Justin Pollard
Sally Pollitzer
Mike Power
Thomas Power
Sally Preston
Eilly Quinlan
Wilma Rekkers
Stevan Rimkus
Alison Roberts
Julian Roberts
Michele Roberts

Lucinda Robertson
Mary Rourke
Derval Royston
Susan Royston
Conrad & JoAnn Ruppert
Johanna Ryan
Mary Ryan
Anna Sage
Jennifer Sharp
Anne Sharples
Eileen Smith
Mary and John Smith
Ruth Smith
Yve Solbrekken
Brigid Speirs
Nyall Speirs
Bernardette Starr
Bruce Stewart
Scott Stickland
Monica Strogen
Keith Sutherland
Sean Swallow
Ann Thomas
Niamh and Liam Tierney
Anita Townsend
Susan Turner
Richard Tyson
Henrietta Usherwood
Lesley Venn
Evelyn Walsh
Denise Walters
Clarissa Webb
Sarah Webb
Naomi White

SUPPORTERS

Ann and Robert Woods
Eithne Wright

Susie Young
IrishFoodGuide Zack